MEN AND MOTHERS

MEN AND MOTHERS
The Lifelong Struggle of Sons and Their Mothers

Hendrika C. Freud

Translated by Marjolijn de Jager

KARNAC

First published in 2013 by
Karnac Books Ltd
118 Finchley Road
London NW3 5HT

The publishers gratefully acknowledge the support of the Dutch Foundation for Literature.

Nederlands
N letterenfonds
dutch foundation
for literature

Translator: Marjolijn de Jager.

British Library Cataloguing in Publication Data

A C.I.P. for this book is available from the British Library

ISBN-13: 978-1-78049-076-2

Typeset by V Publishing Solutions Pvt Ltd., Chennai, India

www.karnacbooks.com

For my son Yuri H.

CONTENTS

ACKNOWLEDGEMENTS

I would like to make a few comments about the genesis of this book. As a young psychoanalyst, I was surprised when, during her treatment, my first patient suddenly threw herself into a sadomasochistic sexual relationship with a man. I asked my supervisor for guidance. He advised me to re-read Freud's "A Child Is Being Beaten", but he considered a person with a sexual perversion to be incurable and suggested I stop the analysis. In the end, I did so, albeit reluctantly. Today, I would handle it differently. In the early 1960s, relatively little was known about therapy with the so-called perversions.

It was purely by chance that during that same period I was reading some of Marcel Proust's work. His accounts and explanation of distorted love relationships spoke to me. From that time on, in addition to Freud and his successors, I would turn to this author for clarification and insight. By reading Proust, I gained a better understanding and greater empathy for my sexually deviant patients. To my surprise, moreover, Proust's ideas were not so much incompatible with those of Freud but were rather a welcome supplement. Without Proust, I would never have clearly understood homosexuality and perversion; psychoanalysis without Proust was no longer sufficient.

I have used these two authors as guidelines. Not only because they are my two greatest mentors, but also because they see through the dark and unfathomable devious paths of love as no other. Besides, in psychological matters, there is no source more eloquent than literature.

The discretion that a psychotherapist must observe often prevents him or her from fully citing details from clinical practice. Every individual is unique and therefore recognisable. Thus I have limited myself to brief outlines and sought greater completeness in Proust's *Bildungsroman*, *À la recherche du temps perdu*, translated as *In Search of Lost Time* (earlier as *Remembrance of Things Past*), which describes a story of the development of homosexuality and perversion.

FOREWORD

About ten years ago, a Dutch newspaper asked me to review Proust's *Remembrance of Things Past*; a new Dutch translation had just been finished. It was my first true encounter with Proust. I had tried him a few times before, but I had always given up after twenty or thirty pages.

It took me a couple of months to finish reading *Remembrance of Things Past*. I even went to Miami Beach to read Proust. For some, probably perverse, reason, I believed that South Beach was the right place for reading Proust.

My reading experience resembled a rollercoaster. Some chapters were extremely insightful and offered me everything I wanted from a novel; other chapters were so dull that even after two double espressos I could not concentrate on the sentences. The article I wrote summarised my mixed feelings about Proust, which did not please everybody in the Netherlands. In certain circles, Proust is still a saint.

This is only one of the many reasons that Hendrika Freud's book on Proust and Freud made me happy. She writes: "Not only Albertine, but the reader, too, is taken for a ride. With so many affirmations and denials following each other, we lose the thread of the story." It was not my fault or lack of intelligence that made me lose the thread of the story several times; perhaps it was Proust's intention.

One of the remarkable feats of Hendrika Freud's book is that she makes the reader (at least this reader) want to read Proust again. She doesn't fall into the trap of preaching in The Holy Church of Proust, nor does she hide behind academic jargon. She is always clear and accessible; she does not talk down.

There have been quite a few prior attempts to explain Proust to the layman, most notably Alain de Botton's *How Proust Can Change Your Life*. But Hendrika Freud goes one step further than just explaining Proust; she makes clear that the distinction between myth (or novel) and science is a false one. We are shaped by myths; we understand the world and ourselves through myths. For this reason, the debate about whether or not Freud should be considered a scientist is completely beside the point. Such a debate is as absurd as a debate about the scientific merit of *Antigone*.

When I was fifteen, I wanted to become an actor, and I refused to finish high school. My parents and my teachers sent me to a psychologist, a rather shy and feminine man who didn't say a word until I started talking. After a few sessions, I started to invent stories. Perhaps I wanted to provoke him, I wanted him to become less feminine, but also because I felt responsible for the situation. I believed that I should offer my therapist something substantial, and therefore I invented a girlfriend who committed suicide. A few years later, I was sent to a psychiatrist who was the opposite of the psychologist. He was manly and asked direct questions, for instance, how often I masturbated. In my opinion, this was an impolite question even for a psychiatrist, so I answered: "I quit masturbating". The psychiatrist urged me to leave my parental home and find a place for myself. I wasn't ready to leave my parents yet, so I invented a life in a small, furnished apartment where I lived to my satisfaction.

The relationships with both of my therapists were based on lies and storytelling. The moment I realised this, I left my psychiatrist. My relationship with psychotherapy resembled my relationship with Proust: interesting but overrated.

Another of Hendrika Freud's feats is that she convinces the reader that therapy can be fruitful for patients. But sometimes reading Proust or Freud or Hendrika Freud is enough.

Her insights about perversion and the mother–son relationship were both shocking and familiar to me, but always a pleasure to read. Any mother, any son, and any other pervert who is neither son nor mother will benefit from this book.

Arnon Grunberg
Glion, July 2012

PREFACE

As regards the sexually mature individual, the choice of an object[1] is restricted to the opposite sex, and most extra-genital satisfactions are forbidden as perversions. The requirement, demonstrated in these prohibitions, that there shall be a single kind of sexual life for everyone, disregards the dissimilarities, whether innate or acquired, in the sexual constitution of human beings; it cuts off a fair number of them from sexual enjoyment, and so becomes the source of serious injustice.

—Sigmund Freud[2]

This book was written for and about sons, but for and about the mothers of sons as well. Yet, I hope anyone will be able to recognise some part of him/herself in it: after all, the general is clarified by the particular. Through pathology, we learn to better understand normality. Many men consult me after reading this book, because they recognise aspects of themselves in it. It is meant for a lay readership as well as professionals. Not only will sexual perversions be discussed, but so will everyday variations such as teasing relationships and "moral masochism".

My interest in perversion was aroused from the moment that my first analytic patient, a woman, unexpectedly embarked upon a masochistic sexual relationship with a man that included bondage—although she already had a strong tendency to experience everything that happened to her masochistically. In the same period, I began reading Marcel Proust and was inspired by his work. Half a century later, I still find perverson a fascinating subject.

I would like to offer two caveats. First: a psychological theory always presents a stylised picture from which any individual variations are missing. Patterns are generalisations. Each individual case must be studied on its own merits. Theories are merely research outlines that need further refinement. Second: rather than being moralistic or judgemental, this study aims at fostering a better understanding of male perversions and some forms of homosexuality. As regards homosexuality, I want to stress that in this book, mainly the more deviant, less successful forms are discussed, often in connection with perversion. However, homosexuality need not at all be considered pathological, as Sigmund Freud already realised roughly a hundred years ago. On the contrary, happy homosexual couples of longstanding duration are sometimes more successful than heterosexual ones. In my opinion, the sex of the partners is not the deciding factor, but the level of mature object relations reached, whether homo- or heterosexual.

This book deals with men who have a particular relationship with their mother, who experience a male development that is different from the classical Oedipal one. It is not about men who compete with their father but rather about men who maintain a symbiotic bond with their mother. "Patricide", the (symbolic) murder of the father, expressed in rivalry with the father, is the Freudian model of the Oedipus complex. Matricide is a less familiar concept; after all, the mother is as holy and sacrosanct as the Virgin Mary.[3] Hate towards the mother is a serious taboo, but taboos ask to be breached.[4]

There are men who avoid rivalry with the father and with other men. Men whose aggression is inhibited and who are afraid of losing their identity, their physical integrity, and the love of their (internalised) mother. This all-too-intense bond leads to stronger identification with the mother than with the father. We shall characterise this excessively strong bond with the (internal) mother as symbiosis, as a "symbiotic illusion" in fact, since everything that does not belong there, such as hostility and aggression, have to be repressed. Quite frequently, this form of symbiosis between mother and son seems to go hand in hand with a preference for a partner of the same sex and/or with perverse sexual scenarios.

I want to emphasise right at the beginning that perversions appear in heterosexuals as well as in homosexuals. Homosexuality and perversion are not to be confused with each other, although they may well exist within one and the same individual.

The people under consideration here come from my practice as a psychoanalyst and psychotherapist. These individuals contact me for every possible emotional problem, not primarily for their so-called perversions specifically. Homosexuality is not a problem in and of itself either. When thinking about "perversions", many people think of behaviour that is morally reprehensible, while such developments can actually present creative solutions for emotional problems. Crude forms of violence fall within the realm of criminality and justice and are outside the scope of this book. Just as it can never be the intention of any treatment to change a homosexual choice of partners into a heterosexual one, similarly it is not my intention to try to rectify an effective perversion between two consenting adults. Usually, perverse variations are too satisfying and indispensable to try changing them. They essentially provide a sense of triumph and superior satisfaction that rise above "normal" sexuality. Perversions consist of variations on conventional sexuality that have turned into a compulsion. These variations, based on strictly private phantasies, have turned into phantasy's rigid limitations. The obsessively repeated fixed scenario is the precondition for satisfaction. Stereotype and monotony have replaced unbound variations.

Dreams, which can also fulfil desires creatively, follow the same psychological principles and laws as perversions do. Neither can be taken at face value but both need to be explained and interpreted in order for their meaning to be disclosed. Freeing the individual from his fears around fusion with and aggression towards the object, the content of the perverse dream scenario has more to do with emotional survival than with sexuality in its narrower sense. Perverse sexual games are often monotonous like addictions. To be able to reach orgasm, the same stereotypical scenario has to be constantly repeated. That is the price that must be paid for protection against fear and ill-controlled rage: such feelings acquire a form by which they can be managed and controlled. Sexuality itself can be an addiction, like watching pornography and other compulsions whereby the object is more a thing to be used than a human being.

On the one hand, the bond with the mother image that is too strong, too intense, and has never been resolved provides a sense of safety and security. However, other than the reassurance it provides, it is a false idyll that causes one to feel a lack of freedom, helplessness, and anxiety. The content and significance of perverse love play concerns fear of fusion with the partner, on the one hand, and, on the other, serves as channelling of anger and frustration. Both love and hate, to be traced back not infrequently to the original relationship with the mother, seek a safe way out, in disguised form and in devious ways. Indeed, during the performed scenario the powerful phallic mother image is stripped of its power. The all-too-intense bond of love has led to the son's excessive identification with the mother. Their symbiosis allows hardly any room for the expression of any opposition or disagreement, and thus leads to his reduced ability to establish himself as a man, to inhibition of aggression, and to a fear of impotence.

The perverse scenario goes coupled with a mind that is split into two incompatible worlds, both of which seem valid: "Mother is dead, mother is alive, women have a penis, women are castrated human beings." During the performance of the perverse scenario, a world with different rules and different laws replaces everyday reality. In an exceptional state of mind, a "magic world" is temporarily created in which a satisfying phantasy can be enjoyed. For a brief moment, daily reality has no hold over the dream scenario, which in turn doesn't form a threat to the everyday reality. That is how, in addition to their ordinary life, often well-functioning and even creative personalities are able to make room for their fears in a dreamlike scenario and thereby render them harmless.

The origin of perversion as well as of homosexuality is open to multiple explanations. Interacting from the very beginning of life, both predisposition and environment probably play a role. I make no claims on putting forward the ultimate truth about homosexuality and perversion. Such labels conceal extremely different realities. Homosexual manifested forms are just as diverse as heterosexual ones. Perversions, too, are manifested in all kinds of forms and varieties. The patterns for loving that each person unconsciously adopts go through a learning trajectory that begins at birth. I am concerned here with one essential aspect in particular, namely the mother–son relationship and its influence on the development of the latter.

A psychological explanation is not necessarily proof of a causal connection. Not every closely bound mother–son pair has the consequences described in this text.[5] Where homosexuality is concerned, it is to a great extent the cultural and social influences that determine what is considered to be the norm.

It is possible that one day there will be solid evidence that every manifestation described in this book can be explained through genetic predisposition and/or brain functions. This doesn't seem probable to me, however, because such complex forms of behaviour cannot be explained by one single factor or cause. The outcome is decided not by nature or nurture but by the mutual interaction of predisposition, environment, and life course.

The structure of my book is concentric rather than linear. This means that the same data are constantly examined from different points of view. Repetition, which is thereby unavoidable, may help in clarifying the complex material.

For an understanding of this text, it isn't necessary to be familiar with the work of Marcel Proust or Sigmund Freud, although to me, the oeuvre of both has been a source of inspiration. The author Marcel Proust is the psychologically subtle "hands-on" expert in the realm of homosexuality and perversion, while Sigmund Freud is the academically trained psychologist who seeks explanations for manifestations with which he is not always particularly familiar through personal experience.

In the first place, I would like to thank my patients, who have taught me a great deal and who, for half a century now, have been a source of inspiration and worldly wisdom to me. Through their reactions, numerous readers have strengthened my conviction that in this book many people will recognise themselves and find support for greater self-understanding.

Notes

1. In psychoanalysis the term "object" refers to the partner of the subject, the love or hate object.
2. Freud, S. (1930a). *S. E. 21*, p. 104. London: Hogarth, 1971.
3. Welldon, E. V. (1989). *Mother, Madonna, Whore: The Idealization and Denigration of Motherhood*. London: Heinemann. Welldon deals with the power the mother has over her child. An emotionally vulnerable mother who experiences her child as part of herself may pervert the latter's lovelife.

4. Wieland, C. (2000). *The Undead Mother: Psychoanalytic Explorations of Masculinity, Femininity and Matricide.* London: Rebus Press. In this book, Wieland deals much more extensively with the concept of matricide.
5. Furthermore, there are also cases of perversion and/or homosexuality that are linked to a threatening father figure.

INTRODUCTION

The perversions are neither bestial nor degenerate in the emotional sense of the word. They are a development of germs all of which are contained in the undifferentiated sexual disposition of the child, and which, by being suppressed or by being diverted to higher, asexual aims—by being "sublimated"—are destined to provide the energy for a great number of our cultural achievements.

—Sigmund Freud[1]

This chapter is intended, first and foremost, to briefly pass in review every topic to be raised. Not only have things changed in the body of psychoanalytic thought since the publication of my previous book on perversion two decades ago,[2] but my own ideas have undergone further development as well. In the classic psychoanalytic model of development, the father holds a central position. In the interim, the role of the mother has become much clearer to me. An important element therein is formed by the "symbiotic illusion", a term I developed as a result of my experience with perversions but that unquestionably has a more general scope.

In addition to clinical examples, I use the oeuvre of Marcel Proust as illustration because, in my opinion, his views are complementary to

Freud's; Proust completes what is absent not only from the latter but actually from psychoanalytic theory as a whole: that is to say matricide, the murder of the mother, in other words. Once again, I make extensive use of this author for the simple reason that he provides the finest examples where perversions and homosexuality, my subject matter, are concerned. In addition, I offer brief sketches from my own practice as a psychoanalyst and psychotherapist.

A different Oedipus

Not every man goes through an Oedipal phase, the Oedipus complex is not as universally applicable as Freud originally thought.[3] Not every man when still a small boy has the phantasy of fighting a silent battle with his father to obtain the exclusive love of his mother, only to relinquish her in the end for the sake of a mature love life with another woman. There are men who take a different course. And for some of them, the (unconscious) phantasy of matricide, with which they struggle throughout their lifetime, is closer than patricide.[4]

Oedipus, hero of the classical Greek tragedy, is ignorant of his origins. In a blind rage at the man who obstructs his passage at a crossroads, he murders his own father, which had been his predestined fate. For as soon as he was born, it had been prophesied that he would grow up to kill his father and marry his mother. This is why his father Laius decided to have him killed immediately after his birth and, although Oedipus survived these murderous intentions, he was unable to escape his fate.

There are many versions and interpretations of this myth. Freud, who discovered the Oedipus complex, relied on *Oedipus Rex*, the Sophocles version. There is one aspect to which he paid no attention, however, namely to the question of infanticide that it contains. In actuality, the infanticide, or its intention, preceded the patricide. Neither did Freud spend much time on the role of Jocasta, Oedipus' mother, who seduced him, married him, and bore him children. And yet, she was the instrument of his ghastly fate. After the oracle declared Oedipus guilty, denial was no longer possible and he grew desperate with anger, guilt, and shame. He wanted to kill his mother/wife before doing away with himself. However, Jocasta was a step ahead of him and committed suicide, whereupon Oedipus gouged out his own eyes with the pin of her clasp.

The myth served Sigmund Freud as illustration of his theory: love for the parent of the other sex as the central motor of human existence; whether successful or not, the dénouement of the fateful childhood Oedipus complex functions as core of all subsequent emotional entanglements.

The validity of the Oedipus complex as core complex is gradually being put into perspective. First of all, Freud was already doing so himself. Towards the end of his life, he discovered the importance the mother has for girls and, with that, the relativity of the Oedipus complex.[5] He realised that women remain more attached to their mother and for a longer duration than he had originally suspected. Subsequently, Peter Blos, Sr wrote about men and fathers in a sense that differs from Freud. He explored the tender relationship between sons and fathers.[6] Finally, my concept of matricide in combination with a symbiotic illusion offers a model that is different from the usual Oedipus story.

To explain this other male development, I will make a short detour via female development. This had always been less clear to Freud than the male one, even though he based his theory largely on the treatment of hysteria in women. He referred to female sexuality as the "dark continent" to which he, as a man, had insufficient access. Subsequent researchers, frequently women, helped to complete his theory on this point. Still, the original Oedipal vision continued to work so forcefully that a revaluation of female development is anything but a redundant luxury. This is the substance of my book *Electra vs Oedipus*,[7] which deals particularly with the question of how girls and women relate to their mother. For the majority of women, the mother turns out to hold a central position throughout their life. This is all the more true when, as occurs all too frequently, the father does not accept his responsibility and remains aloof. It now appears that such a lack of paternal intervention is far more ill-fated for boys than for girls.

A baby's first love object, for both boys and girls, is obviously the mother. A boy must wrest himself free from this primal bond, a necessity that applies much less to girls. In some boys, however, the development resembles that of the girl because they cannot sufficiently break free from their inner maternal image. This unresolved attachment to the mother forms a threat to the masculinity of men who have identified too strongly with a woman. The fantasy of matricide, which can appear instantaneously or can remain unconscious, is one way for these men to defend themselves against a threatening fusion with their mother image. It is not so much a matter of the mother of flesh and blood but of the internalised image the man has formed of his mother.

Thus, the Oedipal theory has its limitations for men as well as for women. Perversions are the most striking example of sexuality's developmental variants. My views of this aspect of male development are intended as a supplement to existing perceptions. After all, every theory has its limitations. There isn't just one single developmental model that can be generalised and that would be valid for everyone. What matters particularly is the individual life story.

We are concerned here with men who have not gone through the Oedipus phase, who haven't experienced a normal Oedipal conflict and unconsciously seek a "different" solution. Their ambition, too, is directed at inner balance, even though at first sight the path that leads there may be odd. Perversions aren't immediately comprehensible. Just as with dreams, the significance of the perceived behaviour cannot be grasped without further interpretation. Furthermore, similar behaviour can represent entirely different meanings.

Consciously or not, certain men remain bound to their (inner) mother and strongly identify with her. This renders their male identifications rather weak, which has consequences for their masculinity, their gender identity, their choice in partners, and their sexual practice. The unconscious phantasy is then less a matter of the longstanding symbolic patricide but much more of matricide, that is, of the elimination of the mother.

This is not to say that every man with a strong mother fixation will necessarily grow up to be perverse or homosexual. Conversely, the pattern of the proverbial "mamma's boy" in combination with a distant father seems to hold equally untrue for all homosexual men. A distinctly passive attitude towards a father seen as threatening (or unresponsive) can also become eroticised. Isay goes so far as to assume in homosexuality a natural bond of love and a primary orientation towards the father. This would appear so unnatural to the mother that she will work zealously to gain her son's love for herself. Hence, the demanding mother of many homosexuals. No decisive proof has been found for this, to me, rather far-fetched, assumption (see Friedman[8]).

In the field of psychology, it is never a matter of a linear cause-and-result chain but rather of a connection between phenomena that affect each other. With psychological characteristics, it is never a question of either/or but of and/and, nature and nurture. Inborn disposition, milieu, and development affect each other; there is always the matter of biology plus environment. Little has been established that incontestably concerns possible physical components, such as hormones, physiology of the brain, and genes. Not only do constitution and sociocultural factors play a role, but so does the family from which the individual originates. In addition, the influence of sibling order should be considered, as should the mother's preference for a specific child.

In perversion, which may or may not be part of homosexuality, we are dealing with complex layered patterns of behaviour and fantasies. Mostly the specific and individual mother–son interaction that has existed from earliest childhood onwards plays a crucial role here, as we will see.

Attempting a definition

It is difficult to provide a culture-free (sound) definition of perversion, also known as paraphilias, neosexualities, or sexual deviation, free of moral judgements.[9] It has to do with fantasies, accompanied by actions or not, with or without a partner. Instead of free choice and variation as a condition for arousal come compulsive behaviour and obsessional thoughts. Intimacy is replaced by stereotypical rituals or thoughts thereof. The formation of visual imagery is an important ingredient, as is generally true with male sexuality. The phantasies are completely idiosyncratic, that is to say that they are connected to the personal life history and difficult to influence, even if the individual in question so desires. With perversions, it is less a matter of authentic sexuality and more of the use of eroticism as a sexual façade behind which other motives, such as psychological survival, lie hidden. Perversion is in essence a defence mechanism protecting the individual against anxiety and a way of sublimating anger and hatred. Certain sexual preferences, such as paedophilia and paedosexuality, are socially unacceptable. Like the more criminal variants, for example indecent assault, sex murder, and other destructive forms, they are beyond the scope of this book.

Proust and Freud

Marcel Proust and Sigmund Freud provide two different and complementary interpretations of the Oedipus myth.

According to Freud, the myth symbolises a universal longing of the little boy to kill the father, albeit only symbolically, and possess the mother: a question of competition with the father for the love of the mother. He explains homosexuality as a negative Oedipus complex, namely a passive homoerotic attitude towards the father. In this view, there is no room for the anxiety that too close a bond with the mother may incite. Though fear of and suppressed anger towards the father may lead to perversion and/or homosexuality, this explains, at least in my experience, only a minority of cases.

Freud considers the Oedipus complex as a universal point of departure to illustrate the (un)conscious tendencies of (all!) men. The first primal law of human civilisation, the taboo on incest, implies that it is forbidden for a man to desire his mother. He who does not respect the incest taboo and does not conquer the Oedipus complex must, like Oedipus, bear the dreadful consequences of his transgression, namely a (symbolic) castration.

According to Freud, some boys back away from the Oedipus complex out of too great a fear of castration. This would hold true for both perversions and homosexuality. They find refuge in the preceding anal phase, which they experience as being more secure. Some take on a passive, aggression-inhibited, and somewhat subservient attitude towards the father. Others are excessively attached to their mother.

So much for the classic psychoanalytic theory of male development. Freud never elaborated any further on the disorders in the mother–son relationship that are so crucial for the understanding of perversion. Hatred for the mother and matricide are missing from his theory.

Freud explains everything in terms of the individual's drives and libidinal phases. Only in more recent psychoanalysis have relationships with parents and the patterns that are thereby formed been applied as bases for the subsequent love life.

In my outlook on both homosexuality and perversions, the mother stands central. In this, I agree more with Proust than with Freud. The traditional Oedipus myth is not automatically applicable. In these cases, as we shall see, the love for the parent of the opposite sex is often altered by a seductive attitude of the mother.

From the very beginning, the secret and indestructible guilt-laden pact between mother and son was a theme of Proust's. The son is allowed to be weak and nervous, in exchange for which the mother will indulge him, and only then will she give him her unconditional love. The price the son has to pay is that of total devotion. It is a mutual blackmail that condemns both partners to a loving, nerve-racking bond, in which overt anger has no place.

I have called this mother–son bond the "symbiotic illusion", in which the mirage of unconditional love can remain intact. But not without a price. A false idyll is created this way to seal the implicit pact between mother and son, an idyll from which conscious feelings of hate are banned. Anger is isolated and translated into a separate reality: the perverse scenario.

In contrast to Freud, the Oedipus myth symbolises for Proust the ambivalence towards the mother.[10] The father is not the rival in the Oedipal sense, but at most an irritant in the collusion between mother and son. The result is not so much an Oedipal love for the mother but a perverted dyad with her. The development of the triangle father–mother–son has been disrupted. Mother and son team up and boundaries are crossed that exclude the father as a troublesome third. The mother is seductive or even eroticising, and the son is her accomplice. At the same time, he is terrified of becoming trapped in her nets. When the mother is intrusive and controlling as well, the son will try to avoid her, without being able to give up the pact he has with her.

Thus a form of incest is generated that is not so much physical as mental, yet no less destructive. Not "A child is being beaten"[11] by the father, as Freud titled his famous article about masochism. In male perversion, as I see it, it is the desecration of the mother that forms the pulsating core of sexual arousal. The complex perverse theatre can be compared to a dream text that needs to be decoded. This scenario, as we shall see, serves to reverse childhood frustrations and traumas and "detoxify" them in an exceptional state of consciousness, in which shame and guilt are temporarily suspended.

Apart from the death wish, Freud is particularly concerned with libido and much less with aggression, while Proust, on the other hand, describes the vicissitudes of both love *and* hate. Freud speaks chiefly about the father, while Proust pays much greater attention to the mother. The distorted relationship the narrator as a little boy has with her leads to his ensuing strongly perverted love relationships. Proustian love is a veritable torment because of jealousy and the fear of loss of love that the narrator had originally experienced with his mother.

Both Proust and Freud are of the opinion that a careful analysis can lead from the particular to principles that concern the general. It fascinates them that an inanimate object such as a fetish can bring about as much erotic arousal as can a person of flesh and blood. Both Proust and Freud are equally convinced that love involves idealisation, the overrating of the object that is the target of our infatuation. On one thing specifically they are in total agreement, namely that infatuation has more to do with phantasy and projection than with the objective qualities of the beloved.

The imagination that dominates in fetishism may be able to clarify how an old shoe can be just as exciting as a pretty young girl. What is needed in either case is converting the beloved by way of the inexhaustible powers of phantasy. We are all familiar with the Grimm fairy tale about the princess who is expected to marry a frog. Despite her protests, she goes along with it. She is rewarded when she shares her bed with him for the first time and he is suddenly transformed into a desirable prince.

Love and perversion

In the nineteenth century, the novelist Stendhal already subjected love to a thorough analysis in his famous *De l'Amour*.[12] After him, as far as I know, Proust and Freud are the first in Western history who dared to broach an unromantic, ruthless analysis and interpretation of love. For the first time, they each make the connection between infatuation and perversion, with illusion as their common root. Sexology was still in its infant shoes. Von Krafft-Ebing's *Psychopathia Sexualis*,[13] published in the early twentieth century, merely describes the different perversions and their manifestations. The cause is attributed to degeneration or masturbation. A psychological explanation of any depth is unfamiliar to the author. Proust and Freud dare to bridge "perverse" and "normal" without any prejudice or moralisation.

After all, the Latin *pervertere* means nothing other than "to turn" or "to rotate". "Perverse" literally means "turned", and then goes to "twisted" or "warped". Human sexuality is supremely versatile and usable for various motives in which phantasy is a welcome aide. Furthermore, sexuality and aggression are easily intertwined because they are both vehement and exciting emotions that touch the roots of our existence.

For Freud, the word "perversion" contains no condemnation whatsoever. Consequently, this is partly the reason why the term has been maintained in psychoanalysis until today, while outside the field it may be considered a term of abuse or condemnation. New terms have been invented, such as "neo-sexuality" or "sexual deviation". The well-known

American sexologist John Money speaks of *paraphilias* and *lovemaps*, special and highly individual patterns and preferences that come into being while the child is being raised, sometimes caused by neglect or abuse of the child.[14] Because a century of psychoanalytic research and practical experience cannot simply be effaced, I uphold the contested word. Any religious or moral emotional value or normative thinking is absent from it, although every designation, every category, and every distinction is bound to time, place, and culture.

I would like to give an example that shows how perverse patterns of interaction are quite frequently not directly connected to sexuality but serve as a defence mechanism. Mieke, a woman approaching fifty years of age, has an extremely turbulent relationship with her male friend. He is morbidly mistrustful and always suspects her of unfaithfulness. He calls her all sorts of ugly names and humiliates her by telling her she is nothing and can do nothing well. She patiently listens to all his verbal abuse instead of telling him to get lost. Like a long-suffering victim, she submits to it all because, in spite of herself, she anticipates the reconciliation that always follows. Her bliss when he shows signs of loving her once again makes up for all her suffering. She is unable to imagine love without this game, for in the end, it is a game with a familiar outcome. She encounters only men who use her and do with her whatever they want. It was exactly the same in the past with her parents. Of course, this kind of sadomasochistic marital relationship is proverbial as well. One only has to remember Edward Albee's *Who's Afraid of Virginia Woolf*.

From Freud to today

For many decades after Freud had published several studies on perversion, almost complete silence reigned where the subject was concerned. Not until the final quarter of the twentieth century did this theme and everything it entails, such as narcissism, gain renewed and copious attention once more. In the past twenty-five years, psychoanalysis has begun to pay increasing attention to the earliest interactions between parent and child. Object relations theory has more or less replaced drive theory. In infant psychiatry, the interaction between mothers and babies has been studied closely, helped by video recordings. All of this has had consequences for the practice of psychoanalysis. Distant mirroring has been gradually replaced by the recognition of what takes place between the two participants in a treatment relationship.

With time, the Oedipus complex has been replaced by the more neutral term "triangulation" as a crucial step of development. What is each individual's place in the triangle father–mother–child? What is the child's position in regard to its parents?

Although there is a fair amount yet to be discovered about homosexuality and perversion, particularly about their female variants, more is known today about gender identity and all that is connected with it. Apart from the interest in narcissism, there is a growing interest in personality disorders, such as the borderline syndrome.[15] Psychoses are somewhat better treatable these days. In psychotherapy, insight and medications appear to support one another, while talking and pill-taking are now often combined. Thanks to family therapy, more is known about family structures and their influence on personality. All of this has had its influence on the theory and practice around perversion.

Masochism

It may seem odd to pay so much attention to a phenomenon seemingly as rare as perversion, a topic that is not of concern to most people. Though the strictly sexual perversions are relatively rare, this is not true for the non-sexual varieties such as sadomasochistic teasing relationships. We are all familiar with the pestering or harassment that may take place between partners. We all know couples that don't coexist in a peaceful, loving way but are constantly on a footing of war with one another; couples that are dismissive of each other, either overtly or in a more subtle, veiled manner, and yet, to everyone's amazement, stay together. No matter how paradoxical it may sound, without that particular relationship, which apparently provides satisfaction as well, those same two people would have long ago abandoned each other. To everyone's surprise, women who are beaten and abused usually persist in staying with their violent men. Sadomasochism often functions as the rigid cement of a relationship.

The tendency to turn the other person into a fetish is equally common. With this, I mean manipulation, or the creation of a false image of love behind which lies hatred and the need to be destructive. Hannah has a male friend who always lies to and cheats on her. He is secretly bisexual. Finally, she discovers something is amiss and realises that her father was just as untrustworthy as her current partner. With the former, she never knew what he was up to or where he was hanging out. Unwittingly she looked for and found a partner who matched her unconscious problem in the vain hope of resolving it. She had never managed to find out the truth about her father; his secret relationships had always remained a mystery to her. Now she has found a perverse partner whom she is trying to break of his lying and cheating, an endeavour that is doomed to fail, of course. It is her way, unconsciously, of still trying to bring to a satisfactory ending the sad and unresolved problem with her neglectful father, who in the interim has died.

Another example of the universality of—the non-sexual form of—perversion is the widespread phenomenon of moral (that is to say, non-sexual but characterological) masochism, which appears in both men and women. It involves the inclination to make ourselves unhappy and feel victimised: "If I just missed the bus, it's because the driver is trying to give me a hard time"; "When a friend doesn't return my call, it's because he really doesn't like me"; "If I apply for a new job, they probably won't hire me". In short, it is a matter of anticipating disappointment, which automatically elicits the expected negative reaction.

The fact that suffering has such an irresistible appeal is a paradox that is as fascinating as it is incomprehensible. Every religion asks for sacrifices that are made to avert the revenge of the gods. The obsession with suffering and the crucifixion in Western culture is a perfect example of this. Why people have a penchant for saddling themselves with trouble has always been a difficult question.

Suffering masochistically and compulsive complaining contain a hidden accusation, replacing overt hostility. Masochism offers many narcissistic advantages. Suffering wrongs instead of openly expressing one's wishes and desires may spare one the risk of being rejected. The masochist's complaints contain veiled accusations as a result of which his opponent will start to feel guilty. That way he indirectly accomplishes what he fears won't work in a more direct manner. The silent accusation implies that the other is the wrongdoer and the aggressor. The masochist salvages his sense of self-worth and prevents disappointment because he is chronically disappointed anyway. By anticipating disappointment, he provokes what he expects and is always right. He draws the suffering he fears closer to him and is therefore the director of his own fate. He poses as a powerless, helpless victim but surreptitiously has (unconscious) power over his partner. He risks nothing because he operates according to a fixed and safe pattern. He thinks he is being dealt with unjustly and thus feels fully entitled to present his unsettled account whether it's appropriate or not. He functions according to the principle of being right at all costs and thereby salvages his vulnerable narcissism.

Why perversion?

Since perverse behaviour has long been seen as a violation of the law and a transgression of the social order, it came under the heading of criminality. Psychiatry wasn't called upon until the nineteenth century, when punishment for deviant behaviour no longer met these needs. That is when research in perversion, the study and categorisation of its various forms, the domain of the new science of "sexology", became a legitimate undertaking.

The little child's fear of being separated from its mother is a major concern of both Proust and Freud. This fear of separation and abandonment is a common human problem. Life cannot be lived without loss and abandonment. Not everyone feels the need to deny the fear of these and to try to invalidate them through manic actions. Proust's episode of the goodnight kiss, the key of his novel, to which I will come back later, is all about the fear of separation and abandonment.

The mother is our first love object, she is indispensable, and the fear of losing her is often accompanied by its opposite, namely the fear of being overrun and dominated by her, and of losing all personal identity. The archaic aggression that is linked to anger around thwarted independence can be played out in a perverse scenario. This then serves as self-esteem regulation and a solution for identity problems. At the same time, the fear of losing oneself or of going crazy requires a barrier against psychological breakdown, and once again the manic defence in the form of perversion is a possible solution.

Perverse scenarios function as support for a weak self-esteem. Perverse sexual actions can give those people whose narcissism is frail the feeling they are masters of their own fate again. Alex is addicted to watch pornographic scenes on his computer and give in to his need to masturbate whenever he feels slighted. That way he can surreptitiously take revenge on his partner. Instead of weakening the sense of self the often bizarre sexual activities provide a feeling of triumph because they represent a manic defence against powerlessness and fear. "Perverse ritual is not devoid of symbolic meaning, but is more like the manifest content of a dream. These behaviours have symbolic functions at a high level of abstraction despite their apparent concreteness"[16]. The perverse scenario also helps as a support for insecurity around one's gender identity. The question: am I a man or a woman, a boy or a girl, can be avoided. In the megalomaniacal conceptual universe, every limitation can be momentarily removed. He or she can be of both sexes simultaneously without having to choose and without the narcissistic affront that the choice comprises an inescapable limitation. By its severely regulated and predictable characteristic, perversion helps a man to deal with his fear of women. It can enable him to function heterosexually and maintain his potency, thanks to games that have the secret significance that nothing harmful can happen to him. Threatening homosexuality can be avoided by performing perverse scenarios with a heterosexual partner. None of this is a conscious choice, of course, and when such a man is asked whether he has homosexual fantasies he is likely to deny it vehemently. Moreover, it should be obvious that "perverse" and "normal" overlap and that both normal and perverse homosexuality exist, just as there is normal and perverse heterosexuality.

The perverse scenario exists to maintain a psychological balance. What does that mean? If I am afraid of fusing with my love object, I can keep him or her at a distance by avoiding intimacy and still engage in sexual relations. When sexuality follows a fixed pattern, it becomes impersonal and the other poses no threat. For a brief moment, he or she is more a thing, an implement, than a love object.[17] My aggression towards him or her can't get out of hand because I am shaping it according to specific, fixed rules of the game. I am not at risk of entrusting myself to an uncontrolled orgasmic experience but have everything tightly in hand. (The impossibility of surrender is compensated for by feigned dependence.) I can make place for my traumas without going under. I can briefly bring my masturbation fantasies to life and thus feel powerful. In other words, I once again have control over my existence; humiliations and threats to my sense of self are temporarily unable to hurt me.

Expansion or curtailment of the erotic arsenal?

The problem of perversion lies not as much in alternative sexuality as it does in its limitation: when one and the same phantasy image imposes itself as an essential condition for arousal. Jacques, a rather feminine-looking man with his hair in a long ponytail, relates that he can only come when he is blown by a Chinese-looking woman with a ponytail, or with sadomasochistic porn scenes involving several men and women. When asked, he declares he has no homosexual experiences or interests. Nonetheless, there is clearly a problem with his male identity. He wants nothing to do with female genitalia. Furthermore, he seems to be looking for exogamous partners: women who do not resemble his mother. Women who remind him of his mother render him impotent. This is an example of a curtailed sexual experience, which troubles Jacques because it includes impoverishment as well. With his bizarre erotic tales, he attempts to excite and seduce the therapist, which could readily herald a perverse transference if the therapist is not prepared for it.

Alternative sources of arousal can be enriching but not when freedom of choice is missing. Stereotypical patterns of behaviour serve to resolve conflicts of another source via sexuality. The problem is separated from the rest of the personality and expresses itself exclusively in the quasi-sexual sphere. Because the perverse scenario keeps fears at a distance, the persona is free to make use of his abilities—often to the fullest extent—in other areas of life. The result, however, is that the stereotypical scenario cannot be missed and this compulsiveness comprises a curtailment of the sexual freedom of choice.

Additionally, there exist forms of perversion that have more to do with power over others than with power over one's own hidden chimeras. The antisocial, socially unacceptable, or psychopathic forms of perversion, of which the individual himself does not suffer but the environment or the society all the more so, are not the subject of this book.

The father

This book deals principally with the role of the mother, although the importance of the father is thereby in no way underestimated. On the contrary, if he doesn't occupy his place in the triangle father–mother–child, the mother's task not only becomes more onerous, but she will also take a more central place in the child's world and thus the balance that two parents can offer is disrupted.

Following in Freud's footsteps, there are authors who attribute an important role to the father in homosexuality. A few authors, such as Richard Isay,[18] point more specifically to the father as the primary object of longing in the little boy as the root cause of homosexuality.

Of course, Freud also indicates the love for the father, the fear of losing his love, and the resulting restraint of aggression. Freud explains male homosexual pursuits in particular by means of this "negative Oedipus complex". It is the so-called female position with regard to the father, prompted by fear and the need to please him. This masochistic attitude does, indeed, appear in sons of strict and authoritarian fathers whom they see as a threat. Alexander has an authoritarian, disciplinary father and grandfather, both military men who had served in the Dutch army in Indonesia. He is married and has two sons but keeps longing for sub-servient positions and a passive role in sexuality. His wife is not will-ing to treat him roughly or violently, and he fears her wrath if he seeks his pleasure elsewhere and is unfaithful. He loves his wife and suffers because of his unsatisfied sexual preferences.

Experience teaches us that a tender relationship with the father leads in no way whatsoever to homosexuality or perversion. On the contrary, it is an important ingredient for favourable male development. The lack of it leads to longings for a kind father, a yearning that can be so strong that it results in homosexual longings. Abel, brought up in the Dutch Bible belt, is one of fifteen children. While his father was strict and rather menacing, his mother, a passive woman, was mostly unavailable. Abel is in his forties now and has never had any relationship, either with a man or a woman. He has hesitatingly come to the conviction that he has a preference for men. He recently met a man he likes but who is as frightened of intimacy as he is. When asked what his phantasies are, he tells me he can get excited when seeing a man urinate. It seems his fear and lack of assertiveness prompts him to look, albeit from a distance, for the masculinity he lacks. The desire for anal penetration is not at all limited to homosexuals. It can be just as much an unconscious desire of heterosexual men, a desire they realise only in their dreams or secret phantasies. The longing to derive strength from the incorporated phal-lus appears particularly in men who lack the masculine support of a father figure. Not all cases of perversion derive from the unresolved symbiotic bond with the mother. However, it is my viewpoint that it is, generally speaking, the mother who forms the linchpin of deviating development.

Most authors agree that the Western world, and that is what this book deals with, is living through a "fatherless" era[19] from which, more than ever before, the father is missing as support and someone to hold on to. In any case, the child has a harder time identifying with him than with the mother because most of his activities aren't visible and thus remain somewhat abstract. All too frequently, he has renounced his authority completely. The empty space that has replaced the patriarchy may have strongly promoted the development of perversion. Many mothers are—willingly or not—alone with their children; single-parent families become ever more frequent. Fathers either work outside the home or are physically present, to be sure, but psychologically absent.

When the father plays no role in the mother's fantasy either, his function is difficult to grasp for the child. That is to say, children often experience fathers as absent, unapproachable, or powerless. That way, the child is left to the care, but also to the need, of the mother, who might commit it to her own purposes and satisfaction.

Psychology and literature

The novelist creates vibrant, psychologically interesting characters. Even the most incisive psychoanalytic case histories, such as Freud's, reveal only a part of the truth, although they are as engrossing as a novel. Rarely are they as rich and profound as the characters in the finest psychological novels. We know Tolstoy's Anna Karenina much more intimately than Freud's Dora.[20] The work of art is a universe all its own that offers insight into the motives of its protagonists.

Freud frankly admitted this novelist's edge in his correspondence with Arthur Schnitzler.[21] I, too, consider *belles-lettres* and familiarity with it as a rich and important source of psychological knowledge and insight, in which psychoanalysis is as plentiful as academic psychology is poor.

Proust's personal preferences sometimes make him one-sided. But he is unrivalled concerning the twists and turns of love, such as masochism. Moreover, Proust himself sees the description and study of sadism, as he called everything having to do with sadism and masochism, as his special field.[22] Here it is especially a matter of the insights that can be gleaned from Proust's work. The peerless beauty of his work must, sadly, be left aside.

Structure of this book

In Chapters One through Six, I introduce the connection between childhood fears and torturous relationships according to both Proust and

Freud. In Chapters Seven through Nine, I dwell upon perversion and sadomasochism in the personal and social arenas. I close with concluding remarks that review the themes of the book.

Notes

1. Freud, S. (1905e). Fragment of an analysis of a case of hysteria. *S. E. 8*, p. 50. London: Hogarth. Where homosexuality was concerned, Freud had liberated views, certainly for his time. Thus he wrote the following letter of solace to a concerned American mother: "Homosexuality is assuredly no advantage, but it is nothing to be ashamed of, no vice, no degradation, it cannot be classified as an illness ... Many highly respectable individuals of ancient and modern times have been homosexuals, several of the greatest men among them. It is a great injustice to persecute homosexuality as a crime, and cruelty too." He also gave an interview to the paper *Die Zeit*, in which he said: "I am convinced that homosexuals should not be treated as sick. (...) Should that not oblige us to consider many great thinkers as sick? (...) Homosexuals are not sick. Nor should they be taken to court as defendants."

   Together with Stefan Zweig, Arthur Schnitzler, Franz Werfel, Jakob Wasserman, Hermann Swoboda, and Moritz Schlick, Freud also signed a petition to the German Reichstag for the repeal of a 1871 law which stated that homosexuality was a crime. The signatories of the petition stated: "Homosexuality has existed throughout history among all peoples. (...) Their sexual orientation is as authentic as heterosexuality. The state has no grounds to propagate heterosexuality and marriage for homosexuals because that would only lead to unhappy human beings. (...) This law is an extreme violation of human rights because it deprives homosexuals of their sexuality, although no one is harmed thereby. (...) Homosexuals have the same duties as everyone else. In the name of justice we request the legislator that they be given the same rights." (In: R. Isay (1989c), *Being Homosexual: Gay Men and Their Development*.)
2. Halberstadt-Freud, H. C. (1991). *Proust, Perversion and Love*. London: Taylor & Francis.
3. Deleuze and Guattari devoted an entire book, *L'Anti-Oedipe* (1972), to the enfeebling of the paradigm of the Oedipus complex. The indomitable yearning that rules the unconscious is like an inexhaustible phantasy machine, much as it is with the schizophrenic. Bourgeois society and capitalism are bent on restraining and curbing phantasy life via the family and the myth of Oedipus and the incest taboo, as if that is the sole and most important taboo.

4. Karl Abraham, a close colleague of Freud's, was the first one to broach the subject of hatred and murder of the mother around 1911 and much against Freud's liking. Abraham explained depression through disappointment in and hatred for the mother, sometimes caused by the birth of a next child. His ideas concerning the good and bad mother were later developed by his student Melanie Klein. See: Ulrike May (2001). Abraham's discovery of the "bad mother": a contribution to the history of the theory of depression. *International Journal of Psycho-Analysis, 82, 2*: 283–305.

5. Freud, S. (1931b). Female sexuality. *S. E. 21*, pp. 223–247. London: Hogarth.

6. Blos, P. (1985). *Son and Father, before and beyond the Oedipus Complex*. New York: The Free Press/Macmillan.

7. Freud, H. C. (2011). *Electra vs Oedipus: The Drama of the Mother–Daughter Relationship*. London: Routledge.

8. Friedman, R. C. (1988). *Male Homosexuality: A Contemporary Psychoanalytic Perspective*. New Haven: Yale University Press. This author mentions identification with the mother as one of the most important determining factors. Additionally, he points to genetic, endocrine, and other factors. Friedman also posits that not every mother–son bond that is too close leads to homosexuality, while on the other hand, not every homsexual turns out to have had such a bond in combination with a distant father.

9. Roudinesco, E. (2009). *Our Dark Side: A History of Perversions*. Cambridge: Polity Press.

10. Moreover, Proust's vision is not couched in a theory. His outlook can be inferred from his novels and other works. Besides, I share this interpretation with various authors. Jean-Yves Tadié, who delivered Proust's work and is his biographer, as well as Michel Schneider, both well-known authors who use biographical data in addition to his work, observe the morbid growth in the mother–son relationship, although, according to them, Proust would have never become a writer without at least a partial identification with his father. Tadié, J. -Y. (1996). *Marcel Proust*. Paris: Gallimard; Schneider, M. (1999). *Maman: L'un et l'autre*. Paris: Gallimard.

11. Freud, S. (1919e). A child is being beaten: a contribution to the study of the origins of sexual perversions. *S. E. 17*: 175–205. London: Hogarth.

12. Stendhal (1957). *De l'amour*. Paris: La Renaissance du Livre.

13. Von Krafft-Ebing, R. (1903). *Psychopathia Sexualis, Zwölfte verbesserte und vermehrte Auflage*. Stuttgart: Ferdinand Enke.

14. Money, J. (1984). Paraphilias: phenomenology and classification. *American Journal of Psychotherapy, 38*: 164–179; Money, J. (1980). *Love*

and Love Sickness: The Science of Sex, Gender Difference, and Pair-Bonding. Baltimore: The Johns Hopkins University Press.

15. Kohut, H. (1971). *The Analysis of the Self: A Systematic Approach to the Psychoanalytic Treatment of Narcissistic Personality Disorders.* London: Hogarth Press; Kohut, H. (1977). *The Restoration of the Self.* New York: International Universities Press; Kernberg, O.F. (1975). *Borderline Conditions and Pathological Narcissism.* New York: Jason Aronson; Lasch, C. (1978). *The Culture of Narcissism: American Life in an Age of Diminishing Expectations.* New York: W. W. Norton.

16. Meyer, J. (2011). The development and organizing function of perversion: the example of transvestitism. *International Journal of Psychoanalysis,* 92: 311–332.

17. Bach, S. (1994). *The Language of Perversion and the Language of Love.* New Jersey: Jason Aronson. Bach considers treatment of the other person as a thing the core of perversion.

18. Isay, R. (1989a). The development of sexual identity in homosexual men. *Psychoanalytic Study of the Child,* 41: 467–489; Isay, R. (1989b). Fathers and their homosexually inclined sons in childhood. *Psychoanalytic Study of the Child*: 275–294. Isay's viewpoint differs from mine. Furthermore, it is striking that he omits the mother from his theoretical argument (such as Freud did), while according to his examples, the mother–son interaction does conform to what I have found in both homosexuality and perversion. Eliminating the mother serves here to support the negative Oedipus complex, the love for the father. The distant, absent, or violent father with a homosexual son is also mentioned, although the interpretation is different. Isay claims that a strong sexual attraction of the small boy with regard to the father lies concealed behind the son's masochistic attitude.

19. Mitscherlich, A. (1973). *Auf dem Weg zur vaterlosen Gesellschaft.* Munich: Piper.

20. Freud, S. (1905e). Fragment of an analysis of a case of hysteria. *S. E.* 7: 5–125.

21. Freud, E. L. (Ed.) (1961). *Letters of Sigmund Freud.* New York: Basic Books. Entry for 8 May 1906: "I have often asked myself in astonishment how you came by this or that piece of secret knowledge which I had acquired by a painstaking investigation of the subject, and I finally came to the point of envying the author whom hitherto I had admired" (p. 251); and 14 May 1922: "Your preoccupation with the truths of the unconscious and of the instinctual drives in man, your dissection of the cultural conventions of our society, the dwelling of your thoughts on the polarity of love and death; all this moves me with an uncanny feeling of familiarity. So I have formed the impression that you know through

intuition—or rather from detailed self-observation—everything that I have discovered by laborious work on other people. Indeed, I believe that fundamentally your nature is that of an explorer of psychological depths ..." (pp. 339–340). In this, I agree completely.

22. Sadism can serve to rescind passivity and find the activity that is missing from the father's side.

CHAPTER ONE

Proust and Freud as taskmasters

*Those passages in which I was trying to arrive at general laws were
described as so much pedantic investigation of detail.*

—Marcel Proust[1]

Proust and Freud were contemporaries but were not familiar with
each other's work.[2] They lived in completely different worlds
but, nevertheless, have much in common. Both Proust and Freud
would rather be judged on their words than on their persona. They are
far too aware that personal shortcomings can detract from the appreciation of their work. All the same, various interesting biographies of each
author have appeared that help us gain a better understanding of their
writings. Although the necessary restraint is required, it is clear that
connecting the biography of the author to his oeuvre can sometimes be
worthwhile. It will serve to better comprehend his vision but also his
limitations.

Both Proust and Freud are incomparable observers of their own
inner worlds, and also theorists about the inner worlds of others. They
analyse themselves in order to be able to plumb the depths of their own
psyches and those of other people. That aspiration forms the basis of

1

their work. Freud's point of departure is a male psychology that isn't always equally compatible with women, or with all men. A female inventor of psychoanalysis would have focused on different aspects. In all likelihood, she would have seen the mother as much more the central figure even then. On the other hand, Marcel Proust, a homosexual male, put a special emphasis on the mother. Freud's and Proust's different psychological insights are fostered by different personalities, each with its own sexual identity and preference. Just as it is more difficult for a man like Freud to find his way on the "dark continent" of female psychology, it is harder for Proust to identify with heterosexual men and women, or with lovers who are not victimised by their jealousy as he is. Proust and Freud are best seen as balancing one another: they complement each other very well. Proust can certainly not be said to be healthy, either physically or psychologically: even as a child, he already suffered from serious asthma attacks, and life was hard for him from the very beginning. Nevertheless, he was able to distance himself sufficiently from his own problematic nature and to arrive at profound psychological insights and discover generally applicable patterns.

The mother–child relationship is Proust's pre-eminent domain, while Freud provides us with special insight into the relationship (rivalry) of the son with the (Oedipal) father. Subsequent developments in psychoanalysis that focus more on the mother have only made Proust's work more modern and, psychologically speaking, more relevant. It is true, of course, that Proust writes about a special kind of man and a specific kind of love. Yet, he arrives at insights that we can all recognise. As we shall see, the complicated and paradoxical interaction between mother and son that he describes prepares the way for a perverse and sado-masochistic lifestyle.

When we compare this to Freud's development and insights, we get a different picture, although his mother was an important and lifelong influence for him, if only because he survives her by a mere eight years. But he didn't become entangled in complicated patterns with her. She didn't claim him and, although she was proud of him, she didn't attempt to force his life into a specific direction, as Proust's mother did. From the very start, Freud had more control over his own life. He lived with his parents until his twenty-seventh year, but not until their death, as Proust did. He was a dutiful son who visited his mother every Sunday. Still, he was far from emotionally dependent upon her, and his ageing father, who was socially unsuccessful, was nevertheless a determining influence in his life. He doesn't admit ambivalence towards mother figures in his writings, and Proust does so only in veiled ways. Although Freud's ambivalence is less vehement than in the case of Proust, he stays away almost throughout his life from scrutinising the mother–son relationship more closely and prefers to focus on the role of the father. The fact that it was not until after her death (he did not attend her funeral) that he would examine the psychology of the woman more closely is, of course, no accident. In short, Freud's masculinity was not directly threatened by his forceful mother even though he lacked the support of a strong father. But, just like the Baron of Münchhausen, Freud would pull himself from the mire by his own bootstraps: the formulation of the Oedipus complex. Freud phantasises about the Oedipus myth and thereby restores his own inner balance. Thus he corrects the desired equilibrium between his father and mother. He simply creates the strong father who is lacking but for whom he yearns. A father with whom to compete, a father who is powerful and successful, and young enough to satisfy his much younger mother so she won't need to seek solace in her son, as Proust's mother does. The mother figure receives remarkably little attention in Freud's work, while the symbolically threatening father figure is the critical one in his blueprint of the development of the male. However, not every male's development fits into this framework.

Models different from those that Freud explores are possible. He never described a single conflict of male patients with their mother. They never hated or desecrated her. On the contrary, their most fervent infantile longings are directed at her without any ambivalence. Freud sees the mother–son relationship as the least conflicted one, as the most ideal bond of love in existence.

In Proust's case, it is very different. He was raised primarily by his mother and grandmother. It is they who determined his tastes and preferences. His father, an extremely successful physician and scientist, remained somewhat detached from the family, as so many men still do today, in part because of his busy professional life. However, his example must also have had an influence on his son. He was a giant with an enormous work drive. His son shares this high level of ambition. The scientific disposition and the interest in medical topics are common to him as well. Still, Proust has a greater affinity with his refined and culturally better-grounded mother and grandmother than with his less sophisticated father.

To a great extent, Proust's life and work run in parallel lines. This is so strong, in fact, that in his great novel, *Remembrance of Things Past*, he twice calls his protagonist, the narrator, Marcel. The novel differs very clearly from the author's real life on one point: Robert Proust, his younger brother, does not appear in his work. Even as a child, Marcel was already jealous of him, as he is no longer the only child. He must have been disappointed that he alone was not sufficient for his mother. He is sickly and asthmatic from early childhood onwards, and, because of this, is also heavily dependent on her care. For her part, his mother finds it hard when her son demonstrates his independence and goes his own way.

Comparing Freud and Proust

Around the same time that Sigmund Freud, the Viennese psychiatrist, published *The Interpretation of Dreams*[3] in 1900, the French novelist, too, prepared to explore the inner self. For the first time in history, the time was ripe for a more thorough exploration of unconscious and/ or innermost feelings and phantasies, although these were not entirely unfamiliar.[4] A few authors before me[5] have already compared the psychological insights of Proust and Freud, but not in any depth nor with a specific concern for their view of male homosexuality and perversion. Some authors admire Proust as a psychologist, but psychology itself never paid him the tribute that, in my opinion, he deserves. Not until 1999 does the journal *Revue Française de Psychanalyse* devote a special issue to this writer.[6]

Freud and Proust, both children of the nineteenth century, the former poor and the latter rich, were born in what were then the two most important cultural centres of Europe, Vienna and Paris. Both were raised with middle-class ideals and Victorian mores. Both were given a classical schooling and neither of them was religious; Freud's education was for the most part a secular one, while Proust was raised as a Catholic despite his having a Jewish mother.[7]

The fact that both men were exposed to two cultures, the Jewish and the Christian, increased their social sensitivity, as did the fact that they were both the eldest sons of mothers with high expectations. Proust and Freud not only have an eye for conflicts in and with the outside world, but especially of interest to them is the inner world as the domain of inner conflicts and contradictory desires. Both describe this psychic reality as an intriguing hidden universe that has to be deciphered. Both try to arrive at generally applicable psychological laws. Their methods correspond to the extent that it is the objective of each to extract more general patterns from the individual case. In Freud, this leads to a theory on psychic functioning, while in Proust it brings forth a psychologically sophisticated introspective novel with an occasional philosophical digression.

In addition to artistic subjects such as music, painting, and literature, Proust recounts a diversity of psychological issues. It strikes me that on many points Proust and Freud develop remarkably comparable insights. They both explore the way memory works, the world of dreams, the unconscious, associative thinking, coping with bereavement, jealousy, and the vicissitudes of love, such as sadism and masochism. Jealousy, in particular, (homosexual) love, and bereavement had never before or after been dealt with in such detail and with such psychological insight as in Proust.

Freud designs a method of treatment that consists of listening with the "third ear" when looking for the meanings behind the words. He tries to understand what his patients tell him, but also what they withhold, intentionally or not. He is a scientist who is looking for a coherent system within the phenomena. In so doing, he designs a completely new language for psychological phenomena for which there had been no vocabulary previously, resulting in an ever-revised theory. Proust, who also attempts to discover and interpret the hidden meaning of what appears to be the obvious, observes: "The function and the task of a writer are those of a translator",[8] in the sense of making comprehensible that which seems dark and incomprehensible or for which there is no vocabulary yet. Thus, just as in psychoanalysis, the reader is given a tool by which to decipher the code of her own psyche. While reading, an intense interaction between writer and reader is established, almost as that which happens between patient and analyst during treatment. The "transference" relationship between book and reader here, too, is complemented, as it were, by the "countertransference" in the sense of the reader's reaction to the book. She understands it in her own way and recognises her own story in it. This way, the reading of Proust may lead to a possible self-analysis. Proust formulates it thus:

> ... it would be inaccurate even to say that I thought of those who would read it as "my" readers. For it seems to me that they would

not be "my" readers but the readers of their own selves, my book
being merely a sort of magnifying glass [...] I would furnish them
with the means of reading what lay inside themselves.[9]

Both authors can be said to articulate the unravelling of the psyche in
a literary fashion. Had Freud, who received the Goethe prize because
of his literary style, been a novelist, he could hardly have given his collected works a better title than *Remembrance of Things Past*, while Proust
could easily have referred to his oeuvre as *Psychoanalysis*.

If we combine the various protagonists, *Remembrance* could be read
as the life story of one person examined from different angles. Ultimately, the childhood years and youth of the narrator lead to the experiences of the Baron de Charlus. The various protagonists can be seen
as different aspects of the narrator and thereby offer us insight into his
development and the origin of the perversions he describes. A case history can never provide us with the wealth of experience, the range of
feelings, the intensity of emotions, the complexity of relationships, and
the nuances of imaginative power that a true novelist with an analyt-
ical mind such as Proust's can bring us. The experience of two individuals in an analysis, the feelings of analysand and analyst that lead
to insights, is nowhere described as extensively as in the interaction
between the protagonists of this novel. Freud readily admits that the
artist has a great advantage over the scientist in exposing the psyche.[10]
And, regarding the "oceanic feeling" about connectedness to eternity
and the endlessness of the Cosmos, he writes: "It is not easy to deal
scientifically with feelings".[11] If the metapsychological terms that Freud
uses sound somewhat dated today, it is because he wants to emulate
the language and exactitude of the nineteenth-century natural sciences.
At the time, it was the only scientific language available to him. In his
case studies, he employs a much more direct language and a style that
contains nothing formal or distant and thus has an immediate appeal.

Both Proust and Freud are enormously intrigued by the psychology
of love,[12] which includes perversion and homosexuality. We are accustomed to giving love an exalted, romantic connotation without being
aware that ambivalence, and even hate and anger, also belong to the
domain of those feelings we tend to refer to as "love".

Moreover, love is essentially a product of personal development
and social environment. The form in which we experience love is also
determined by the culture in which we live and is transformed over the
course of history. Human longings are by nature extremely malleable

and only acquire their definitive form during the lengthy development from child to adult. We don't act according to our instinct; the forms our longings take are the result of constitution and experience. What and how we love also depend on the interactions with our first love objects and on the way in which we learned to love from our parents.

Thus, I do not use "love" in the conventional romantic connotation of the word, but as a more all-encompassing concept. Especially with perversion, we ought not to shrink from connecting hate and fear with love. Stoller actually posits that there can be no sexual excitement without phantasies in which hate plays a role.[13] Thus we can see how the concepts of love and perversion begin to overlap imperceptibly.

At the same time that Freud treats his patients, he also wants to test and illustrate his new ideas. According to him, the existing moralistic theories on perversion do not coincide with everyday clinical practice. For Proust, perversion and homosexuality seem very closely related to his personal life experiences. He draws material from these in order to write what he calls an "introspective novel" with occasional theoretical digressions, although "a work in which there are theories is like an object which still has its price tag on"[14].

For both Proust and Freud, self-analysis is the first step on the way to insight. The exploratory expedition begins with their own psyche.[15] Where love and its wanderings are concerned, sadism, masochism, and fetishism have their particular attention. Masochism is probably the most common and most puzzling perversion, while it also plays a role in all other forms of perversion. Not only is social life permeated with it, masochistic features also play a role in every neurosis.[16] Why do we torture, taunt, and humiliate the one we love? And, even more puzzling, how can you enjoy your own suffering? Proust writes about sadism and Freud about masochism, but they are driving at the same thing: sadomasochism. The contraction indicates that they are two sides of the same coin that tend to go together. Both Proust and Freud examine their own motives as well as those of other people. Their insights frequently correspond but their emphasis is different, and thus they complement each other.

Freud and Proust do not only seek hidden meanings. In plumbing the depths of the psyche, the passing of time and the course of the life story play a primary role for both.

Freud nurses the ambition of designing a scientific psychology. Having started out as a neurologist, he bases his theoretic model on the example of physiology and physics of his time. As he listens to himself and to his patients, he discovers the importance of psychic reality, the inner mind's theatre. Discovering inner reality is also the ambition of Proust. His specific sensitivity makes him able to expose the earliest, archaic experiences of the child with its mother. However, it would still be a long time before psychoanalysis was to discover the true importance of the very first years of life.

Proust describes the mother as the dominant influence in the young child's life, although he moves the events to a slightly older age. He describes the narrator in *Combray* as a child of about eight years old. In his earlier, more straightforwardly autobiographical, unpublished novel *Jean Santeuil*, the protagonist is younger. The feelings and experiences he depicts are those of the small child concealed inside an adult man.

Proust shows us a great deal of the unwholesome dyadic interaction with the mother, which excludes the father. The Oedipal triad hardly plays a role in Proust's writings, and therein he complements Freud seamlessly. Proust is the psychologist of perversion who is preoccupied with the mother–son dyad, while Freud pays more attention to the inner image of the symbolic father as Oedipal rival.

Proust discovers a different Oedipus complex at the same time as, but independent from, Freud.[17] Just like Freud, Proust does careful research in order to find commonly applicable patterns via the so-called details of life—such as slips of the tongue and other errors that have gone unnoticed. Just like Freud, he is particularly fascinated by involuntary memory. Well known is the story of the Madeleine (a French type of biscuit) that the narrator dips in his tea, the taste of which then brings back images from his youth. We have all had occasion to experience such smells and tastes that bring back memories of our childhood. Proust is the first to verbally articulate sensual perceptions and the feelings linked to them. This writer considers intuition without any intellectual processing to be as worthless as a writing style that fails to express the content with precision. No *art for art's sake* here. He detaches himself from what is the novelistic style of his time to the same extent that Freud distances himself from academic philosophy and psychology.

Proust makes a distinction between the conscious, voluntary memory that remembers facts and the involuntary memory that suddenly and unexpectedly announces itself. Like a scent that can resurrect a past experience. Without warning, we then relive that past very intensely and, by focusing on this sensual perception with the help of associations connected to it, we are able to retrieve memories into our consciousness. This spontaneous, not wilfully guided memory may be accompanied by feelings of great bliss. Reliving a sensual perception is capable of revealing the essence of a past experience. That past, pulled from the boundaries of time and space, not only brings greater joy than the event itself, it can also become the source of inspiration for a work of art.

Freud discovers that thinking in dreams follows different laws, characterised by "condensation" (whereby a single image or person may symbolise several situations or individuals) and "displacement" (whereby a character trait may have shifted from A to B from those that are in force during our waking life). Proust's involuntary memory roughly follows the same patterns as the thinking style of Freud's "primary process" that prevails in dreams. In both cases, the unconscious is revealed. Both dream-thinking and involuntary memory are timeless and are not governed by the laws of physical reality.

Proust's voluntary, consciously directed memory and Freud's "secondary-process" thinking also correspond. Both are governed by the laws of time, logic, and reality, contrary to what happens with involuntary memory and primary-process thinking.

Both involuntary memory and primary processes represent a "different" reality that, as a rule, is not accessible to consciousness. It concerns the personal psychic reality grounded in one's individual history. This is our "inner theatre" where imagination is autonomous and key figures from our past surface under different guises.[18] Only a contextual interpretation, whereby the individual life story is taken into account, can reveal its meaning. The perverse scenario is precisely such an inner theatre, a stage on which the various protagonists from the past come to play their respective roles.

Both Proust and Freud wonder how the involuntary, the primary-process thinking, can best be resuscitated. Both authors discover that it is in dreams and daydreams that the most appropriate gateway to the unconscious part of our psyche is to be found.

Combray, with which Proust's novel opens, begins with a description of how the narrator used to fall asleep and the visions that go along with it. Here Proust illustrates how during sleep, or in the psychic dusk between sleeping and being awake, the unconscious is more readily revealed than in an awake situation. As we dream, we regularly return to the years of our childhood. We wander through our parental home, see family members who are long dead back again, and satisfy our most childlike yearnings. Our forgotten past, of which we are presumably no longer conscious, reappears brightly and clearly before our mind's eye.

Like Freud, Proust believes that habit formation has an adverse effect on memory. When we unexpectedly leave our daily routine, we discover things about ourselves that we had thought were long forgotten. According to both Proust and Freud, the unconscious can more easily become conscious under unusual circumstances or via unanticipated sensual perceptions. Free association, while the individual lies on the analyst's couch, is part of this. Or for the first time in a long while nibbling on a Madeleine dipped in a cup of linden-blossom tea.

According to Proust and Freud, important memories of childhood never vanish. It merely seems that way because they are not freely accessible at every moment of the day. For Freud, inner conflict or trauma leads to suppression of memories. In Proust, on the other hand, the passing of time plays the principal part. That alone makes us into a different being than we used to be. We no longer understand our former self. Who still understands the passionate love for someone to whom we have become indifferent? Who remembers the fervent feeling that went along with it? The fact that all our experiences cannot be called upon at any given moment renders them unconscious. With this observation Proust arrives at an extraordinarily modern definition of conscious versus unconscious.[19]

"The intermittencies of the heart" Proust calls the sudden flashes of conscious realisation; the surfacing of quasi-forgotten memories or lost parts of ourselves, often as a result of a sensory sensation. Proust gives the example of the narrator suddenly weeping profusely a year after his grandmother is dead and buried because he sees her in his mind the way she was: sweet and caring. He feels unwell and only then does he realise she is really dead. Although he had spoken about her often, he never felt anything when he did so. Now, suddenly, in an accidental gesture that resembles the time when his beloved grandmother was consoling him during an asthma attack and helping him to undress, her image comes back to him.

Not only does Proust reveal how earlier memories, detached from time and space, can be experienced anew in the present, but also how discordant relationships from childhood are reactivated in later adult love relationships. Proust discovers "transference" at the same time as

Freud: he often compares his feelings for Albertine to those he used to have for his mother when he was a child. The latter is precisely what Freud achieves during an analysis and which he refers to as "transference neurosis". Thereby he means that old feelings for intimates, like parents or caregivers, are reactivated towards the therapist during analysis or psychotherapy. The analyst gratefully makes use of this repetition compulsion: the reliving of old feelings is his most important tool for effecting change.

Both Proust and Freud are in quest of the essence of our existence: what is it that drives us? Both are of the opinion that we are driven and guided not by conscious but by unconscious ideas and phantasies. It is a matter of feelings, longings, phantasies, and personal myths that are nurtured by our most individual life story.

Both Proust and Freud are fascinated with the vicissitudes of love. Proust mainly extols unhappy love, which in his opinion is a pleonasm, since we are bound to suffer anxieties around jealousy and loss. "*Il n'y a que des paradis perdus*": the only paradise is a lost paradise. It has only existed in our imagination. Essentially, Freud agrees with him: finding a love object is an attempt at finding the original love object, the mother again. Besides, "[…] something in the nature of the sexual instinct itself is unfavourable to the realization of complete satisfaction".[20]

They each acknowledge the necessity of strengthening the love stimulus in order to prevent it from being extinguished. For Proust's narrator, jealousy is the indispensable ingredient to generate excitement when in love. Marcel, or the narrator, locks up his beloved Albertine like a prisoner in his apartment so that she will not be able to fuel his already fierce jealousy any further. He feeds his imagination with heated phantasies about what she might have done, whom she might have encountered, if she were free.

According to Proust, we love only as long as we are jealous. To be sure, though jealousy is not the sole condition for love, it is definitely universal, as Freud agrees: "It can easily be shown that the psychical value of erotic needs is reduced as soon as their satisfaction becomes easy. An obstacle is required in order to heighten libido".[21]

Similarly, Freud reminds us of the importance of jealousy in "A special type of choice of object made by man".[22] For some men, a woman becomes attractive only when she belongs to another man. Women who stir up jealousy because they belong to another or are sluttish may become an obsession for precisely that reason. Not until he has grounds to be jealous does such a man's passion reach its height and the woman gain her full worth. Maintaining love relationships with these women can take such psychic energy that it undermines all other interests. According to Freud, all of this has to do with the infantile fixation on the mother, that is to say, the mother complex. Both the narrator and Swann are readily recognisable in this. After all, Swann, a kind of double of the narrator, suffers from a similar kind of inconsolable love as the latter does.

Actually, Proust is more preoccupied with envy, which is a more archaic feeling, than with jealousy. It's not the Oedipal rivalry that is at stake but rather Hamlet's "to be or not to be", a ruthless struggle of life and death.

The fear of not being the only and the most beloved one is central to the narrator throughout life; it is as central as it is to a small and helpless child, dependent on his caregiver for his survival in the dyadic or symbiotic early phase of life. Proust's work presents us with the phantasies of a young child in an adult man. A child that imagines himself magically disposing of his rivals. In perversion, such a world, with which everyone is somehow familiar, is an extremely lifelike, ever-present reality.

Erik, an adult man, is in a sadomasochistic relationship complete with the sexual rituals that go along with it. He cannot tolerate it when his therapist leaves on vacation. Although he habitually complains about everybody treating him badly, his usually passive attitude becomes negativistic and destructive. He, the victim, becomes reproachful and accusatory. Everything the therapist says is wrong now, nothing makes sense any more, treatment is totally pointless, he doesn't want to see anyone any more, and so on. There is no happy medium between being accommodating and fierce raging (repressed in therapy, overt at home) whereby he wants to smash everything and everyone within reach. When he does not receive enough attention, his jealousy, or rather envy, is boundless.

Proustian "love" is always closely linked with jealousy and therefore can only make one unhappy. The choice of a partner can, by definition, only be a bad choice, he writes. Love's paradox is that the one we cannot do without when we are in love is at the same time the very one who causes us the unbearable anxiety of losing her. What is essential in love relationships is dictated by everyone's past, such as a fierce dread in childhood of losing mother, or her love.

Proust describes in sombre tones that the desirability and loveliness of our beloved carries less weight than the reliving of what Freud calls "separation anxiety". For his part, Freud also mentions overrating the beloved, seeing her through rose-coloured glasses. Even more significant is the fact that our longings can never really be satisfied. Longing is infinite by nature since the first separation can never be undone again. The blissful symbiosis is based on an illusion.

Proust's almost exclusive interest in sadomasochistic love is most certainly familiar to Freud as well, as is clear when he writes: "The man almost always feels his respect for the woman acting as a restriction on his sexual activity, and only develops full potency when he is with a debased sexual object; and this in its turn is partly caused by the entrance of perverse components into his sexual aims, which he does not venture to satisfy with a woman he respects. He is assured of complete sexual pleasure only when he can devote himself unreservedly to obtaining satsifaction [...]".[23]

In my opinion, Proust rightly attributes perversion to conflicts and complicated, perverted interactions between parent and child. When the child feels forced to repress his longings, when he doesn't dare show fear, and cannot vent his rage about frustrations, when his mother shows him the opposite of what she truly feels, when she replaces tenderness with harshness, it is perverted love that leads to masochism and sadism and to pleasure by means of torturing and being tortured.

The sadomasochistic narrator, Proust says, has learned to connect desire and cruelty because he was a lonely child who was made to pay dearly for every smidgen of love and who feels guilty when he experiences pleasure or desire.

Like Freud, Proust shows us how sadism and masochism go hand in hand. An individual who feels that during his upbringing he was the victim of a strict morality and heartlessness can process this in his phantasy life and/or his sexual scenarios by taking on the role of executioner or victim.

The relationship between a cruel upbringing and criminal sadism is not the subject of this book. It is important to determine the similarities but, above all, the differences between psychopaths, torturers, and war criminals, on the one hand, and private perversions, on the other. The same cruel phantasies may be at the basis of either. However, perversions are usually innocent flights of ideas that cannot do any real harm. Furthermore, criminal sadists are not likely to seek treatment, nor are they motivated to examine how they came to commit their acts. They do not seek imaginary but rather very real power, whereas people with perversions are powerless and vulnerable instead.

There are two things we are quite certain of: first of all, that a cruel upbringing spawns cruelty; and, second, that perversions aren't necessarily the result of actual cruelty but rather of how the child experiences being treated. Projection of his own aggression can play a role in his perception of his parents. The deciding factor is not the parents' behaviour or the child's unconscious desires, but the way he has interpreted and experienced their treatment of him. Every child in the same family with the same parents has different perceptions of them and consequently has very different parents. Despite Jean-Jacques Rousseau's memory of being beaten as a child, masochists are rarely beaten by their parents in their childhood.[24]

A disrupted love relationship between parent and child is frequently the result of the projection of a parent's unconscious conflicts and the role in which he casts the child in his inner theatre. A father who thinks he sees his own hated father back again in his son may act harshly towards him. A mother who believes she recognises the mother she feared or hated in her daughter may be unable to love her.

It is certainly not true that in perversion, as is the case with psychopaths, conscience, or superego formation, is flawed. Perverse individuals often have a strong, even a very strict, superego, from which their inner theatre helps them to escape momentarily. Proust really suffers from his moral scruples and is afraid that his preoccupation with sadism requires justification.

What I learned from Proust

Without Proust, I would not have understood the more bizarre forms sexuality can take. Nor would I have been able to understand the subtleties of transference interactions and the hidden manipulations and the secret excitement one often encounters in people in therapy. Just like Freud, Proust is able to meticulously express what he observes in human interactions. He is a master in listening with the "third ear", in the interpretation of body language and reading facial expressions. For him, a single glance speaks volumes, a slight slip of the tongue tells him an entire story. He is a master in detecting concealments behind which secret phantasies and emotions are hidden.

Not only did male homosexuality and perversion become clearer to me after reading Proust, I gained a much better understanding of the intricacies of mother–daughter interactions, a subject brought by many of my female patients. As I reflected upon the complicated relationship some men maintain with their (inner) mother, it struck me that women can have exceedingly intricate relationships with their (inner) mother, without consequences for their gender identity.

Not only has the forming of the theory around perversion been hampered and delayed by the too rigidly conceived Oedipal model, devised with respect to male development; for a long time, the mother–daughter relationship, too, did not receive the attention it deserved.

Explicit sexual perversions are mostly a male affair, although a penchant for perverse scenarios and interactions is certainly not absent in women.[25] Traditionally, perversion has been connected with castration fear, which currently is interpreted in a wider sense. It involves feelings of powerlessness and fear of injury, applicable to both sexes. For men, this includes a threat to their potency and, consequently, a fear of women. Perversion in women expresses itself somewhat differently. They are less focused on the compulsive repetition of sexual acts as a form of reassurance. They often participate in the man's sexual scenarios, frequently while denying their own perverse desires. The dominatrix, *la dame sans merci*, and the whore with a whip are phenomena of all times.

While men regularly use sex as a solution to their problems, women regularly avoid sex to solve theirs. Detachment from the mother is of vital importance to the male child and much less necessary for the female. Some men never attain the Oedipal triangle but remain stuck in the preceding anal phase (if we even want to speak of phases rather than object relations, as is usual nowadays). Holding on to anality implies dwelling in a magical world where idealisation makes the unappealing appealing. A world in which a turd can stand for a penis or even a baby. The symbolic level that belongs to the Oedipal phase has not, or not completely, been attained. Anal sadism stems from a stage in which empathy for the love object does not yet count. Peter cannot stand the fact that his therapist is going on vacation. It makes him so angry that he has nothing further to say. He discontinues any meaningful interaction on the symbolic plane where therapy takes place. He becomes extremely concrete and wants to have it his way, end of story. Reality is to be bent to his will, just as a baby will continue to cry until its mother gives in. While he denies any dependency on his therapist, it is replaced by a peremptory attitude. Talking about the pain of interruption is not an option; he wants actions not words.

In contrast to what is the case in male development, the gender identity of women is not compromised by too close a connection with their mother. The girl can suffer from separation anxiety and fear of retribution when she chooses her own way of life and aspires to autonomy, but the psychological consequences are different. Women can experience a lack of autonomy and independence from their mother. Their sexual experience can suffer from inhibitions and qualms, such as "my pleasure will distress her", without their gender identity being affected. These same qualms are an ever-returning theme in Proust, detracting from his narrator's male functioning. He is trapped between his longing to explore his own sexuality and the pressure to relinquish his personal desires for the sake of his mother. It is a dilemma that many women will recognise. Among female problems, there often lies concealed a life-and-death battle with the mother and murderous phantasies *vis-à-vis* her, which I only really understood after reading Proust. This became one of the themes of my book *Electra versus Oedipus*.[26]

The unsuccessful struggle for independence combined with a longing to please the mother may play a role in male homosexuality, but especially in perversion where sexual identity is at stake.

Not until the last quarter of the twentieth century did it become clearer what it is that determines the development of gender identity. It was discovered that gender identity is irreversible once established. When the sex is incorrectly designated at birth, as with children whose genitals are not evident (hermaphroditism), the felt gender is no longer reversible after the second year.

In addition, the wish or expectation of the mother and/or the father with regard to the sexual identity of the child is strongly decisive in the latter's psychosexual development. It was discovered that a mother who wants a daughter instead of a son and treats her son like a girl plays a decisive role. He may become less sure about his gender identity and possibly even harbour the desire to be a woman, as is the case with transgender problems.

Furthermore, a distinction must be made between one's gender identity (which for homosexual men in no way means that they do not feel themselves to be male) and sexual orientation—preference for a partner of the same or the opposite sex—and, finally, the sexual role a person fulfils. A feminine man isn't necessarily a homosexual at all, and a virile man can be either homosexual or heterosexual. Gender is more than sexual identity; it also comprises the psychological significance that one's own sex has for every individual. Too close a bond with his mother image can threaten a man in his sexual identity. Masculinity is more difficult to acquire than femininity. Girls can continue to follow their mother as a model, while boys really have to avoid doing so if they wish to become a man. When regression and fusion with the mother are a threat, what will also be generated is fear of domineering phallic women. Thereby a man may tend to avoid female love objects altogether, or else he may attempt to combat his fear for the power of women through tricks such as perverse scenarios that help to protect his threatened sense of gender identity and potency from destruction.

When the symbolic father is totally absent from the child's inner world, his role and the difference between the sexes and the generations grow blurred.[27] In perversion, it is the phallus, the symbolic source of strength and power, that is missing or denigrated as a point of reference, whereby the symbolic order cannot, or only incompletely, come into being. Thus, we might need a new and more refined theory on perversion, since we now know more about the development of gender identity, thanks to the close observation and analysis of children.

Because of Freud's version of the Oedipus complex, it is my opinion that divergent male sexuality has remained mysterious for all too long. Proust's vision, where not the father but the mother is the core of the conflicts, offers better possibilities for insight into this matter.

Notes

1. Proust, M. (1981). *Remembrance of Things Past, Time Regained*, Vol. 3, pp. 1098–1099. New York: Random House.
2. Philip Kolb, the bearer of Proust's letters, verbally confirmed to me that Proust had never read anything by Freud, which, according to him, only makes their points of similarity all the more remarkable.
3. Freud, S. (1900a). *S. E. 4 and 5.*
4. See Ellenberger, H. (1970). *The Discovery of the Unconscious: The History and Evolution of Dynamic Psychology.* New York: Basic Books. The history of dynamic psychiatry in which France plays an important role and where the name Proust also appears. Proust and Freud were familiar with the work of Charcot. Proust's father and Freud were colleagues.

Adrien Proust wrote on hysteria just as Freud did in 1890. "Marcel Proust's work is of particular interest because its subtle analyses were not influenced by Freud and the other representatives of the new dynamic psychiatry" (p. 167).

5. Rivière, J. (1972). *Quelques progrès dans l'étude du coeur humain*. Paris: Librairie de France; Miller, M. (1956). *A Psychoanalytic Study of Marcel Proust*. Boston: Houghton Mifflin; Girard, R. (1978). Narcissism, demythified by Proust. In: A. Roland (Ed.), *Psychoanalysis, Creativity and Literature*. New York: Columbia University Press; Kristeva, J. (1994). *Le temps sensible*. Paris: Gallimard; Bowie, M. (1987). *Freud, Proust and Lacan: Theory as Fiction*. Cambridge: Cambridge University Press.

6. Halberstadt-Freud, H. C. (1999). Pertinence psychanalytique de Marcel Proust. Perversion et homosexualité: patricide ou matricide?, *Revue Française de Psychanalyse*, Vol. LXIII: 285–602.

7. Gay, P. (1987). *A Godless Jew*. New Haven: Yale University Press.

8. Proust, M., *Remembrance of Things Past, Time Regained*, Vol. 3, p. 926.

9. Freud, S. 1960. The Letters of Sigmund Freud, Selected and edited by Ernst L. Freud, transl. by Tania & James Stern, Basic Books, New York.

10. Freud, S. (1960). *Briefe 1873/1939*. Selected and re-edited by Ernst and Lucie Freud. Frankfurt am Main: S. Fischer Verlag GmbH. (See note 21 in the Introduction [Schnitzler].)

11. Freud, S. (1930a). *Civilisation and Its Discontents, S. E. 21*, pp. 59–149.

12. Proust was the first creative writer who dared to openly examine the negative feelings that play a role in love. In 1910, in *Contributions to the Theory of Love*, I, "A special type of choice of object made by men", Freud wrote: "Up till now we have left it to the creative writer to depict for us the 'necessary conditions for loving' which govern people's choice of object, and the way in which they bring the demands of their imagination into harmony with reality. The writer can indeed draw on certain qualities which fit them to carry out such a task; above all, on a sensitivity that enables him to preceive the hidden impulses in the minds of other people, and the courage to let his own unconscious speak. But there is one circumstance which lessens the evidential value of what he has to say. Writers are under the necessity to produce intellectual and aesthetic pleasure, as well as certain emotional effects. For this reason they cannot reproduce the stuff of reality unchanged, but must isolate portions of it, remove disturbing associations, tone down the whole and fill in what is missing. These are the privileges of what is known as 'poetic license.' Moreover they can show only slight interest in the origin and development of the mental states which they portray in their completed form. In consequence it becomes inevitable that science should concern itself with the same materials whose treatment

by artists has given enjoyment to mankind for thousands of years, though her touch must be clumsier and the yield of pleasure less. These observations will it may be hoped, serve to justify us in extending a strictly scientific treatment to the field of human love", *S. E. 11*, p. 165.
13. Stoller, R. (1979). *Sexual Excitement, Dynamics of Erotic Life*. New York: Pantheon Books. This book discusses—with her knowledge and approval—the perverse masturbation fantasies of Belle, who was in analysis with Stoller.
14. Proust, M., *Time Regained*, Vol. 3, p. 916.
15. Baudry, J. -L. (1984). *Proust, Freud et l'autre*. Paris: L'écrit du temps, Éditions de Minuit.
16. Kristeva, J. (1993). *Proust and the Sense of Time*. London: Faber and Faber. "The sadomasochism of Sodom and Gomorrah is the truth underlying eroticism and feeling and, on a deeper level, sadomasochism is the very bond that brings society together" (p. 13).
17. Zilboorg, G. (1939). Discovery of the Oedipus complex: episodes from Marcel Proust. *The Psychoanalytic Quarterly, 8*: 279–302. Zilboorg demonstrates how Proust and Freud discovered the Oedipus complex at the same time and gave it a different meaning.
18. McDougall, J. (1985). *Theaters of the Mind: Illusion and Truth on the Psychoanalytic Stage*. New York: Basic Books.
19. Proust, M., *Remembrance of Things Past, Cities of the Plain*, Vol. 2: "More than a year after her burial, because of the anachronims which so often prevents the calender of facts from corresponding to the calender of feelings—that I became conscious that she [my grandmother] was dead. [...] At any given moment our total soul has only a more or less fictitious value, in spite of the rich inventory of its assests, *for now some, now others are unrealisable*. [...] For with the perturbations of memory are linked the intermittancies of the heart. It is, no doubt, the existence of our body, which we may compare to a vase enclosing our spiritual nature, that induces us *to suppose that all our inner wealth, our past joys, all our sorrows, are perpetually in our possesion*. Perhaps it is equally inexact to suppose that they escape or return. In any case *if they remain within us, for most of the time it is in an unknown region where they are of no use to us, and where even the most ordinary are crowded out by memories of a different kind, which preclude any simultaneous occurrence of them in our consciousness*. But if the context of sensations in which they are preserved is recaptured, they acquire in turn the same power of expelling everything that is incompatible with them, of installing alone in us the self that origunally lived them" (pp. 783–784); "For as the dead exist only in us, it is ourselves that we strike without respite when we persist in recalling the blows that we have dealt them" (ibid., p. 786). Compare this with

Freud in "Mourning and Melancholia" (1917e). *S. E. 14*, pp. 237–259. The self-reproach of the grieving melancholic are reproaches directed at the love object, with whom he has identified after the loss suffered. The loss of the love object brings the ambivalence of the love relationship to the fore and via self-chastisement revenge is thus taken on the original love object.

20. Freud, S. (1912d). On the universal tendency to debasement in the sphere of love, in *Contributions to the Psychology of Love II, S. E. 11*, p. 188.

21. Freud, S. Ibid., *S. E. 11*, p. 187.

22. Freud, S. (1910h). *Contributions to the Theory of Love*, I, *S. E. 11*, pp. 163–177.

22. Freud, S., Ibid., *S. E. 11*, p. 185.

24. Rousseau, J. -J. (1914). *Les Confessions*, tome 1. Paris: Georges Crès.

25. Chasseguet-Smirgel, J., 1985. Creativity and Perversion, Ch.1. Free Association Books, London. See also Françoise Dolto, Le cas Dominique. Editions du Seuil, Paris, 1971.

26. Freud, H. C. (2010). *Electra versus Oedipus*. London: Routledge.

27. Chassequet-Smirgel, J. (1985). *Creativity and Perversion*, ch. 1. London: Free Association Books. See also: Dolto, F. (1971). *Le cas Dominique*. Paris: Editions du Seuil.

CHAPTER TWO

Love's illusions

The whole problem of perversions consists in viewing how the child—in his relationship with his mother, a relationship established in the course of the analysis, not because of his dependence on her for his survival but because of her love, that is a dependence on the desire of her desire—identifies with the imaginary object of this desire, which the mother herself symbolises by the phallus. The phallocentrism produced by this dialectic is the only thing to be taken into account here.

—Jacques Lacan[1]

The world of illusion goes back to the earliest bond between mother and child, in which the child is able to imagine himself existing in an inextricable, symbiotic dyad with his mother. The baby doesn't yet realise that he is completely dependent upon his mother for survival, while the reverse does not apply to her. The awareness of this factual inequality is the first narcissistic blow the child is made to bear and must overcome.

Conversely, when the mother does need her child for her own psychic survival, they have an unhealthy relationship: a symmetrical symbiosis is a parasitical relationship, based on a mutual illusion.

As the examples of Margaret Mahler demonstrate, even in the average symbiotic phase of the baby, not everything is always equally smooth, and is far from idyllic.[2] The supposedly idyllic baby period does not unambiguously exist; from the very start, there are all kinds of frustrations, especially in less than harmonious families or with emotionally unstable parents. Mahler's examples clearly point out that problems can even set in as early as during the rapprochement crisis—the period between symbiosis and separation—in which the toddler distances himself with little steps from the mother, always looking back to her for her approval. During that phase, the child learns to experiment with distance and proximity, which can create discomfort even for the average mother–child pair. Some mothers cannot tolerate it when their toddler shows signs of independence and crawls away from her. She is sorry to let go of her child when he goes to bed. Such a mother keeps going back anxiously to see if her child is still breathing, is still alive. Some mothers have a hard time accepting that they aren't continuously indispensable. Unresolved problems during these first phases of life influence the Oedipal triad and everything that follows it. They shape the adolescent period and, in the end, the emotional state of the adult person.

The child's self-esteem is undermined by an unresolved symbiotic phase in which a mother attempts to satisfy her own narcissistic needs through her child. The mother of the narrator in Proust's work had her personal plans with him, which did not take her son's talents and wishes into account. Perverse interactions often consist of misplaced attempts at behaving the way the other would like you to behave, a kind of "mirror, mirror, on the wall" instead of authenticity. The child loses the ability to follow or recognise his own desires because he has to fulfil his mother's wishes in order to obtain her love. If she unconsciously wants her child to be sickly and therefore dependent on her, if the child senses that his or her sex is undesirable, or if a homosexual son is the mother's favourite, he will have a good chance of becoming what the mother craves for her own unconscious reasons. The earliest training ground of emotional life teaches the child how to manipulate others as well as himself in order to safeguard the satisfaction of his emotional needs.

Using my concept of the "symbiotic illusion", I will try to show how a two-sided dependency in the mother–child dyad can lead to perversion. For the sake of clarity, I will sketch this combined interplay in its most extreme form. The crumbling of the symbiotic phantasy after the first year of life is a difficult stage in every child's development, all the more so when the mother is incapable of supporting her child in relinquishing his megalomania and, instead, unconsciously conspires with him to maintain the delusion. If she needs the child so as not to feel desperate, lonely, or unloved, she will tend to treat him as a part of herself. A child is then going to function as an extension of her, as a projection screen, a toy, or a fetish of the mother. She cannot permit herself to see him as a separate individual with a will of his own. She therefore unconsciously reinforces him in the conviction that he is capable of satisfying all her needs, that he is even more important to her than her husband; indeed, that he is crucial to her emotional wellbeing. In this way, she seduces him and flatters his sense of self-worth.

She steps outside all the normal boundaries of a mother who is fond of her child. She will make him believe in an imaginary world, as if he were grown up enough to satisfy even her erotic needs. Thus, with the aid of his phantasy of being one with his mother, a child can overcome his unwelcome feelings of helplessness. Any form of separation is resolutely denied in this closed dyad between mother and son.

Max, a homosexual man, has difficulty acknowledging an approaching separation when his therapist is going on vacation. He is in denial about the interruption, which therefore always comes as a complete surprise to him. During such periods, he regularly develops a delusion, namely that he will be infected with AIDS, although this is impossible since he is not involved in any intimate contacts with anyone. In other words, the lost proximity of the therapist is being replaced by the imaginary intimacy with a partner, which will result in a life-threatening infection. That infection is then subsequently to be blamed on the therapist who has wilfully abandoned him, whereby he is tempted to hand himself over totally to others at random. He has to avoid this most dangerous temptation of losing himself, his independence, his personal integrity, by keeping his distance from the object, in which the delusion of infection assists him. At the core of his problem lies fear of closeness, which for him has always implied surrender to his mother. There was no confidentiality or real intimacy between them and yet, paradoxically, he did have a feeling of being one with her. This is what I encounter over and over again in such symbiotic relationships, which can exist in women as well as in men. There is no true intimacy, no exchange of feelings or thoughts, but rather an avoidance of these in order to steer clear of any conflicts. Being one with the mother is merely an illusion, sometimes coupled with conscious but unadmitted hostility and/or avoidance of her. Max lived in a symbiotic relationship with his mother and, because he was one with her, it was unthinkable that she would ever not be there. Even long after she had died, in his phantasy she was still there for him, and that way he never actually felt alone. After her death, he does not go through any grieving process. He totally denies both the imaginary dyad and the possibility of a separation. At the same time, his dependency is too great to be acknowledged, and it had never been necessary since his mother had always truly been there for him. Their relationship was quasi without conflict. Max has never expressed any criticism of her yet. She, in turn, idolised him, which flatters his vanity.

To make sure that the symbiotic illusion is not broken, hostility must be denied; a reversal of any trace of hate into love must take place. Only then can the "blissful" symbiosis with the mother, the indispensable dyad, flourish. The lack of freedom and the vast, unacknowledged dependency cause damage to the feeling of self-worth. This results in unconscious hostility and anger, which—in a perverse scenario—is expressed in the erotic form of hatred.[3]

One pays a high price for denial of the differences between mother and son, such as sexual difference and generational difference. It threatens the son's sexual identity, and expressing masculinity may become taboo. The child wants to please his seemingly omnipotent mother while, at the same time, this secretly makes him rancorous. He tries to satisfy her phantasies and wishes by adapting his behaviour to her. He tries to think and feel like her, adjust his preferences to hers. As is the case for Proust's narrator, he can do nothing better than show his mother how dependent, weak, and sickly he is.

Even the mother's death doesn't change anything in this false idyll because it is not the real mother but the inner, imaginary mother who monopolises the son's emotional life. "The law of the father", in Lacan's words, is not applicable here, exactly as in psychoses, where reality can be totally destroyed and normal rules are no longer valid. The difference with perversion lies in the fact that the loss of reality here is only partial and momentary.

Thanks to his mother's complicity, the son can create his own laws and, if necessary, transgress Oedipal norms and boundaries. His conscience does not prohibit him from offering himself as the object of his mother's desire to the exclusion of the father.[4] The perverse world of illusion is a Sadean universe where values are turned upside down and the law of the father, the Oedipal law, is for the most part excluded. Everyday shame—which is most definitely present in everyday circumstances—and feelings of guilt do not play a part in the perverse game, which is played by its own rules in a separate state of consciousness. "I enter a different world where I have my partner, dressed in lacy underwear, beat my penis with a whip until I reach orgasm", says Tom. Feelings become distorted or perverted, certainly in phantasy if not in reality. The illusion of being large, potent, and powerful, albeit with the aid of indispensable, perverse scenarios, is intended to protect the subject from fear—fear of either being swallowed up by the powerful mother figure or of destroying her. One or the other will succumb in the case of conflict.

The closed mother–child dyad is more readily developed when a mother has not detached herself from her own mother. She then runs the risk of choosing a man who is just as weak as her father. As a result, she will continue to need protection from her intrusive inner mother image. Unconsciously, she sees her male child as a helper for, and guardian of, her sense of self-esteem. We can picture her (unconscious) phantasy about him as follows: "If he demonstrates his love for me, it means that I am a good mother"; "I can be proud of him as a part of myself, and I therefore have a right to exist"; "I hate him when he goes his own way, becomes independent from me, needs me no longer, abandons me"; "He hates me because I prevent him from functioning apart from me, so I have to bribe him, claim him, demand his attention, cause him to feel guilty, make him responsible for my well-being. Anything to keep him close to me. But I can't show that I need him, instead of which he must get the feeling that he can't survive without me."

This situation finds its counterpart in the unconscious phantasy of the child: "When I show that I want to be independent, my mother hates me"; "I'm better off just remaining a small, dependent, needy child"; "She only loves me when I need her, she gives me her love on the condition that I prove I cannot do without her"; "I have to show that I agree with everything she wants or thinks, that I feel the same as she does, and have no opinions of my own". In other words: "I am threatened with abandonment and destruction if I don't have the ability to satisfy my mother's desires."

John is a striking example of the symbiotic illusion whereby conflicts between mother and son are avoided. He has never rebelled against her influence; he remains in a position where he must please her. That is why he is incapable of acquiring a separate identity and keeps yearning for confirmation. The uncomfortable feeling he is a failure brings him to me. Once he is in therapy, in his search for confirmation, he tries to please the therapist by behaving as her mirror.

John is a young married man, the father of three children, for whom fetishism and transvestitism have to be combined with family life. He is able to split his consciousness and live in two entirely different worlds. John says he is seeking treatment because of sexual problems with his wife (who is frigid) and regular episodes of transvestitism that disconcert him.

Through the splitting of the ego, two separate personalities are created that help to maintain irreconcilable realities. When he wears women's clothing, he imagines that he is a woman with a penis; in his usual everyday identity, he is a frightened, insecure man and his wife is the powerful woman. The two concepts of a woman with a penis and a woman without a penis can thus effortlessly coexist. Because of his transvestite episodes, John maintains a separate house, thereby attempting to keep his two lives apart as best he can.

At the same time, transvestitism is an appropriate metaphor for his personality: his entire existence could easily be described as a single, continuous role-playing. He is geared primarily towards manipulating anyone he meets in order to obtain confirmation or affirmation of his viewpoint. He is always worried about the impression he makes on other people. His wife has to repeat many times a day that she loves him, and when she utters any doubts he feels acute anxiety, but when she tells him what he wants to hear, he doesn't believe her. He is heavily preoccupied with what others think of him. He frets over how he can influence them so they will always assure him he's right. He fights a continuous battle to preserve his sense of self-worth and his male identity. He resembles a Don Quixote who must eliminate invisible adversaries in order to survive psychologically.

John tries as best he can to exclude his mother from his daily life, but where his inner reality is concerned, he is unable to do so. She continues to preoccupy him. He believes the world is filled with people who do not take him seriously and only seek affirmation of their own position. Thus it is his feeling that the entire world behaves like his mother. In this sense, everyone resembles the mother who never listens to him and always makes sure she gets her way. Every year she gives him the same Christmas present: socks that he thinks are ugly. He receives what he doesn't want, and what he wants he doesn't get. This is characteristic of perverted mother–child interactions, as is the fact that he never dares, or can, call her to account for this. He has to be grateful and thank her for things she wants to give and he doesn't want to receive. His wishes do not matter. His mother regularly delivers critical comments on the way he dresses, and often makes clothes for him, as well as for his wife and children—clothes they do not need and which they find atrocious. This is characteristic: clothing seems to occupy a special place in the phantasy of these mothers about their children. John tries to stay away from his mother as much as he can because standing up to her is impossible for him. When he asks her for something to drink at her birthday party, she answers him as if he were a child: "No, don't be impatient, you have to wait, you'll get some later." He cannot react because he is speechless and dumbfounded every time he is overruled.

John has always been a passive child, loved by his mother because he was so docile. He did everything she wanted him to do, think, believe, and feel. In the family, his weak father stood on the sidelines. He left the raising of the children primarily to his wife. Furthermore, he hardly plays any role in John's inner life and never has. Mother set the rules and, in all her narcissistic vulnerability (she might just have a nervous breakdown if you were to resist her), she was extremely domineering. By identifying with her and becoming a woman himself when he puts on women's clothes and, dressed this way, then masturbates, he can temporarily triumph over her. During those rare moments, he feels relaxed and sure of himself. But John is ashamed to come to me as a transvestite, and not until one of the last sessions does he dare to appear in this attire. In his everyday life, he feels depressed, tense, and lonely. He talks a lot but feels no real contact with me, and often I don't with him either, no matter how hard I try to reach him. When I broach this lack of reciprocity with him, he grows sad and helpless. He tries to say what I want to hear because he has no core self and a weak ego. He is an "as-if" personality who behaves more like a mirror and an echo than a partner and interlocutor.

The boy who must do without the necessary identification with the father, because of the latter's absence (in the child's inner world), may start to feel he is the object of the mother's desire, that he is a part of her. This family constellation apparently appears more frequently in homosexuality and is likewise typical of perversion.[5] A subtle and inscrutable mother–son interaction goes hand in hand with this, in which he constantly keeps trying to strike a bargain with her. The normal Oedipal development, where the father has a say and can interfere in case of an unhealthy intimacy between mother and child, is missing. The child realises early on that it is not his father but his mother who has power over him, and he imagines it is she, not the father, who possesses the symbolic phallus and is all-powerful.

The term "phallus" is used here to indicate power and potency, not in the sense of the penis as a physical body part. Men and women can both have phallic characteristics. When a son feels he lacks the phallic might, he stands a good chance of developing a fear of women and their power, a power that threatens to devour him. His dread includes the fusion, both desired and feared, with the love object that can destroy him. Instead of consciously fearing the vagina, John dreams of falling into a ravine. He would rather not be reminded that beings without a penis do exist, which would be a threat to his imaginary "unisex" world. Therefore, he creates a world in which both sexes have the same genitalia whereby fear of bodily harm can be avoided.

When individuation and identity development are thwarted, there are consequences for a person's self-esteem. It makes one helpless, desperate, and lonely. Just as in the dream, a sexual scenario that renders fears harmless and makes wishes come true may bring relief. It is a manic defence against feelings of depression, by means of a phantasy scenario where the subject is triumphant and, moreover, feels superior compared to people with a "normal, boring, ordinary" sex life.

In the previously mentioned mother–son relationships, the child experiences the mother as someone who asks for more than he is able to give without becoming untrue to himself. The son finds himself in a quandary when he has to relinquish his individuality to be one with his mother in order to deserve her love. Involuntarily, these mothers are involved in double-play: on the one hand, they seduce their son; on the other hand, when it suits them, they turn into the wife of their husband. That way, they undermine the son's sense of self-worth.

The symbiotic illusion doesn't necessarily exist exclusively with regard to the mother. At times, there is a father–son symbiosis. Mario had a mother who was paralysed because of polio and a father who kept him as close as he possibly could, probably needing him for solace and support. They never spoke together about the frustration of having an invalid mother and wife; anger or protest of the son against his father or mother was utterly unthinkable. Most girls with anorexia suffer from an excessively involved and intrusive mother. But occasionally, there is one who has a more than usually intimate bond with an overanxious or intrusive father. One of my anorexia patients had a father, a gynaecologist, who wanted to do the internal examination of his daughter himself.

"*Le désir de l'homme est le désir de l'autre*", writes Lacan ("Human longing is to fulfil the longing of the other"). Although not rare, a mirror-like existence in which a person can only be that which the other wants him to be, is pre-eminently true in perversion where it concerns mother and son. Donald Winnicott, the famous English paediatrician and psychoanalyst, invented the term "false self" for pleasing and mirroring the other.[6] The core of the personality, the individual with his own wishes and desires, can be entirely absent. The unresolved continuation of the child's early relationship with his mother, without an (inner) father to protect him from fusion with her, can produce psychotic fear. Perversion may serve as a defence against emotional breakdown. In his work, Proust illustrates the genesis of the fears from which the narrator suffers and he connects them to the mother–son relationship.

Perversion serves to guard the emotional equilibrium. In that sense, it is a defence mechanism that helps to prevent a breakthrough of fear. Without this creation, the individual might disintegrate, lose his points of reference, in short become psychotic. The perverse scenario makes use of various mechanisms. One of these is the splitting of the ego: what holds true for one part of consciousness is not valid in a different compartment of the mind. Triangulation, where father, mother, and son occupy their respective positions, has not been successfully achieved. Genital sexuality has not been firmly established. The anal world that replaces the phallic one is idealised, as occurs in Sade. Everything in Sade has to do with filth and excrement, but, instead of being dirty and putrid, it is on the contrary marvellous and exciting.

Splitting up reality helps the individual to endure it: "woman has a penis" is both true and untrue. The child does not give up his phantasy of omnipotence. "I can choose which sex I want to be, I am both sexes simultaneously", whereby the narcissistic insult of being limited and belonging to only one sex at a time is denied. The feelings of omnipotence during the perverse act serve as a defence against feelings of helplessness, hopelessness, and emptiness in a narcissistically vulnerable personality.

We need to imagine an individual who feels threatened in his psychological survival, something that entails narcissistic vulnerability and a weak gender identity; an individual who needs to struggle with destructive longings and archaic fears. He does so with the aid of a sexual ritual that has a fixed, extremely idiosyncratic scenario. Each time he feels he is emotionally in danger, he feels compulsively driven to perform a magical or phantasised act, by means of which he can escape from his fear of destruction, disintegration, and loss of identity.

Perversion enables him to sexualise aggression, particularly the fear of his own aggression, as well as fear in general, instead of succumbing to it psychologically as happens in psychosis. Through the creative magic of the imagination, everything dangerous instead turns erotically coloured and thus exciting.

Both Proust and Freud emphasise the strong connection between feelings of guilt and the development of sadomasochism, the most frequently recurrent form of perversion, both in moral and erotic form. Freud makes the link between an unconscious need for punishment and masochism. Proust writes about insurmountable guilt feelings. The exceedingly docile, polite, and obedient child (his Mlle Venteuil, for example, see Chapter Six), represses her rage and jealousy because she feels guilty about it.[7] Sadistic phantasies are denied access to consciousness by being changed into masochism. The latter will eventually take control over sexual life or lead to moral masochism. These feelings of guilt do not refer to "the superego, the heir of the Oedipus complex", as Freud's theory demands. In perversion, that stage is not, or only incompletely, reached. Guilt and fear are far more archaic in nature: phantasised destruction of the self or the other through jealousy and murderous rage. I repeat: in perversion, physical and psychological survival are both at stake.

In Proust's work, perversion is very narrowly intertwined with homosexuality. Although homosexuality and perversion are most definitely not synonymous—if only because heterosexuality can also be coupled with sadomasochistic or fetishist sexual scenarios—it is a fact that they quite frequently appear together. Proust sheds light on the problems that are a result of this combination through the Baron de Charlus, who is both homosexual and a masochist.

Proust seeks to analyse sadism, which is obviously a psychological mystery he wants to clarify. Perversion teaches us that one's own cruelty and destructiveness can come back to oneself like a boomerang.

There are advantages in projecting that destructiveness onto the other. Consequently, the other will be experienced as a sadist. Uncontrollable problems in the individual's regulation of his aggression can become manageable by giving them free rein in a compulsive sexual ritual. That way, split off from consciousness, they can be denied and rendered powerless. Sacher-Masoch makes his wife Wanda, "Venus in fur", beat him as if he were her victim. But not before he first gave her extremely detailed instructions about the correct amount and the manner of abuse that are essential for his gratification.

Perversion clarifies that the mother–child relationship, which unfolds there, is paradigmatic for women as well. My insight into the unresolved symbiotic bond between mothers and daughters, which I encounter on a regular basis in female patients, came to the fore only after studying male perversion. To be sure, female development doesn't very readily lead to perversion as the result of a similar symbiotic illusion, but a lack of separation and individuation certainly has negative consequences for her and her offspring as well.

Although sexual perversion is primarily a male phenomenon—the equivalent of the drag queen does not exist in women—moral masochism appears more frequently in women. The difference between men and women has to do, among other things, with the difference in the mother–child relationship. Mothers have fewer erotic longings where daughters are concerned and are more frequently seductive with sons. Obviously, the sexual difference plays a role in the attraction of the child for the mother. In Proust, we can read very extensively what such a distorted mother–son relationship looks like. Women can have a distorted relationship with their mother as well, which can lead to all sorts of complications, as described in my book *Electra versus Oedipus*. Of course, sexual perversion appears in women, too—one need only think of the lady with the whip in SM clubs. In addition, she fulfils her role as a participant in heterosexual male practices. To what extent she finds this pleasurable, or how willingly she does so, has not been sufficiently researched yet.

The frustrations and hostility that are engendered in the earliest dependent phases of life are expressed in a great variety of ways, of which perversion is only one.

A child can feel herself to be the victim of her parent, from which a preference for moral masochism then develops. Every one of us is occasionally engaged in sadism or experiences it, albeit usually in non-sexual ways. This may vary from straightforward cruelty to a more-or-less innocent form of teasing. The relationship between partners can have a perverse character in a sexual way, but it can also display a morally sadomasochistic interaction. It is easily noticeable in everyday life that people do not only make others suffer but themselves as well. This does not mean, however, that it is easily understood psychologically.

Moral sadomasochism, that is to say, psychological dependency and tyranny, appears much more frequently in the work of both Proust and Freud than the sexual variant. Moral masochism is more or less part of every neurosis in which fate can play the role of a sadistic partner. Moral and sexual masochism can appear simultaneously in one and the same individual. Several perversions do in fact frequently appear together in one person. For instance, a masochist can be a fetishist, a transvestite, and a voyeur all at the same time. The psychological splitting of the mind enables a person to live in two wholly separate mental worlds. In addition to the perverse world where everything is topsy-turvy, reality continues to be valid as well. That this ability is quite normal can be seen in the exalted situation commonly known as being in love. The most thriving and successful people may show a very different picture in their private life. Their perversion may be helpful in packaging problems so that they can continue to function satisfactorily. According to Freud, the child is in origin "polymorphously" perverse. Perversion is a normal phase in every child's development before mature sexuality sets in. This view, currently expanded, for the first time in history made insight in perversion possible, making it comprehensible instead of morally reprehensible.

Notes

1. Cited by Janine Chasseguet-Smirgel, in *Creativity and Perversion* (1985). London: Free Association Books, p. 85.
2. Mahler, M. S., Pine, F. & Bergmann, A. (1975). *The Psychological Birth of the Human Infant: Symbiosis and Individuation*. London: Hutchinson. Mahler and co-workers were the first to do empirical research in the development of very young children, beginning with the symbiotic first phase. Mahler describes the various sub-phases of the separation–individuation process. The first is the period when the child still feels more or less one with the mother. Then, around fifteen months, he discovers that his mother can manage without him. She is a separate person and the child needs her. His initial narcissistic delight in being

the centre of the world is over. He recognises his powerlessness, and the dyad has been broken. Negativism makes its entrance. Feelings of depression, anger, and fits of rage are the result. The fear of strangers returns.

The toddler then has a tendency to split his love objects; the good and evil mother, almost as two separate individuals. This is when language development sets in, around the same time as toilet training. Gender identity is formed and sexual difference is discovered. Step by small step, the child experiments with moving away from mother, and on this crucial development a great deal depends. Will experimenting with independence be successful or does the mother find that threatening?

A rapprochement crisis may develop that will remain an unresolved conflict. Approval and disapproval become extremely significant, ambivalence raises its head, and anger is suppressed in order for the child to be loved.

3. Stoller, R. (1976). *Perversion: The Erotic Form of Hatred*. New York: Harvester Press/Random House.

4. Rosolato, G. (1967). Etude des Perversions sexuelles à partir du fétich-isme. In: *Le désir et la perversion*. Collection dirigée par Jacques Lacan. Paris: Éditions du Seuil.

5. Friedman, R. C. (1988). *Male Homosexuality: A Contemporary Psychoana-lytic Perspective*. New Haven: Yale University Press.

6. Winnicott, D. W. (1972). Ego distortion in terms of true and false self. In: *The Maturational Processes and the Facilitating Environment* (pp. 140–152). London: Hogarth. The article originally appeared in 1960.

7. Although the personal life of Marcel Proust is not the subject of research here, it is interesting to learn something about his symbiotic relation-ship with his mother from his correspondence with her. (See Proust, *Selected Letters 1880–1903*, Ed. Philip Kolb. London: Collins, 1983.)

On 22 October 1896, when he is twenty-five years old, he writes to his mother (salutation: "My dear little Mama") that he is so depressed because of thirty francs he has lost. It makes him feel so guilty towards her that he is considering suicide.

On 6 December 1902, at the age of thirty-one, he writes to her that he cries every night because he finds his mother's attitude so incompre-hensible. He was feeling so nervous because of her that he burst into a rage at a friend and threatened to beat him with his fists. He tram-ples on the latter's new hat and rips it apart. He was so angry with his mother and his father that he no longer knew what he was doing. He proves it by sending his mother a piece of the silk lining of the tram-pled hat. The fact was that his mother had forbidden the servants to listen to his orders any longer: "You seem to think you're pleasing the servants and punishing me at the same time when you put me under interdict and tell them not to come when I ring or wait me at the table, etc. You're very much mistaken." "You know what a keen psychologist I am and what flair I have, and I assure you that you are quite wrong." "What afflicts me—though in my present distress these petty quarrels leave me indifferent—is not finding the moral comfort I thought I could expect from you in these truly desperate hours." (The maid had been told not to light the fire for him any more, and his mother had threatened to fire her if she were not to heed that order.) "The truth is that as soon as I feel better, the life that makes me feel better exasperates you and you demolish everything until I feel ill again. This isn't the first time. I caught cold last night; if it turns to asthma, which it's sure to do in the present state of affairs, I have no doubt that you'll be good to me again. But it's sad, not being able to have affection and health at the same time" (p. 281).

On 9 March 1903, at the age of thirty-two, he writes:

"My dear little Mama, Even with a mother's keen inverse prescience, you couldn't have devised a more untimely means than your letter of nipping in the bud the triple reform which was supposed to go into effect the day after my last dinner out. [...] But you should have realised that if I had any intention of changing it was enough to say: 'change or you'll be deprived of your dinner', for me to immediately abandon all thought of doing so—thus showing myself to be not frivolous and capricious but serious and reasonable. [...] As for the dinner itself, to which you refer with so much delicacy as a dinner for cocottes, [...] I cannot do otherwise and the importance to me [...] outweighs the damage the bankruptcy into which it will throw me can do. For I shall inevitably give the dinner at a restaurant, since you refuse to give it here. And I am under no illusion: though you say you are not trying to punish me for giving it in a restaurant, you will not provide me with a sum equivalent to what it would cost to give it here. [...] Calmette for one, is as important to me as Lyon-Caen to Papa, or Robert's chief to him. The disorder you complain of does not stop you from giving dinners they desire. And the state I happen to be in does not stop me, however ill, from attending those dinners when the day arrives. So you won't easily make me believe that this isn't punishment, since what's possible for them becomes impossible for me. [...] So I fail to see why such dinners, which are possible when they are useful to Papa or Robert, and for which I have never withheld my cooperation, though harder for me to give in the state of my health than yours is for you, become impossible when they would be useful to me. Or rather I understand, but my interpretation is different from yours. [...] I remember telling you, early in December, when you complained of my intellectual inactivity, that you were really too impossible, that confronted with my veritable resurrection, instead of admiring it and loving what had made it possible, you insisted on my starting to work at once. But I complied and took up just the work you wished. [...] and I did manage, crushing as it was for me, to attend Robert's wedding. All this isn't enough for you, or rather it's nothing to you, and you'll continue to disapprove of everything I do until I fall ill again. [...] I won't get much pleasure [...] thanks to you [...] But I don't aspire to pleasure. I gave up hope of that long ago. Instead of sleeping just now, I write to you and I'm racked. [...] You can't do me any positive good, and you're not on the way to learning how. [...] I would like to live in separate quarters. [...] [but] I resign myself to life as it is. I can't deny that the unhappiness of my life provides me with a good deal of philosophy. [...] I do my best to please you. I can't say the same for you. [...] but I'm not reproaching you, I ask you only to stop writing me ......

A thousand loving kisses,
Marcel" (pp. 309–312).

CHAPTER THREE

The fateful goodnight kiss

Everything in the sphere of this first attachment to the mother seemed to me so difficult to grasp in analysis—so grey with age and shadowy and almost impossible to revivify—that it was as if it had succumbed to an especially inexorable repression.

—Sigmund Freud[1]

The well-known episode of the goodnight kiss[2] in *Remembrance of Things Past* deserves our particular attention. It lies at the core of the narrator's later development. Proust comes back to this episode over and over again to explain how the narrator's love life came to be perverted.

Not only does the episode tell us how the child suffers because he experiences the way he is treated by his parents as cruel. This episode also explains how the child gets even with his mother by in turn rendering her powerless, too. The only way he can soften his mother is by relinquishing his individuality for a symbiosis with her.

This crucial episode seems to have the function of a "screen memory", an image behind which a similar, older memory lies hidden.[3] The goodnight kiss episode represents previous, comparable but forgotten painful memories, and symbolises the desperate need for the mother's love. The narrator, a frightened little boy, is sent to bed by himself without his mother's customary goodnight kiss and the ritual that goes with it. In an early small novel, *La confession d'une jeune fille* (The confession of a young girl), Proust already explains how a mother abstains from giving love to her child, fearing she will spoil him too much. When the child shows that he needs a bedtime ritual including a goodnight kiss, his mother will deliberately withhold it from him. He has not deserved this extraordinary favour because he is resisting her iron will.

And yet Proust repeatedly excuses the mother's uncompromising attitude towards the narrator: she acts this way because she cares about the child's wellbeing and she only wants what's best for him. He must be toughened up, he must become a real man instead of the weak, feminine child that he is. The father's irritability and lack of sensitivity, or the inadvertent cruelty of the paternal grandfather, are brought in as explanation and excuse for the mother sticking to her guns. If there's anyone who deserves criticism, it surely is the son, who, by behaving in a way of which she disapproves, is hurting his mother. She cannot be seen as someone who wrongs her child and is hard or cruel. The image of a blissful pact between mother and son must remain intact. The only reason that the intimate bliss between the two of them is not attained is because the father, depicted as coarse and insensitive, wouldn't tolerate it. This father can hardly be called a threat in the sense of the Oedipal rival. He is more of a spoilsport who is to be kept outside the beatific mother–child dyad. Mother and son have to be able to play their ill-fated little games without being disturbed, games the father, in his naïveté, doesn't understand at all. Mother applies a regime that involves withholding love alternating with compliance, on the condition of her son's complete surrender to her demands. The unpredictability of this regime binds the child to his mother all the more. It contains the promise that he is his mother's most cherished companion, and it suggests that mother and father share less intimacy with each other than mother and son do.

The implicit message is this: if father were not there, mother would be loyal only to him. (When fathers are physically or emotionally absent, such a pact only becomes more unbreakable.) Thus she seduces him, although she must also reject him on a regular basis when reality intervenes in the guise of father. Then the illusion is briefly interrupted. After all, she is married and has to satisfy her husband as well.

Ultimately, the little boy is not an adult man and cannot satisfy her in all respects. The romance between mother and son is above all a product of phantasy, based on an illusion.

Proust safeguards mother and grandmother from any suspicion that they might want to frustrate the child Marcel on purpose, even if involuntarily. It is not out of maliciousness that the mother perverts her son and ties him to her as much as possible. These mothers do so because they badly need their child as support for their own psychic survival. Proust never explicitly states that the mother ties the narrator more closely to her by denying him the satisfaction of his personal desires, although he shows time and again that she demonstrates her love and consideration to him only on the condition of his being sick and in despair. Yet, the narrator keeps up the definition of his mother as good and pure like a sacred Madonna. That she can also be extremely domineering and intrusive, that she tries to impose her will, is repeatedly excused. Hatred and aggression, or even mere ambivalence, are not tolerated in a symbiotic illusion, or a peaceful unity, as Proust calls it. The narrator can't do without the customary bedtime ritual: it protects him from his violent, indefinable fears. But when his parents are dining with guests, he is sent upstairs by himself. His father is embarrassed in front of the guest (Swann) about the demonstrative scenes with the kisses and hugs with both parents that the narrator so much craves before going to bed. On the evening in question, father sends the boy to bed by himself and mother withholds the goodnight kiss for which he yearns. It is not mother or father whom he calls cruel, but the "hated stairs" to his room. Going to bed alone throws him into profound despair, and he tries to master his fears with the aid of all sorts of compulsive bedtime rituals. However, this event will not be without consequences, it is the key episode of the novel in which all subsequent developments are already contained. His childhood anxieties will pursue the narrator throughout his life.

> Once in my room I had to stop every loophole, to close the shutters, to dig my own grave as I turned down the bedclothes, to wrap myself in the shroud of my nightshirt.[4]

When he feels rejected by his mother, he falls victim to mortal fear. Every time he is separated from her, he misses her and feels it signifies his psychic destruction, his total annihilation. As regularly happens in

Remembrance of Things Past, the blame is shifted to the maid Françoise; the narrator's hate for the mother is projected onto the housekeeper.

> On the subject of things which might or might not be done she
> possessed a code at once imperious, abundant, subtle, and uncom-
> promising on points themselves imperceptible or irrelevant, which
> gave it a resemblance to those ancient laws which combine such
> cruel ordinances as the massacre of infants at the breast with pro-
> hibitions of exaggerated refinement against "seething the kid in his
> mother's milk", or "eating of the sinew which is upon the hollow
> of the thigh".[5]

Here Proust is citing some of the nutritional Mosaic laws, with which, thanks to his Jewish mother, he is apparently quite familiar. Here these irrational laws are an indirect reference to her rigidity and ruthlessness.

After long hesitation and an increasing fear of punishment, he nev-ertheless decides to have the maid Françoise ask his mother to come upstairs.

> My mother did not appear but, without the slightest consideration
> for my self-respect, told Françoise to tell me, in so many words:
> "There is no answer."[6]

When little Marcel hears this, he feels like a rejected lover who can't admit that there is no further hope. And some time later, when he calls for his mother again, he fears that he's done for. He will be severely punished, maybe even sent away from home, and that thought imme-diately makes him even more desperate. His mother decides to keep him waiting, letting him dwell in uppermost uncertainty. That peda-gogical approach works like a double-edged sword: on the one hand, it makes him more persistent, while, on the other, it causes him to be even more dependent on her. She deliberately goes to bed later than usual and pretends to her husband that she isn't sleepy yet because of the cof-fee she had. In the end, when his mother comes upstairs and he sees her barely suppressed anger, the child is struck with dread. He is terrified of displeasing her and in an attempt to soften her heart, he lapses into a scene that is as vehement as it is pathetic in its misery and helplessness. Thus he demonstrates the suffocating dependency that she implicitly demands of him, making it clear that he surrenders to her. Mother refers to father's authority and to his irritation as the reason she is forcing her son "to behave". Father is used as bogeyman.

The scene that father is expected to make does not ensue. Although he never shows his feelings, it turns out that he has a more tender heart than mother. He warns his wife in words that go something like this: "What have you gained if you make the boy sick by refusing to take him to bed (he suffers from asthma)? You'd do better to spend the night with him; go ahead and comfort him now."

When at last his mother comes upstairs and sees him standing there in such a state, she doesn't immediately understand what's going on:

> Then her face assumed an expresion of anger. She said not a single word to me; and indeed I used to go for days on end without being spoken to, for far more venial offences than this.[7]

The narrator, who is dying a thousand deaths and hoping for deliverance, finally falls sobbing into his mother's arms. This is his unhappiest childhood memory, which will determine his subsequent love life.

> A similar anguish had been the bane of Swann's life for many years, [...] the anguish that comes from knowing that the creature one adores is in some place of enjoyment where oneself is not and cannot follow—to him that anguish came through love, to which it is in a sense predestined, by which it will be seized upon and exploited; but when, as had befallen me, it possesses one's soul before love has yet entered into one's life, then it must drift, awaiting love's coming, vague and free, without precise attachment, at the disposal of one sentiment today, of another tomorrow, of filial piety or affection for a friend.[8]

Here, Proust gives a perfect description of what we psychoanalysts commonly refer to as transference: earlier feelings for the parents are re-experienced *vis-à-vis* the beloved or, during treatment, the analyst.

The narrator's relationship to his mother, who will disastrously determine the course of his love life, is manifestly ambivalent. She is both cruel and indulgent, she promises and denies, and never shows any unconditional affection unless it is as a concession to his despair. When he repeatedly asked his mother to come upstairs to kiss him goodnight, this is what runs through his head:

> I was well aware that I had placed myself in a position than
> which none could be counted upon to involve me in graver con-
> sequences at my parents' hands; consequences far graver indeed,
> than a stranger would have imagined, and such as (he would have
> thought) could follow only some really shameful misdemeanour.
> But in the upbringing which they had given me faults were not
> classified in the same order as in that of other children.

After all, the most severe punishment usually follows:

> Yet I could easily recognise this class of transgressions by the
> anguish of mind which preceded as well as by the rigour of the
> punishment which followed them; and I knew that what I had
> just done was in the same category as certain other sins for which
> I had been severely punished, though infinitely more serious than
> they. I should not be allowed to stay in the house a day longer,
> I should be packed off the next morning ... had I been obliged, ...
> to hurl myself out of the window, I should still have preferred
> such a fate.[9]

Every time he shows his need for consolation, his mother complies with
his wishes and whims, on the one hand, while she is very angry with
him, on the other. Her rage and contempt for weakness terrify him to
such an extent that he needs all the more comfort from the very one
who threatens him with separation and loss of love.

His mother never means what she professes, but rather its opposite.
When she is stern with him, he senses she is forcing herself into this
attitude. When she is comforting, he senses her suppressed rage. This
is a characteristic attitude for the interaction between a mother and the
weak asthmatic child the narrator is: stimulating non-verbal dependency and passivity, but expecting verbal masculinity, and always having the one accompany the other so that an insoluble double bind is
created. In either case, any true satisfaction is out of the question. Marcel
develops shortness of breath and in such situations full-blown asthma
attacks generally follow. One already perceives the perverse relationship between mother and child that the son will transfer to the sadomasochistic relationships with his partners later on. Indeed, he never
manages to see the world in a different light: not only does every love
relationship display a sadomasochistic character, but so do all relationships Proust describes.

The narrator believes he has had an extremely miserable childhood. His parents were hard on him; precisely because he was a nervous child, they chose to give him a Spartan upbringing. He was severely punished, especially for weakness, sadness, and fearfulness, while, at the same time, a nervous breakdown was the only thing that could bring his mother to pamper him and show him her love. She is always afraid of spoiling him and so, we are told, she steels herself and avoids ever showing him her true feelings. This seems to be a rationalisation for her coldness towards him when he does not comply and her rejection of him when he doesn't do what she wants. When he doesn't act like the son she wants him to be and has the nerve to do what he desires, she unconditionally drops him.

She must conceal the negative pole of her ambivalence towards her son, just as she hides her love, unless he behaves according to her rules. In her attitude, mother is Victorian, physical functions are shamefacedly obscured, sexuality doesn't exist, and the body can only be given attention when it is sick and needy.

The narrator believes his upbringing differs from that of other children in that it is far stricter and includes serious punishments for minor transgressions of the rules of masculinity that his mother imposes. Although cruelty is always attributed to father, this turns out to be untrue; while Marcel expects his mother to reject him completely under the assumption this happens on his father's orders, in reality it is father who takes his side and requests mother to spend the night with their child. Father is inconsistent in his approach; he can be softhearted, although more often he tends to be insensitive. Even though he can scare the daylights out of people with his outbursts of rage, he is actually more vacillating and inconsistent than his wife, whose iron principles he does not share. As so frequently happens, she can use her husband as bogeyman while she plays the role of the timid wife. Mother protests father's words in ways like this: "We shouldn't let the child make a habit of this, after all." And father: "Who's talking about habits? Can't you see the boy is miserable, we aren't bullies, in the end! You'll just make him ill if you keep this up."

Once adult, the narrator's feelings do not change; he is still the frightened child who fears separation from and rejection by his mother.

> But of late I have been increasingly able to catch, if I listen attentively, the sound of the sobs which I had the strength to control in my father's presence, and which broke out only when I found myself alone with Mamma. In reality their echo has never ceased.[10]

He can be brief about his father, whose intentions are fairly transparent and simple, not at all distorted but consistent with his feelings. He is not complicated (perverse) as is the mother with her topsy-turvy utterances:

> Mamma spent that night in my room: when I had just committed a sin so deadly that I expected to be banished from the household, my parents gave me a far greater concession than I could ever have won as the reward of a good deed. [...] And perhaps even what I called his severity, when he sent me off to bed, deserved that title less than my mother's or my grandmother's attitude, for his nature, which in some respects differed more than theirs from my own, had probably prevented him from realising until then how wretched I was every evening, something which my mother and my grandmother knew well; but they loved me enough to be unwilling to spare me that suffering, which they hoped to teach me to overcome, so as to reduce my nervous sensibility and to strengthen my will.[11]

To mother, giving in means letting go of her pedagogical strategies and treating her son permanently as a weak and neurotic boy. The story takes place in an era when little was understood yet about child psychology. Thus far nobody had heard of basic trust and separation anxiety, and children were supposed to be deterred from their erroneous tendencies with inflexibility and sternness. Understanding the child's soul had to wait for researchers like John Bowlby and Anna Freud. In her War Nurseries after the Second World War, the latter welcomed and observed children who had lost or were separated from their parents. In Proust's time, children were raised on the basis of principles, laws, rules, and religious precepts. Their personality was not yet appreciably taken into account. This demonstrates what a gifted psychologist Proust was: he writes as no one had done before him about the intimate emotional perception of a child in relationship to his mother, true to life, subtly, without theorising.

At this fateful moment in the narrator's life, the future relationship with his mother is sealed forever when she gives in to his despair. For the rest of his life, he will have to be sick, desperate, or completely helpless if he wants to get anything done from his mother, or later on from his lover.

And thus for the first time my unhappiness was regarded no longer
as a punishable offence but as an involuntary ailment which had
been officially recognised, a nervous codition for which I was in no
way responsible: I had the consolation of no longer having to mingle
apprehensive scruples with the bitterness of my tears; I could weep
henceforth without sin. [...] I ought to have been happy; I was not.
It struck me that my mother had just made a first concession which
must have been painful to her, that it was a first abdication on her
part from the ideal she had formed for me, and that for the first
time she who was so brave had to confess herself beaten. (Notice
the word choice: "beating" is the pre-eminent key in *La Recherche*
in the various sexual phantasies and games that Proust passes in
review.) It struck me that if I had just won a victory it was over
her, that I had succeeded, as sickness or sorrow or age might have
succeeded, in relaxing her will, in undermining her judgement; ...
her anger would have saddened me less than this new gentleness,
unknown to my childhood experience.[12]

He feels guilty about this Pyrrhic victory that hurts his mother once she
decides to yield to his wishes hereafter. This silent pact will make her
prematurely wrinkled and grey because her son's pleasure is her sorrow and her sorrow is his pleasure.

This thought redoubled my sobs, and when I saw that Mamma,
who had never allowed herself to indulge in any undue emotion
with me, was suddenly overcome by my tears and had to struggle
to keep back her own.[13]

The narrator identifies excessively with his mother and feels guilty
when he imposes his wishes at her expense. Giving in to feelings is
taboo in the narrator's family and is considered to be inappropriate
emotionalism. This rigidity leads to the withdrawal of love: endless
days of angry silence towards the narrator, not allowing him to go outside when he wants to, or threats of sending him off to boarding school.
The greatest of all sins, as he discovers in puberty, is masturbation and
giving in to homoerotic tendencies. Disapproval is expressed through
indirect hints, for sexual themes cannot be discussed openly. To the
narrator's mother, mentioning sexuality in any direct sense is totally
inappropriate. As a nineteenth-century woman, she shows her disapproval of this only indirectly.

But the narrator is not wholly under his mother's spell. He has a secret life of his own that consists primarily of harbouring the most amazing masturbatory phantasies. When the family spends the summer in Combray, he surreptitiously retires to the humid, ivy-covered toilet to satisfy himself on the sly, as Proust describes in veiled terms. That is how he attempts to keep his sexuality under his own control. Mamma does not consider her son's body as his private domain but rather as the battleground between the two of them and as the source of his anxiety. He is not supposed to touch his body, let alone play homosexual games with his friends; his body and its functions must be disciplined and curtailed.

In the nineteenth century, homosexuality, nervousness, and perversion were associated with degenerate physical traits and faulty inheritance. Masturbation was the great taboo of the nineteenth century. It was then still generally assumed that masturbation could lead to death due to a "weakening of the spine", a medical term of the time that is as cherished as it is meaningless. A fanatic crusade against masturbation took place, which can be seen in the upbringing of the narrator as well.[14] Withholding the goodnight kiss and struggling not to give in to improper tendencies are only the beginning of the emotional and physical discipline that is aimed against spontaneous expressions of sexuality.

After the goodnight kiss episode, mother decides to abandon her attempts at raising her son according to her strict moral norms and principles. She agrees to abdicate her throne like a queen. From now on, she will comply with her son's whims. From now on, he is allowed to ask for tender care when he feels ill and weak. This signifies that he is to pay a high price for her love, namely renouncing his independence, even his health. Moreover, he is henceforth condemned to feel guilty because he is spoiling his mother's dreams for his future. Hereafter, her growing old and grey, and even her death, are his fault. After this episode, and for the rest of his life, he will feel the culpability of a would-be mother-murderer weigh heavily upon his shoulders. Matricide will continue to play a role in his sexual excitement, as we shall see. In order to feel aroused, he must momentarily escape from his mother's constraint. His mother has been vanquished by the narrator. From now on, she will be beaten, even murdered, at least in his phantasy, as a condition for his pleasure and erotic exploits.

However, besides the loss in this unwholesome pact, there are indirect advantages involved for both parties. For him, there is a secondary gain in being ill. He becomes powerful through his suffering. And for his mother, his sense of guilt gives her the right to demand docility. A sadomasochistic, exceedingly complicated interaction has been put into effect. Love, sickness, and guilt are forever soldered together. He has succeeded in driving his parents apart and keeping his mother for himself. But instead of the Oedipal rivalry with father, it is the passive dependency on mother that prevails. At the end of the complete novel cycle, Proust writes:

> Was not that evening when my mother had abdicated her authority, the evening from which dated, together with the slow death of my grandmother, the decline of my health and will? All these things had been decided in that moment when, no longer able to bear the prospect of waiting till morning to place my lips upon my mother's face.[15]

Finally, and out of sheer necessity, his mother tolerates not only his weakness of will, but she even turns a blind eye on his homosexuality, as Proust suggests between the lines. The narrator is burdened by guilt feelings around his sexuality because he can long only for that which hurts his mother. The compromise that mother and son together implicitly decide on is the bartering of loving care for illness and frailty. She is no longer overtly angry, although he sometimes perceives her quiet exasperation. He is grateful to his mother and usually suppresses his irritation when she minds his business. They continue their existence in a quasi-symbiotic illusion whereby ambivalence and anger are thwarted, suppressed, and exchanged for feelings of guilt. From this moment on, there is a pact at work that runs something like this: "As long as you won't show when you hate me, I will suppress my anger." This is the common, perverse bartering behind the feigned idyll between mother and son, from which the father is excluded.[16]

Thus mother and son can tranquilly continue their dyadic relationship. The law of the father has been removed, dividing lines between generations and genders fade, and mutual seduction is permitted. This pact allows no overt hostility from either side. All rage is methodically suppressed, turned upon the self, indulged through masochism, or projected onto an arbitrary third party. However, this is not the only source upon which the sense of victimisation feeds: from his earliest life on, the overly sensitive narrator already feels himself to be the passive victim of his parents. He has always felt helpless in the face of his mother's and grandmother's demands. His masochism is nourished by the fact that he feels dependent and defenceless towards a mother whom he experiences as sadistic. After all, she doesn't take the individual, personal needs of this oversensitive child into account, but only her image of him. His masochism is the result of an archaic rage that he turns onto himself because he is afraid to show his frustrating and frustrated mother any sign of hostility whatsoever. His fate as an aggression-inhibited man, in whom many men will recognise themselves, is sealed this way:

> My aching heart was soothed; I let myself be borne upon the current of this gentle night on which I had my mother by my side. I knew that such a night could not be repeated; that the strongest desire I had in the world, namely to keep my mother in my room through the sad hours of darkness, ran too much counter to general requirements and to the wishes of others for such a concession as had been granted me this evening to be anything but a rare and artificial exception. Tomorrow night my anguish would return and Mamma would not stay by my side.[17]

The pivotal example of masochistic sexual pleasure is exemplified by the Baron de Charlus, tied to a bed and beaten, in a male brothel, as we shall see later on. It is typical of masochism that enjoying intimacy, sexuality, or tenderness is taboo unless forced onto one. Only then is pleasure allowed without guilt feelings, namely by enjoying it helplessly, as it were. Hence all the masochistic games that must include bondage. Openly admitting desires and longings is seen as unforgivable weakness. Dependency is denied and being weak is considered life-threatening and thus can only be experienced by being forced. A goodnight kiss, wrested through blackmail from his mother and later from his partner, is the maximum in love and tenderness in which the narrator can indulge. Being sad and then being comforted by a mother substitute is what he eternally and insatiably yearns for.

Proust indicates over and over again that it is impossible to find in love the happiness and satisfaction that we seek. Love is like a vicious circle, broken through only when one's fear is calmed by the one who caused it: in the narrator's case that is the mother and later on his lover. Similarly, fear of loss of love is what tormented Swann, the narrator's alter-ego, during his unhappy amorous longing for Odette.

Showing tenderness is forever connected with fear of loss of love; asking for tenderness is linked to fear of punishment. Such fears can be resolved by ritualising them in a perverse scenario. Thereby, they are magically detoxified and transformed into part of the gratification, resulting in a feeling of triumph that leads to orgasm. The erstwhile victim ridicules and desecrates his mother by saying, as it were: "You want to punish me? Well, see how I enjoy my punishment and my suffering to the point of orgasm." That's how he strips the iron lady, the phallic mother, of her power.

Proust emphasises to what extent our childhood experiences with our parents or caretakers determine our subsequent (love) life. In this regard, he is in complete agreement with Sigmund Freud. Earlier love relationships leave their stamp on subsequent experience and—by the repetition compulsion—are transferred to it flawlessly. In Proust's narrator, we find the experiences of the boy who simply cannot separate himself from his mother, a mother who wants to realise her ideals through him and thus uses him for her own narcissistic purposes. In order to have pleasure, he must not only undo himself of her image but desecrate it as well and, in turn, use it for his enjoyment, which becomes synonymous with his revenge.

In my opinion, it seems less probable that perversion and sadomasochism are a defence against Oedipal aspirations, as Freud assumed. I believe that they are a defence against a demanding, assertive, and perverting parent, usually the mother, as Proust so aptly demonstrates. Hostility and accompanying guilt feelings, caused by forbidden hatred for the mother, must be forcefully warded off and driven from consciousness.

Perversion arises from a more primitive, earlier level of development than the object relationships of the Oedipal phase. The baby period, partially experienced as a symbiosis, the dyad between mother and child, which normally comes to an end by itself, can become a parasitical developmental stage that continues into adulthood. When the mother views her relationship with her partner as unsatisfying, it can lead to a warped triangular relationship. She misses the emotional and erotic fulfilment, which she will then seek in her child. In turn, he will be unable to imagine two loving parents with a satisfying sexual relationship. He cannot internalise an image in which the sexes and generations are clearly distinguishable because, after all, he seems to belong more to his mother than she to his father. Instead, the child will try to fulfil his mother's longings in order not to be rejected by her. If the mother cannot fulfil her feminine role in regard to the father, and the father doesn't occupy his rightful position with regard to mother and child, the difference between the sexes and the generations risks becoming blurred. The phantasy that many young children have of their power-ful mother not needing father because she is half man, a kind of phallic woman, remains intact. In Lacanian terms: if the child must symboli-cally stand for his mother's phallus, he himself cannot enter the phallic phase, and even less experience the usual Oedipal triangle. This for-mulation refers to a stereotypical relationship, which is the prototype of perversion.

This twisted development comes into being when the mother lacks the resources of narcissistic satisfaction—such as her husband, her work, her interests—other than laying claim to her child. Frequently these mothers are themselves still involved in a symbiotic union with their own mother, and consequently have not become truly independ-ent individuals. In extreme cases, all they know is a fused, barely dif-ferentiated existence. Under such circumstances, it is hard for mother and child to develop a separate psychic identity.

Finding ways by which to defend the integrity of the self is crucial. The feeling of being "your own boss, no one can tell me what I have to do or be" remains an ideal that is not attained in perversion. When a parent is experienced as intrusive and threatening to the personal integrity and identity of the child, a perversion such as the need to be beaten becomes more comprehensible; namely as an attempt to magi-cally turn what one has had to endure from passive suffering into active lust. It becomes an attempt to demarcate the ego and the non-ego, to separate oneself from the threatening other.

Differentiation of self and object is particularly precarious under cir-cumstances that are already regressive by nature, such as arousal and orgasm. In order to avoid the feared fusion with the object, the physical closeness has to be surrounded by appropriate security measures such as a previously fixed ritual.

The goodnight kiss episode is strongly reminiscent of the first period of life[18] as described by the American child analyst Margaret Mahler, but in the sense of a pathological symbiosis which cannot be concluded because of the mother's parasitical needs.

The narrator's feelings are the result of the way in which mother and child have dealt with one another. A young child still fears losing sight of his mother. When a mother doesn't support him by her approval of his independence, he becomes frightened and insecure, and this will leave its marks. That might happen during the so-called "rapprochement phase", the transitional period from symbiosis to greater self-sufficiency. The symbiotic phase may then not automatically come to a harmonious resolution. In pre-puberty, symbiotic features might repeat themselves. This can be recognised by a greater sensitivity in girls and greater unruliness in boys. During adolescence, the child must again, and this time more drastically, detach himself from his parents. Not only a repetition of, but also a second chance of correcting, whatever has gone awry during earliest childhood can take place. This second separation-individuation chance is not realised in case of perverse and other aborted developments towards independence.

In the described relationship between parents and child, the mother's attitude in particular is emphasised. She spends the majority of the time with her child, so that recriminations generally affect her. But it is clear that the narrator, an oversensitive child from birth, experienced his upbringing as especially painful because of his physical and mental hypersensitivity.

It is not the actions of the parents as such that are formative, but the way in which the child experiences them; the child develops an inner image of a parent that he carries with him for the rest of his life and that, objectively considered, does not have to coincide with the actual parent. Different children in the same family with the same parents experience these parents differently, and in fact have different parents.

The relationship between the narrator and Albertine will provide us with the opportunity to take a closer look at the bargaining and manipulation that take place between lovers.[19] We will encounter the relationship between parent and child from which subsequent intimate relationship patterns emanate many more times.

Notes

1. Freud, S., *S. E. 21*, p. 226.
2. This episode appears as a theme for the first time in "La confessions d'une jeune fille",in the 1896 collection *Les plaisirs et les jours* (Paris: Gallimard, 1971), when Proust was twenty-six years old. The theme returns in *Jean Santeuil* (Paris: Gallimard, 1954), the more or less failed novel of youth that Proust himself never published. Jean is seven years

old, he is a sickly child and, according to the doctor, his mother expects and demands too much of him. Jean is supposed to grow up to become a diplomat or magistrate, not an artist. She is just as uncompromising as her father, who is the boss and for whom she has greater respect than for her more lenient husband. This family constellation, in which the mother puts her own father, her ancestry, above her husband and consequently denigrates the latter, is not infrequent in homosexuality and/or perversion. *Jean Santeuil* is more openly autobiographical than *Remembrance of Things Past*, in which the sharp edges concerning the parents have been somewhat softened. Here the mother is cruel, she punishes his need for tenderness by making him ashamed, and her son suffers acutely from this. Proust reveals how important are the experiences of childhood and how they remain so for one's subsequent love life.

3. Freud, S. (1899a). Screen memories. *S. E. 3*, pp. 301–322.
4. Proust, M., *Remembrance of Things Past, Swann's Way*, Vol. 1, p. 30.
5. Proust, M., *Remembrance of Things Past, Swann's Way*, Vol. 1, p. 30.
6. Proust, M., *Remembrance of Things Past, Swann's Way*, Vol. 1, p. 34.
7. Proust, M., *Remembrance of Things Past, Swann's Way*, Vol. 1, p. 38.
8. Proust , M., *Remembrance of Things Past, Swann's Way*, Vol. 1, p. 33.
9. Proust, M., *Remembrance of Things Past, Swann's Way*, Vol. 1, pp. 35–36.
10. Proust, M., *Remembrance of Things Past, Swann's Way*, Vol. 1, p. 40.
11. Proust, M., *Remembrance of Things past, Swann's Way*, Vol. 1, p. 40.
12. Proust, M., *Remembrance of Things Past, Swann's Way*, Vol. 1, p. 41.
13. Proust, M., *Remembrance of Things Past, Swann's Way*, Vol. 1, pp. 41–42.
14. Schatzman, M. (1976). *Soul Murder: Persecution in the Family*. Harmondsworth: Penguin.
15. Proust, M., *Remembrance of Things Past, Time Regained*, Vol. 3, pp. 1102–1103.
16. In his book *Présentation de Sacher-Masoch, La Vénus à la Fourrure* (Paris: Éditions de Minuit, 1967), the French philosopher Gilles Deleuze supports my position and writes: "The father is excluded, he doesn't hide behind the role of the phallic mother, as psychoanalysis claims. He is denied and rendered powerless. The pre-oedipal mother must be seduced to a rebirth of the son without a father, compare Jesus Christ.
17. Proust, M., *Remembrance of Things Past, Swann's Way*, Vol. 1, p. 46.
18. Mahler, M. S., Pine, F. & Bergmann, A. (1975). *The Psychological Birth of the Human Infant: Symbiosis and Individuation*. London: Hutchinson.
19. Khan, M. M. R. (1979). *Alienation in Perversions*. London: Hogarth. Masud Khan discusses the *bartering* between mother and son.

CHAPTER FOUR

A new perspective on perversions

It is perhaps in connection precisely with the most repulsive perversions that the mental factor must be regarded as playing its largest part in the transformation of the sexual instinct. It is impossible to deny that in their case a piece of mental work has been performed which, in spite of its horrifying result, is the equivalent of an idealisation of the instinct. The omnipotence of love is perhaps never more strongly proved than in such of its aberrations as these. The highest and the lowest are always closest to each other in the sphere of sexuality: "From heaven, across the world, to hell" (Goethe, Faust).

—Sigmund Freud[1]

In order to develop a modern view of perversion, we need to go back a little into the history of the concept.

Before Freud created his theory of development, perversion was observed primarily from a moral point of view. It was behaviour that diverged from the religious norms and values then current. This centuries-old tradition is still present in that loaded word today.

For the first time, Freud makes the connection between normal sexual development and perversion. He discovers that the roots of sexuality

53

go back to the beginning of life. He considers man as an historic being with an individual developmental history. That personal story makes possible a totally new perspective where opinions around perversion are concerned. Since Freud, object relations theory has for the most part replaced the older drive theory he uses in order to explain perversion.

Freud still explains perversion as regression and fixation, as a being stuck in, or a return to, a previous, more comfortable, and therefore safer, developmental phase. He reasons that the love for the parent of the other sex, the Oedipus complex, is laden with guilt and can lead to fear of punishment. It leads to the boy's renunciation of rivalry with the father out of fear of retaliation, the so-called fear of castration.

In the later development of psychoanalysis, the emphasis not only falls increasingly on the earliest phases, but the relationships within the family gain greater importance. The child's psychological birth starts as soon as he comes into the world and develops in interaction with his environment. All the patterns that will determine his emotional life are laid down from the first days of life onwards. Today, perversion is seen more and more in terms of the earliest bond with the first love object, the mother, and the archaic fears that may be engendered with regard to her.

The beginning and the basis for classical psychoanalytic theory on perversion is Freud's epoch-making *Three Essays on the Theory of Sexuality* of 1905. In his vision on perversion, the Oedipus complex and the role of the father are central. But psychoanalysis is not a static, abstract science; on the contrary, there is a constant evolution at work, nourished by a hundred years of clinical practice. Quite a lot has changed since Freud. There is a growing interest in the role of the mother, whereas for Freud the father remains central. However, it appears that in perversion, the father is often excluded and devalued. His image and his role bear a greater resemblance to those of a disparaged figure than that of an Oedipal rival.

Due to the increased interest in the initial years of life, it has become clearer that the child's earliest experiences are strongest and have greatest impact. They form an indispensable blueprint for later relationships with intimates.

A homosexual man, Mark, is referred to me for psychoanalysis. He is feeling depressed and lonely. This is not that surprising considering his history as a sole surviving Jewish war orphan who lost his entire family, including father, mother, and sister. Before the war and before he had to hide out with strangers, his first few years with his parents seem to have been secure. So far his Oedipal development might have been undisturbed, as I suspect because of his later return to heterosexuality. After the war, he ended up in a foster family with a domineering foster mother for whom he felt fear and envy. She managed to monopolise all her husband's attention so that he felt there was nothing left for him. Mark craved the love of his foster father who was, however, far too busy with his own affairs, while his foster mother preferred her daughter, to whom he felt she gave preferential treatment. While, on the one hand, she bound Mark firmly to her own person, on the other, she constantly frustrated his need for love and tenderness. He would only be kissed goodnight if he had shown himself to be sufficiently docile and subservient to her wishes. His foster mother would only comfort Mark if he cried after a scene in which she had humiliated and punished him.

Mark and his male partner have a torturous rather than a loving relationship. They quarrel constantly and fight over who first shows his emotional needs: whoever takes the first step towards the other to ask for attention and love has lost the struggle for power. This way, they avoid making themselves vulnerable out of fear of rejection, from which each of them suffers. They compete over who is the best cook, for he is the one who can then order the other around as his helper. Both partners wait in vain for the other's praise and admiration: be it of his wonderful, large sex organ or of the small chores he does in the house. They rarely support each other but rather envy the other one's position as the most admired, just as Mark envied his foster mother whose husband showered her with presents. No wonder, then, that giving a birthday gift is an insuperable problem for him. Showing spontaneous feelings might make one vulnerable because it involves a higher risk of rejection. The one who first displays love and thoughtfulness is automatically the weaker one, the loser, and the other triumphs as a "prima donna". Having your fate in your own hands, anticipating rejection, is a prerequisite for these vulnerable men. Only thus can narcissistic blows be intercepted and warded off, leading, alas, to a sadomasochistic relationship.

Masochists prefer being attacked, prefer being victimised, to exposing themselves and openly displaying any yearnings for love and tenderness. They anticipate disappointment and are therefore often suspicious. Masochistic characters are quick to feel wronged. They are always on their guard for a phantasised rejection that they thus actually bring onto themselves.

Mark was a lonely man and when the relationship with his friend was over, he regularly frequented public urinals for anonymous sex. His problems originated in the phase when he lost his parents as a small boy and had to go into hiding. His parents loved him and, as the only son, he was the one who had to survive. So when offered a chance to save one child, they decided that he was the one to go into hiding. He landed successively with a whole series of families who provided hiding places. His analysis, one of my first, went rather well: he started his own business and, to my surprise, a few years after his psychoanalysis, Mark, who had had an occasional girlfriend, went back to being heterosexual and married a charming woman.

Let us return briefly to the beginning of life, to the baby. The baby forms a unity with the mother and initially experiences a symbiotic relationship with her. Gradually, the child discovers he is not one with the mother but a separate being. He sees his mother coming and going, experiences her absences, and learns to discern his own image in the mirror. If all goes well, a first separation and individuation are established. But because so much is happening in the earliest childhood years, a great deal can go wrong, too. A child's early development can already pursue aberrant paths. The possibly perverted interaction, generally with the first object, the mother, has a decisive influence on the way love relationships are experienced in later life. A child who is afraid to lose his mother can become a jealous and coercive lover later on, claiming constant attention. Proust's narrator Marcel interrogates Albertine about her presumed unfaithfulness at such lengths that it makes her desperate. Their intimacy comes down to sadomasochistic interactions that gradually degenerate into a fierce competition and struggle of wills. The issue is that of separation and loss, with a winner and a loser. This life-and-death struggle has to end in an act of lovemaking that serves as expiation.

Sexuality is anything but a simple, uncomplicated, and unambiguous expression of love. It can be in the service of assuaging all sorts of feelings and anxieties, such as fear of abandonment, or it can be a way of venting hostility. Sadomasochism, for one, can help in keeping fear of fusion and symbiosis at bay.

Erik, a divorced man, son of an extremely cool and aloof mother who is afraid of intimacy, regularly goes to sex clubs. There, he meets a woman who is his master in their sadomasochistic games. This woman becomes his new partner, a way for him to be sure of a partner with similar inclinations. She, like himself, needs elaborate sexual rituals as a condition for finding gratification.

Another patient of mine, Mariëlle, had an exceedingly seductive father who crossed the lines and involved her in all his intimacies. She falls in love, and it turns out that her new partner is someone who oversteps all boundaries. His paranoid jealousy reminds me of the way that the narrator in Proust suspects and interrogates his girlfriend Albertine. It appears that Mariëlle's friend becomes highly excited by spying on her, being suspicious of her, and accusing her, even calling her abusive names. Without this incentive, he is impotent. She recognises her sexually preoccupied father in his obsession, and for a long time finds her partner's behaviour reassuring rather than bizarre.

All these perverted emotional relationships serve to maintain the best possible psychic equilibrium. It is essential to know the life history of an individual in order to be able to understand and make sense of his or her sexual preferences.

Freud had a great interest in perversions from the very start. Masochism interested him because it seemed to contradict the "pleasure principle". Nietzsche already had put on his gravestone the words: *"Alle Lust will Ewigkeit, tiefe tiefe Ewigkeit"* (All pleasure wants eternity, deep, deep eternity). How then is it possible that we are so aggressive and destructive, not only towards those closest to us, our partners, but to ourselves as well? Does masochism issue forth from "inner-directed" sadism, or is it an independent, primary drive? We owe a number of speculative metapsychological studies to Freud's struggle with this problem, such as in *Beyond the Pleasure Principle*.[2] It is here that he develops the concepts of life and death instincts (drives), called Eros and Thanatos. After 1920, he assumes that masochism doesn't necessarily originate in sadism, as he had previously supposed, but that it is a primary drive. This death wish is a destructive force that can be aimed at the personal self as well.

Not until the end of his life does he return to the subject of perversion.[3] He discovers that "disavowal", the total rejection of a part of reality, is the most important defence mechanism of the fetishist. This amounts to the total denial of an apparently shocking part of reality, namely that the woman does not have a penis. Denial, creating a new personal reality, is a defence mechanism that today is seen as a characteristic of perversion in general.

Let us return briefly to Freud's libido theory. He draws attention not only to infantile sexuality, which he characterises as "polymorphous perverse", he advances the revolutionary idea that the "perverse" tendencies of small children form the basis for both normal and deviant adult sexuality. Small children visibly enjoy beating or pinching other children until one of them starts crying. The same behaviour in an adult would be considered sadistic. This also holds true for exhibitionism and voyeurism, which is totally normal behaviour in children.

Freud posits that in perversion a kind of pleasure fulfilment is indulged in that is precisely what is repressed in the case of neurosis. That is why he calls neurosis the negative/reverse of perversion. We now know that perverse sexual fulfilment, such as having your partner beat you in order to reach orgasm, does not in the least exclude repression in other spheres of life. Thus it is no longer tenable that in perversion everything is randomly expressed, which in neurosis has been repressed. Rather, the ritual sexual scenario is a defence mechanism, developed to help channel forbidden rage and repress undesirable feelings of fear and anxiety.

As stated: Freud considers that sexuality has an aim and an object. Both the aim, being the action, and the object chosen can vary and diverge enormously:

> Experience of the cases that are considered abnormal has shown us that in them the sexual instinct and the sexual object are merely soldered together [...]. We are thus warned to loosen the bond that exists in our thoughts between instinct and object. It seems probable that the sexual instinct is in the first instance independent of its object; nor is its origin likely to be due to its object's attractions.[4]

This quotation draws our attention to the endless versatility and variability of human sexuality. Not the biological but the psychological factors are decisive. Like Freud, Marcel Proust believes more in the power of the imagination than in the objective appeal of the love object. At the end of his love affair with Odette, he has Swann exclaim that he has wasted years of his life on a woman whom he didn't even find attractive.

Freud denotes homosexuality as "inversion", that is, a reversal of the preferred gender, certainly not as a perversion. Here we should emphasise once again that homosexuality neither implies perversion by definition, nor can it be equated with perversion, just as heterosexuality doesn't exclude perversion. Nevertheless, it is clear that homosexuals can have one or more forms of perversion in their repertory, as Proust's work demonstrates.

Tom, a homosexual man, only enjoys anonymous anal sex after being beaten, much like Proust's Baron de Charlus. He has always been afraid of irritating his guilt-provoking, complaining mother whom he can never please. His most important affective goal in life is to escape from her and from women in general. He derives sexual pleasure from what she would find most horrifying, and in that way he ridicules her and momentarily conquers his fear of her. Thus he can triumph, while at the same time enjoying the passivity and dependency that he cannot possibly allow himself in his normal existence.

For some mothers, it is not sufficient to be treated warmly, kindly, or in a friendly manner. These mothers, who are themselves narcissistically vulnerable and therefore easily offended, need proof that they are good mothers and will do anything to achieve this goal. Such a mother will ignore a warm gesture or the account of a success in which she plays no role. She handles manifestations of affection badly and will always ask for more. That is how she attempts to provide herself with the security and self-confidence she needs. If you refuse her something, she will—overtly or surreptitiously—continue to ask for it and make it clear to you, be it non-verbally, that she is disappointed in you. If you do not like a gift, she will be offended and will try to force it on you anyway. She will phone you and ask in a hurt voice whether you're still alive. When you visit her, she'll wonder why you didn't come any sooner. If you visit her regularly, she will still ask why you don't come more often. Inducing feelings of guilt has a prominent place in all of this. A mother who is afraid that her child doesn't love her will try to bind him to her through feelings of guilt. That which doesn't work voluntarily has to be obtained under duress, with the result that both parties feel they're being forced. She remains deaf to his wishes and tries to artificially strengthen her sense of self-worth while she makes her child just as insecure as she is herself.

This interaction is so frustrating that it engenders profound suffering and depression. The accompanying rage is repressed or displaced to a third party and generally remains for the most part unconscious. This is not the kind of mother to whom you can convey aggressive feelings. None of the individuals in my examples has ever been able to show her any overt criticism, let alone hostility. They never even considered resisting; none of them has gone through the normal rebellious phase of puberty. From early childhood onwards, all of them felt obliged to fulfil or endure the mostly unexpressed wishes of their mother. They are docile and their suppressed rage only very gradually appears during treatment in the transference relationship to the analyst. Then it comes out that they are continuously suspicious and are afraid of being taken for a ride. Masochism serves, as it were, to express: "I can only give free rein to my rage and only express my anger if I receive a serious beating, which I experience as lustful." This way the original feelings of rage and frustration become perverted and directed at the self. Powerlessness is thus converted into lust and triumph: "I am not in pain, on the contrary, I find pleasure in humiliation."

Every good, positive, and loving interaction risks being abused. A beating from the partner can help to escape from annexation, symbiosis, and fusion. It produces a symbolic separation where this had failed with the mother. Avoiding intimacy is a prerequisite for reaching orgasm. The danger of an emotional invasion is warded off by being oneself the initiator and stage-manager of the beating. In normal sexual relationships, passivity and tenderness serve a healthy regression, which is not possible for those who are afraid of fusing with the object.

A complex paradox in masochism goes as follows: "I am triumphant while I obey." Being intimate and loving with a partner, showing emotions, would signify perilous submissiveness and loss of control. Tom and his mother treat each other in a stereotypical manner, while neither of them shows their true feelings, but rather the opposite. When he visits her after a long trip, she doesn't welcome him, but says reproachfully: "Why didn't you come any sooner?" or "Here you are for a change. Why don't you come more often?" And when he leaves, she invariably comments: "Are you leaving already? I always only see you for such a short time." She ignores his homosexuality, allegedly knowing nothing about it. If something comes up that is taboo in her eyes, she wraps herself in a telling silence. She withdraws to the kitchen to cry and then sulks for hours on end. Their encounters are one long enactment of mutual manipulation. They frustrate each other and keep the other under control by painstakingly hiding both their tender and hateful feelings. Rage and destruction are floating in the air, while the symbiotic illusion of the "crown prince" and his mother is being protected like a pseudo-idyll.

What it comes down to is that Tom would rather be beaten by a stranger than seduced by his mother, and he is actually able to turn this event into gratification. Thus dependency and passivity may still be permissible by acting these feelings out in a safe ritual.

Both in homosexuality and heterosexuality, the attained level of object relations, that is to say the level at which love relationships are played out, is more decisive than the sex of the love object. The ability to love, the degree of empathy with the other, the possibility of having independence instead of fusion, are decisive. As Sartre writes about sadism in L'être et le néant[5] (Being and Nothingness), it is the hallmark of perversion to see the other as a thing instead of a person. Most modern authors consider this to be the core of perversion.[6] Sometimes desires are not directed at the whole person but at a part object, such as a breast or penis, that is to say, a form of fetishism. Heterosexual relationships are not exempt from perverse solutions; on the contrary, fear of the other sex can often render these rituals indispensable.

Peter, a married man, has his wife tie him down and whip him. She has to penetrate his anus with a dildo, after which she masturbates him until he reaches orgasm. He is afraid to be laughed at because of his weak potency and worries about a penis he considers too small. He rarely penetrates her for fear of impotence. He cannot attain orgasm via penetration, as it causes him to lose his erection. He would much rather just look at her vagina and then have his wife chastise and curse him, which is part of their ritual game. His fear centres around being devoured by her (vagina), while his secret hatred for his wife is balanced by his love for her. She reminds him too much of his mother. He is unable to vent his destructive phantasies about her and prefers to be her victim rather than the sadistic perpetrator. She has to humiliate him, she is the executioner who has to torture him, all according to his directions. That way, he is able to project his rage onto her, identify with her, and experience through her what he himself dare not express. She consents to his requests for a sadomasochistic sexual relationship, as her fear of men and of sexuality mirrors his problem and makes it comfortable for her to respond to his wishes.

This masochistic man has always been afraid of his mother. He feels she is disparaging towards him, she doesn't listen to him, or hears something different from what he says. She twists his words until they are in keeping with her wishes. His preferences don't count as she fails to see him as a separate person. She knows what he likes to eat but prefers treating him to something she likes. He can never win, in the sense that his mother has no respect for his identity and personal integrity. She demands proof of his love, and if he doesn't visit her often enough, she broods so insistently that he cannot help but feel guilty. Although in his forties, he is still afraid to be rejected by her. In the sexual ritual, the rejection is dramatised in the form of a game. The cunning of perversion is that it succeeds in turning sorrow and trauma into lust, solace, and triumph.

Taking fate in your own hands, changing fear to self-confidence even when it concerns a rejection, being a step ahead of disappointment, these are important motives in masochism: "I'm not afraid of you, your threats, or your punishments. I don't feel guilty. On the contrary, see how I'm enjoying myself and am having an orgasm from what should frighten me. You see, you can't hurt me at all!" By instructing his wife to command and beat him, Peter forces the threatening partner to obey him; at the same time, he proves to her that she has no hold over him. He need not fear rejection because that is precisely what he is asking for. He, his mother's only child, had to make up for her narcissistic vulnerability and lack in feelings of self-worth. Any sign of independence and autonomy, no matter how slight, is a highly dangerous threat to the narcissism of such a mother. The son's own self-image suffers from the symbiotic bond with her. Fathers of sons like these are no support; they don't intervene to protect them from the stifling bond with the mother. If, in addition, the father also conceals his weakness with outbursts of rage and causes the son to be afraid of him, it almost forces him into a passive and masochistic position.

Avoiding intimacy out of fear of being annexed is, as we have seen before, characteristic of perversion in general and of sadomasochism in particular.

In 1905, Freud still defines perversion based primarily on behaviour, such as sexual actions, and not yet on unconscious intentions. Neither does he make connections with family constellations or with the interaction between mother and child:

> Perversions are sexual activities which either (a) extend, in an anatomical sense, beyond the regions of the body that are dsigned for sexual union, or (b) linger over the intermediate relations to the sexual object which should normally be traversed rapidly on the path towards the final sexual aim.[7]

In other words, getting stuck in foreplay and not reaching the sex act, or only after stringent conditions have been met. Although Freud refers to heterosexual relations when discussing "normal adult sexuality", and this definition may contain a moralistic pitfall, his theory is a revolutionary new way of thinking about sexuality. It is clear that Freud is not yet thinking of a more specific personality structure, responsible for the phenomena seen in perversion. He simply defines perversion based on objective behaviour, which he links to various component instincts. These days, the concept of "drive" or "instinct" is of lesser concern to us, and particularly the "component instincts" have, for the most part, lost their meaning as explanation. As if a human being is composed of a set of drives that motivate him and determine his actions. As if a drive were a cause and behaviour a direct result thereof. In the interim, this way of thinking and conceptualising, which is so obviously nineteenth century, has become obsolete. The object relationships that are primarily scrutinised today don't occupy a major place in Freud's thinking yet. On the other hand, he did believe that too much narcissism, defined as "self-love", and too little object love can predestine an individual to homosexuality and/or perversion, and that the early bond with the mother has a great deal to do with both.[8] However, in his era, little was known yet about the development of gender identity,[9] or the importance of the separation-individuation phase during the first two years of life.[10]

Still, an important step forward is taken after Freud's *Three Essays* (1905d). From then on, perversion can no longer be considered simply as morally reprehensible. As early as 1905, Freud writes on fetishism:

> No other variation of the sexual instinct that borders on the pathological can lay so much claim to our interest as this one, such is the peculiarity of the phenomena to which it gives rise [...]. The point of contact with the normal is provided by the psychologically essential overvaluation of the sexual object [...]. A certain degree of fetishism is thus habitually present in normal love ... .[11]

In 1927, he returns to perversion, albeit only in passing, in two important articles, "Fetishism"[12] and "Splitting of the ego in the process of defence".[13]

The splitting does not occur, as with neurosis, between ego and id. By contrast, the person lives with two separate realities, alongside each other. One part denies the perception of reality, albeit unconsciously, while the other, conscious, part functions normally. This is not as strange as it may seem: one only needs to think of a grieving person who imagines she sees the deceased walking past in the street. In these two articles, denial and splitting—still of utmost importance for the understanding of perversion—were connected for the first time with fetishism:

> Probably no male human being is spared the fright of castration at the sight of a female genital. Why some people become homosexual as a consequence of that impression, while others fend it off by creating a fetish, and the great majority surmount it, we are frankly not able to explain.[14]

The little boy, contrary to his expectations that all beings have a penis like himself and fearful from having discovered that his mother does not have this organ, reacts with denial. He rejects the idea that women have no penis and, from that moment onwards, he recognises two separate and split realities at one and the same time.

Freud describes this mechanism of the splitting of the ego for the first time. The perception "a woman has no penis" is acknowledged by one part of the mind while, at the same time, it is denied (as is usual in little boys). In an unconscious part of the ego, the idea that "a woman has a penis" is still valid. This denial is an active but unconscious rejection of the unwanted reality of the difference between the sexes.

What remains of this infantile way of thinking is a more or less conscious disgust with the female sex organ, which according to Freud all men with perversions (and certainly not they alone) have in common. In the case of fetishism, a fetish is sometimes created to help deny reality. The fetish represents the missing penis and is thus a protection against fear or even threatening psychic disintegration, which could lead to psychosis. The fetish has far more meaning than Freud attributed to it by focusing especially on the fear of castration. Just like a stuffed animal or "blankie", a fetish is a transitional object. It helps in denying the absence of, separation from, and abandonment by, the mother, besides the lack of a penis. That which is missing is symbolically represented. With the aid of lacy and ruffled lingerie, the fetish can serve to mask the "terrifying" female genital and magically change it into something beautiful and aesthetic. The beloved becomes a "thing" over which you have power and that won't play unexpected dirty tricks on you. Insisting on having his partner dress up helps the fetishist to cover up an imaginary state of castration, ugliness, dirtiness, or anality, in order to turn it magically into something beautiful, the lady's slip as an idealised lady.[15] The mechanism of the consciousness splitting not only helps to explain fetishism but also renders psychotic delusions, whereby reality is also denied after all, more comprehensible.

When the little boy has grown into adulthood and still denies the difference between the sexes, he is using a mechanism that is characteristic not only of fetishism but of all forms of perversion. This attitude is illustrated by Hans, who has to look obsessively at women's shoes. He gets excited when he sees high heels, which undoubtedly serve as a substitute for the missing penis while, at the same time, he knows perfectly well the latter really isn't there. This idea, which provokes aversion, is banished by actively, even compulsively, looking for the missing body part, this time in the form of high heels. Others will do the same, but as a voyeur in a sauna, by admiring as many penises as possible, whereby the male sex organ itself becomes a fetish.

Denial of the differences between mother and child can be produced when the boy lives in very close connection with her while the father is excluded, so that the boy will start to identify too closely with the mother and with femininity instead of with his own sex. Denying the difference between the generations can become an additional source of confusion here. This occurs when the mother treats her son as a quasi-substitute-partner. The boy has to separate himself from his first object, the mother, in order to develop his male identity and become a man. He has to abandon his infantile tendencies towards his mother, although he might succeed in continuing those with the woman of his choice. But with her, he cannot limit himself to passivity. A man has to prove his masculinity; he has to show his potency and conquer his fear of impotence. Total denial of his feminine side would result in a lack of empathy and tenderness—and always wanting to be pampered and coddled by his wife will not work either.

The girl doesn't have the same problems. Her original infantile and dependent tendencies can continue to exist without great risk. She doesn't have to relinquish her feminine identity as the boy must do. Because the mother, a woman, happens to be the first love object for both sexes, and boys initially identify with her, they have to "de-identify" in order to acquire a male sexual identity. In that regard, the boy has a more difficult trajectory towards masculinity than the girl has to femininity.

In all likelihood, the development of homosexuality in women often goes back to the same unresolved, conflict-laden symbiosis, or rather the lack of it, with the mother. She accuses her mother of lack of love, which she seeks in another woman. This can happen when she feels she has missed the symbiotic gratification she craved as a child. Or else she might be looking for an uninterrupted continuation of this infantile gratification.

De-identification with, and separation from, the mother are rendered even more difficult when the father doesn't support his son and doesn't intervene between mother and child to resolve the symbiosis. When the son sees him as a threat, which is not uncommon in perversion, and/or as distant, this will be unfavourable to the development of his sexual identity. When he is not, or not sufficiently, available, there is no father image with whom to identify. When the child is made to serve the mother's emotional needs through a mutually experienced symbiosis between mother and child, we have to be concerned about the development of pathology. If the mother rejects or disapproves of men and has no internal mental picture of the father's role, she cannot communicate it to her son. This makes it more difficult for the little boy to imagine what masculinity consists of. His sense of self-worth is then weakened and he will not, or only insufficiently, reach the Symbolic stage, which coincides with the Oedipal phase. The first and most important precept, the incest taboo, mediated and symbolised by the father, does not apply to him. He will deny the (symbolic) castration (only achieved by renouncing the wish to take the place of the father). He will hold on to a deep-seated fear of castration (in the widest sense of fear of powerlessness) and of physical injury and will remain stuck in the imaginary omnipotence that he shares with his seductive mother.

This theoretical outline is a schematic representation of the issues, which offers a multitude of variations. In alternative lifestyles, where lesbian or male homosexual couples have or adopt a child, it is not necessarily the case that his or her gender identity will be affected. At least, as far as present understanding goes, very little effect on gender identity seems to be noticeable. The final outcome, namely male or female identity, is largely determined by the intrinsic development of the individual's sexuality. The father need not be physically present to have him represented in the inner experience of both mother and child.

A deceased father can still be very strongly represented in the mother's inner experience and thus in the child's as well. But if the mother, albeit unconsciously, denies the difference between the sexes and the man's role in procreation, she summons the imaginary world in which women are all-powerful creatures who can impregnate themselves without any intervention from a man. Thus, the mother can alternately seduce and reject her son endlessly as a substitute partner so that her position as a powerful phallic woman will remain untouched in his childish phantasy. The perverse world is a world in which signals are turned around, in which God and laws must be destroyed, as illustrated in De Sade's *Les 120 journées de Sodome*. Perversion, certainly sadism, is the erotic form of hatred.[16]

The child who lives in an unresolved symbiosis with his mother has to repress his feelings of hatred and fear. He has to support her by giving her the feeling that she is a good, even ideal, mother. Mothers who are unsure of themselves can be both overpowering and vulnerable. When her narcissistic wellbeing depends on her son, she will pervert him because he has to validate her through his passivity and submissiveness. He is afraid she will have a nervous breakdown should he contradict or oppose her. This makes her strong and weak at the same time, a combination that is confusing for a child.

The schematic picture of the development story outlined here will certainly not pertain to everyone. There are many roads that lead to Rome, and there are as many forms of perversion and homosexuality as there are heterosexual variants. Nevertheless, those to whom it applies may well recognise a few things in these generalisations.

I have focused on the relationship with the mother in particular, but other emphases are possible as well. Where homosexuality is concerned, the previously mentioned author Isay focuses exclusively on the father, although in his case representations he does mention a number of mothers who would fit my picture perfectly. However, he assumes that some male children have a natural disposition to direct themselves primarily to the father in order to receive his love instead of the mother's. According to Isay, this genesis of homosexuality is quite common and is not preceded by a conflict with the mother.

Some cases remain a mystery. A homosexual man, Derek, a farmer's son with a Calvinist upbringing, recounts that he has had very little love from his cool and extremely religious parents. Both his father and mother were distant people. In addition, his father didn't appreciate him as a future farmer. Derek was in psychoanalysis but continued to be hard to reach. He had a long-term relationship with a man, who did have the well-known intimate bond with his mother. He was present at all her naked and dress-up sessions and had to listen to all her complaints about her husband—his father—like a true mama's boy. Both men have since died of AIDS. Derek performed the terminal care of his friend, for whom he felt a great deal of compassion, with love and tenderness. In the transference relationship with his psychoanalyst, however, this narcissistic man continued to be cool and distant, almost haughty. He was as unapproachable as he was unassailable, and hostile in a repressed way, though he never openly expressed his feelings of hatred. Derek used to go to saunas and male brothels where he had himself fist-fucked or had blowjobs through a peephole without seeing or knowing the other man. He was a profoundly unhappy man who functioned beautifully at work, where he was highly cherished. He never succeeded in resolving his rage about the lack of love and appreciation in his youth. Certainly, Derek never had the kind of excessively intimate and seductive relationship with his mother that is under discussion here. It was more a matter of an eternal quest due to a lack of symbiosis than of an excess of pampering and seduction.

Notes

1. Freud, S. (1905d). *Three Essays on the Theory of Sexuality. S. E. 7*, p. 161.
2. Freud, S. (1920g). *S. E. 18*, pp. 7–67.
3. Freud, S. (1927e). Fetishism. *S. E. 21*, pp. 149–159.
4. Freud, S. (1905d). *Three Essays on the Theory of Sexuality. S. E. 7*, p. 148.
5. Sartre, J. -P. (1943). *L'être et le néant*. Ch. III. Paris: Gallimard.
6. Bach, S. (1994). *The Language of Perversion and the Language of Love*. New York: Jason Aronson.
7. Freud, S. (1905d). *Three Essays on the Theory of Sexuality. S. E. 7*, p. 150.
8. Freud, S. (1914c). On narcissism: an introduction. *S. E. 14*, pp. 67–105; (1910c). *Leonardo Da Vinci and a Memory of his Childhood. S. E. 11*, pp. 63–139.
9. Stoller, R. J. (1968). *Sex and Gender*. London: Hogarth.
10. Mahler, M. S., Pine, F. & Bergman, A. (1975). *The Psychological Birth of the Human Infant: Symbiosis and Individuation*. London: Hutchinson.
11. Freud, S. (1905d). *Three Essays on the Theory of Sexuality. S. E. 7*, pp. 153–154. See also J. Lacan & W. Granoff, "Fetishism: The Symbolic, The Imaginary and the Real" in *Perversion*, Eds. Sandor Lorand and

Michael Balint (London: Ortolan Press, 1956). In fetishism and other preversions, the subject has not sufficiently entered the symbolic order of language, law, and the Oedipal triangle. On the contrary, it remians in an imaginary world in which fear is stronger than guilt, and fear of castration takes the place of the symbolic castration (that means the perception of one's own inability, one's own imperfection and powerlessness). Lacan also makes it clear that in perversion, there is no question of an object in the real sense of the word. The love object is the subject him/herself that has remained stuck in the mirror phase of his/her development. He performs an auto-erotic game that is externalised with the aid of a quasi-object. Perversions are characterised by a form of circularity to which the other is not allowed any access.

12. Freud, S. (1927e). Fetishism. *S. E. 21*, pp. 149–159.
13. Freud, S. (1940e). Splitting of the ego in the process of defence. *S. E. 23*, pp. 271–279.
14. Freud, S. (1927e). Fetishism. *S. E. 21*, p. 154.
15. Tournier, M. (1983). The Fetishist. In: *The Fetishist and Other Stories*. London: Collins: "I realized that men could be some use too, that they too could have meaning" (p. 200). Tournier gives a touching description of the experiences of a fetishist. The protagonist marries, continues to collect underwear compulsively, which he snatches from laundry lines everywhere, suffers enormous fears, becoming psychotic in the end.
16. Stoller, R. (1976). *Perversion: The Erotic Form of Hatred*. New York: Harvester Press/Random House.

CHAPTER FIVE

A different adolescence

Unless we can understand these pathological forms of sexuality and can coordinate them with normal sexual life, we cannot understand normal sexuality either.

—Sigmund Freud[1]

... unmixed purity which mankind has never been able to find in pleasure since the First Sin ...

—Marcel Proust[2]

Instead of analysing the creative writer, there is much to be learned from him, as Freud already acknowledged in his correspondence with Arthur Schnitzler.[3]

The youngest of love's victims whom Proust describes in his youth is a sickly boy of about ten years old. He is in love with an older girl for whom he longs terribly in his phantasy.[4] In his disillusionment, he jumps from a window, after tormenting himself at length with the idea that his beloved is unattainable to him. This story heralds the themes of love, guilt, and death that would continue to play such a central role in Proust's work. Either you murder your mother by having a private love and sexual life without her permission, or you perish from fear, rage, and depression which are the result of love's frustrations, is roughly how Proust explains his basic view of love.

He offers marvellous examples of the torturous relationship between an adolescent and his parents. Sadomasochism reaches a climax during adolescence. Pleasure, and sexuality in particular, are strictly curbed in the narrator's youth, to such an extent that chasing after pleasure is changed into its opposite and becomes torture. But that is not the end of the story. The Jean in *Jean Santeuil* and the narrator in *Remembrance of Things Past* manage to magically alter the limitations imposed on them into forbidden pleasure and secret gratification. Via a mysterious mental process, discomfort is changed into lust and excitement. I derive the way this functions from the relationships that Proust's characters have with their parents, both in his earlier work and in his *chef d'oeuvre*. The author teaches us how feelings between parents and children become perverted. The narrator and his mother tend to feign the opposite of what they feel and really mean. Even before Proust truly became a writer, he had already fully analysed what it was that so confused him: the perverted interaction between parent and child, mainly mother and son, and how that is expressed in his love life.

The only distraction granted to the narrator as an adolescent is that of playing outside on the Champs-Élysées with a girl of whom he is especially fond.[5] He suffers from asthma, which his mother seizes as the reason for not allowing him to go outside any more. She claims that playing with the girl in question makes him just as unhealthily anxious and excited as the goodnight kiss used to do earlier on. She implies that it concerns undesirable sexual excitement, which makes him ill. He had better stay home with her, do his homework nicely, and be a good and obedient son. From the very start, neglecting his duties and wasting time, the reproach his mother makes, constantly play a role in this author's work. It will even provide him with the title of his great novel—*À la recherche du temps perdu*, *Remembrance of Things Past*.

A perfect example of the way in which the narrator is raised can be found in *Jean Santeuil*, Proust's early work. Jean's parents watch contentedly as he does his homework assignments. To his annoyance, they tell each other, full of self-satisfied pleasure, how diligently and obediently he is working. Thus they take away his own initiative, as if he were working solely to please his parents. The only way to escape from their judgement and coercion, which he experiences as humiliation, is to completely ignore their wishes. Only by disobeying and refusing to do his homework is he able to safeguard his free will and independence. Only by not submissively doing what his parents want can he hope to be his own master and escape from their definition of his persona, which infuriates him. Just as an angry daughter told her therapist: "The worst thing is when my mother wants the same thing as I do, for then it is as if she's taking my plan away from me and I don't feel like going on with it any longer."

When the narrator goes out again and a tickling game with his little girlfriend excites him to such an extent that he falls ill, there is the devil to pay. Jealous of his contacts outside the home, his mother demands that for her sake he give up his love for the girl. With her continuous pressure on her son, she can become sharp and ironic. When critical and sarcastic remarks don't have the desired result, she falls back on moral pressure and blackmail. His "nervousness" is no excuse for irritating his parents, she says. Nero, too, may have been nervous, but that doesn't make him any better.[6] When he doesn't knuckle under, she increases the pressure and blackmails him. She imposes more and more prohibitions on him, and when he resists she comments that it can't be that difficult to refrain from doing something for the sake of one's mother. "You're deeply hurting your mother, who loves you so much. If you really loved her, you'd abide by her wishes, which would come before anything, and you would never hurt her."

Internally, the narrator is spitting with fury and surreptitiously kicks the furniture. At that moment, he can only think of how much he hates his parents. But it doesn't take long for him to have remorse and then he feels all the more guilty.

In this intractable power struggle, the guilt feelings that mother and son are able to stir up in each other are the primary weapons. He blackmails her by falling ill, and she does the same through her distress and accusations. The one who suffers most wins. Until that battle is decided, mutual torment continues. Usually it ends with an idyllic reconciliation and the narrator yields in tears.

Their strictness, narrow-mindedness, and moralising attitude is proven by their condemnation of misalliances. Swann, their family friend, is married to the courtesan Odette, and although they do receive him, it is only under the tacit condition that he not speak about her. In their home, he acts as if he were unmarried and as if his daughter Gilberte does not exist. When he leaves, they take this comedy even further by discussing him as a pitiful bachelor who is heading for a shamefully lonely and abnormal old age.

So far, we have discussed the ambiance at home. But what about life at school for adolescents such as Jean Santeuil? Adolescents who are insecure and timid, who are in doubt about their sexual identity, feel quite differently from the ordinary schoolboy. This feeling of being different is described beautifully in several novels, among others in *Maurice* by E. M. Forster.[7]

Jean is uncertain about the impression he makes on others. His schoolmates hate him because he doesn't fit in with the peer group; they harass him and always pursue him after school; every boy is his enemy. He is a masochistic dandy who elicits negative attention and acts like a victim. He is so supersensitive, so excessively friendly, obsequious, and submissive just to be liked that he only exasperates his classmates. They think he is a hypocrite and ridicule him. His maladjusted behaviour and his contrite attitude display his tendency to ask for punishment, which consequently does, indeed, follow. His sense of self-worth suffers greatly from his lack of masculinity. Just as he was a lonely child, he is now a lonely adolescent.

Homosexual men who look back on their youth tell a similar story. They don't belong in the group because their gender identity is unclear to themselves and their peers. They don't go in for sports and rough games, and that makes them feel different from other boys.

Jean has one close friend, Henri, with whom he likes to spend time. Jean's parents smell a rat and disapprove of the friendship. They demand that he drop his friendship with Henri, since they suspect that the two of them are involved in forbidden and unwholesome activities. Henri, who seems to be the leader, instigates the more passive Jean not to do his homework, and worse. Proust calls their relationship "perverse", whereby he suggests their homosexual relations without spelling them out.

But there is more. With their erotically exciting boyish pranks, they desecrate Jean's parents. This is reminiscent of Mlle Vinteuil in *Remembrance of Things Past* who defiles her father's photograph during sex play with her lesbian girlfriend (see Chapter Six). This profanation, as Proust calls it, will continue to be a *leitmotiv* throughout his work.

When Jean visits a brothel together with his friend Henri, he has the frightening phantasy that he is in danger: he might be murdered. In his imagination, he is a helpless victim in a slaughterhouse. In a flashback, he recalls that his mother was once struck by a woman servant who later turned out to be a murderess. Today's prostitute closely resembles the maid of previous days. He calls her villainous, mean, and common, but that's precisely what makes her so exciting. The phantasy that this whore could be his mother's murderess gets him very heated while frightening him at the same time. He is projecting his phantasies towards his mother onto the whore and suspects her of murderous intentions.

This same association pertaining to his mother being struck, which we encounter in *Jean Santeuil*, returns in *Remembrance of Things Past*. Intense guilt feelings and self-reproach follow sexual excitement. Jean is both perpetrator and victim: in his phantasy, it is all about murdering or being murdered. He identifies with the mother who is hit and enjoys the phantasy of being the passive victim of a sex murder that is as delightful as it is violent.

The images presented here as quasi-coincidental phantasies stand for the desecration of the parents, particularly the mother: the "profanation" required for sexual enjoyment and its subsequent punishment are equally laden with lust. This adolescent masturbation phantasy is later completed in *Remembrance of Things Past* when in *Sodom and Gomorrah* the Baron de Charlus visits a brothel and has himself flogged by a couple of boys from the slaughterhouse who are made to play the role of cruel rogues. Humans have been feeling guilty since they were expelled from Paradise. Just like the narrator, he must come up with all sorts of cunning schemes in order to be allowed to feel pleasure and at the same time soothe his conscience.

Several violent and sordid domestic scenes are the result when, in Henri's presence, Jean's mother forbids him to see his friend ever again. In his fury, Jean slams the doors so violently that the glass panes fall to smithereens. Once he is alone in his room, Jean calms his pent-up rage onto his mother's fur cape as if it were she herself. A bout of insanity supposedly leads to ejaculation on the object of this desecrated fetishlike garment. Then Jean's mood switches, rage is replaced by self-reproach and pity for his poor little mother.

On a different occasion, in a furious outburst of rage Jean breaks the precious Venetian vase his mother once gave him as a present.[8] He himself is quite shocked by it but, to his great surprise, his mother forgives him for this heinous deed. She manages to exploit the occasion and binds her son even more strongly to her by not growing angry but rather by reacting lovingly. Each time she succeeds in fuelling the "symbiotic illusion" between mother and son even more. She says that breaking the vase is like breaking the glass at the wedding ceremony in the synagogue, which stands for an eternal bond. With this statement, she suggests that her son has married his mother.[9] Thus, rage brings him no results and only leads to reinforcement of the galling symbiotic bond with his mother. Mme Santeuil succeeds not only in bypassing her son's rage but also in suppressing her own anger, just as we saw in the goodnight kiss episode.

Their reconciliation always consists of his mother spoiling him on the condition that he yield to her wishes; he has to be passive, ill, or show himself to be contrite in order to earn her loving attention.

The reader already understands that it is not the father who carries the day, but the persevering mother. In every household he describes, Proust subtly but unequivocally manages to portray the women as dominant.

The mother manages to turn hatred into sadness and reproach, which causes her son to feel guilty. In Jean's family, the inability to show any emotion goes back to previous generations. Mother's mother never displayed her feelings either. Mother's father was hard and firmly believed in strict pedagogical principles. He used to tease his daughter with ironic comments, just as she does with Jean, and treated her harshly rather than lovingly. But, Proust writes, she has forgiven him for that. Is it because she can now do the same thing to her son? He often repeats that it is extremely difficult for the mother to be strict, as if he has to apologise for her. According to him, she hides her tender feelings and shows the contrary of what she actually feels. This view of her behaviour makes it more difficult to hate her: after all, she means so well. Even when he feels she is treating him cruelly, the narrator moulds it as if it's not her true intention. Pleasing the other is always overtly shown while tormenting the other must be kept concealed as much as possible. And yet, Proust renders clearly visible the hidden hatred that is implicit in the coercive mother–son relationship.

With feigned abandonment, Jean admits to all sorts of misdeeds he has never committed, merely to provoke his mother. The same thing will occur later between the narrator and Albertine. She drives him to despair with her confessions. Jean feigns the opposite of his true feelings, suggesting remorse in order to disguise secret lust. His emotionally crooked ways are extremely sophisticated. There is no spontaneity whatsoever between mother and son for fear that it would be abused.

He reminds me of Evan, a homosexual man who will never tell his mother what he truly thinks. He plays up to her so as not to offend her. He doesn't tell her he is a homosexual and never talks about his male friends. He assumes she is completely ignorant and tries to please her, afraid of emotional scenes and reprimands. Worse, he fears for her life should he be honest with her; she would weep, complain, fall ill, and finally die of grief. When I suggest that she has long suspected his homosexuality and that it might pay off to confide in her, thereby normalising their contact, he initially doesn't dare. It takes a long time and much pondering to conquer his fear of his mother. When he finally decides to put his cards on the table, there is no reaction at all from her end. The contrast between his expectations and phantasies regarding his mother is revealing and challenging for him. His mother hardly seems interested and probably knew all along what she wasn't supposed to know. The attitude of mothers of homosexuals is frequently ambiguous. For a long time, they deny the facts and then, when they are finally, inescapably confronted with their son's homosexuality, they are not surprised. They do not, or only barely, react, and act as if they knew it right from the start and find it perfectly normal.

A revelatory scene from the mother–son drama has to do with Jean's desire, and later on the desire of the narrator in *Remembrance of Things Past*, to see La Berma (Sarah Bernhardt) in her famous performance of Racine's *Phèdre*.[10] His mother won't allow him to go to the performance, arguing that the risk he will fall ill again is too great. He cannot accept this command and an endless verbal battle ensues with arguments pro and con. He goes on and on until in the end his mother relents. Indeed, he is now allowed to go out but his guilt prevents him from enjoying the performance to which he had so fervently looked forward. He is afraid that his determination to get what he wanted is hurtful to his mother. The fact that he went out against her will is spoiling his pleasure. While at first he thought of his parents as cruel, now, because of his remorse, they are suddenly doubly precious to him again.

Jean's choice, between going out against his parents' wishes and restraining himself by staying home, turns into a true obsession. Depression follows upon every outing because he blames himself for causing his mother's unhappiness. La Berma, in his eyes a wise deity whom he idolises boundlessly, changes into an evil seductress and his mother turns into a saint. He splits the good and evil mother into two individuals and projects the latter onto La Berma, just as children do with fairy tales about the evil stepmother.

When he does go out, the narrator is always warned that he will surely become sick again. Thus he is made responsible for his own health: if he falls ill, it will be his own fault. Sickness is now equated with punishment for disobedience and for admitting the desire to become an independent person. Once he is sick, he reverts completely to his mother's power, and she subjects him to a strict regime. He is not allowed to eat anything and once a day he has to have an enema. When he is ill, he is given only milk to drink until the fever is completely gone. This regime is not prescribed by a doctor, but is entirely his mother's initiative. For him, the anal penetration by his mother via the enema is an experience that is as intrusive as it is erotic. The anus becomes a receptive vagina, whereby homosexual feelings are stimulated. The symbolism of this intervention means that the child is not master of his own body. He is the passive victim of an intrusive, phallic mother figure instead of being a belligerent adolescent. His mother enjoys making him into a helpless baby, carefully controlling everything that enters and exits his body.[11]

The same measures follow in *Remembrance of Things Past* upon his having romped around with Gilberte on the Champs-Élysées. He gets very excited, supposedly, resulting in his first spontaneous ejaculation, and then falls ill. It is in no way a coincidence that shortly thereafter his grandmother has a stroke on the very spot where the narrator has his first sexual experience. He phantasises that her illness and death are his fault. Sexuality, suffering, guilt, and punishment are increasingly linked together.

For the narrator, illness, adolescence, and sexual maturation go hand in hand. One is punishment for the other, as it were. When Jean gets into a fight with his classmates because they are harassing him, mother is ready to discourage physical violence: "You shouldn't fight, especially when you're as weak as you are, you shouldn't even defend yourself." Other than making good grades, she systematically and with the best intentions squashes any initiative, thereby frustrating his masculinity.

When just a child, the narrator already learns to phantasise about everything that is forbidden to him in reality. Being bedridden in adolescence is a goldmine for the erotic phantasies of a writer, as Alberto Moravio experienced during his youthful tuberculosis as well. The experiences of the narrator, who feels imprisoned and oppressed by his parents and grandparents, are repeated when he is an adult. The "repetition compulsion", or *Wiederholungszwang*, which plays such a major role in Freud's work, is equally well known to Proust. Later on, the narrator will reverse his passive role into an active one when he is with his beloved Albertine.[12] He will forbid her to go out and have fun, just as his parents used to prohibit him when he was young.

Jean's mother is dissatisfied when his father, who is described as both more lenient and more irascible, doesn't remind him to do his homework often enough for her liking. According to her, Jean presumably lacks the discipline that she, true to family tradition, would like to have pounded into him. She is extremely unhappy when the father notes that his son has no career ambitions and puts up with that. Nevertheless, she still attempts to deploy the father's authority in order to realise her ideals concerning her son. When Jean does not obey and she feels that some show of strength is required, she calls father in to play the ogre. This illustrates the father's role in perversion. He tends to be a cowardly man who is emotionally or physically absent. At times, he is a brute or else the mother calls upon him to act as the ogre. Thus it is in Proust. The father has to display the anger that the mother conceals since, after all, she and her son love each other so intensely. If she is unable to make her son obey her through her own measures, the father has to intervene. The father understands little of all the mother and son's subtle games. He fulfils the role of the outsider who would much prefer to be left in peace. The hypersensitive, bizarre exchanges between mother and son merely annoy him. He is typical of the father in his study who may be disturbed only under exceptional circumstances. When he is called in, he obliges with a terrifying outburst of rage. He is crude and clumsy in the realm of subtle emotion in which mother and grandmother excel, who admire him but surreptitiously look down on him as well.

The erudite and well-read mother and grandmother introduce the narrator to the world of books by reading to him and quoting the utterances of their favourite writers. While they instil love for literature in him, they disapprove of his wish to become a writer. He had better aspire to a social career. The father doesn't disagree with that, as he is well aware that such a career wouldn't make his son very happy. He believes that one ought to enjoy one's profession. Such a concept is wholly lacking in the plans the mother fosters for her son's future. While she wants to shape him into a specific mould, father says: "He's not a child any more, he knows himself what he wants to do with his life." The narrator doesn't ever succeed in pleasing his parents and, into the bargain, they always disagree among themselves.

A revealing dream divulges Jean's feelings. His parents are victims of an accident from which they soon recover, although they were dead. They're trapped like rats in a cage, and while they are holding Ciceronian discourses, their tiny bodies are being pierced with bloodstained pens. Thus he is taking revenge on his parents by torturing and rendering them powerless in his dream. The rat theme is closely linked with Proust's father, according to Jean-Yves Tadié.[13] He was a physician who specialised in combating cholera and the plague. Tadié assumes that dinner table conversations often had rats as their subject. The father's influence is not absent in Jean Santeuil nor in the narrator of *Remembrance of Things Past*. This impressive man, with his high ambition and unprecedented enthusiasm for work, served as Proust's example.

The never-ending pressure exerted upon the narrator, namely that he must not waste any time, must do his homework, mustn't be lazy, must show his willpower, conveys the autobiographical source of the title of Proust's great novel. In the end, the narrator manages to turn every reproach from which he suffered as a child into its opposite. Proust's genius enjoys the lost bygone time as a blessing in disguise. The reflection and phantasies, for which he took all the time he had, helped him to develop his authorship. Furthermore, what we see here is how defeat is turned into triumph: shaping a demand, a prohibition, or a torment into its opposite, an enjoyment, and deriving pleasure from it. Therein lies the secret of perversion.

When the summer season begins, the narrator is sent off to the Normandy coast with his grandmother. He so annoys his parents that they prefer travelling without him. The usual problem is repeated: either you do what we like or we wash our hands of you and leave you to your own devices.

Dread of separation and abandonment, just like dreading the loss of love, are the greatest fears in ambivalent relationships. Anger and hatred have to be repressed, with the result that these feelings are expressed at unexpected moments.

The semblance of the symbiotic idyll must be maintained at any cost. In perversion, there is frequently a deeply hidden but no less vehement dread of separation. The fear of no longer being allowed to be one with the (inner) mother can result in a fear of rejection and even profound depression.

A vacation with his grandmother does not bring any relief since she shares with his mother the same passion for a strict regime for her grandson. His grandmother will not allow him to go his own way freely any more than his mother will. When Marcel isn't feeling well, she locks him up in a darkened room in the Grand Hotel (in Cabourg, which is called Balbec in the novel) until he is fully recovered. For her, everything revolves around his frail health and the anxiety it arouses. The mutual torment takes place non-verbally and semi-unconsciously. He worries his grandmother, and she "pampers" him until he almost suffocates for not being able to breathe. After a while, when he is permitted to have some leeway again, his remorse throws him into a depression. He is afraid his grandmother will die if he goes off by himself to seek his forbidden pleasures. His sexual escapades will be the death of her. He feels obliged to keep returning to her as quickly as he can. The game of separation and abandonment that he will later play with Albertine can be recognised as a repetition of these interactions with mother and grandmother. Experimenting with distance and proximity goes back to earliest childhood when the toddler dares take a few steps away from mother and she signals that this is disagreeable to her. The anxious, worried mother must be spared by the child in order not to be deprived of her affection.

The slightest bit of freedom, every step away from the (grand) mother, is coupled with a feeling of guilt and fear of loss of love, so that he derives no pleasure from it, unless he can transform his fears through perverse creativity into their opposite, by secretly ridiculing and desecrating the hated and feared parent. When he displeases his grandmother, she leaves him to his own devices all day long, and out of revenge he does the same to her.

The narrator never openly shows his feelings of sadness, frustration, or rage, and neither does his grandmother. Just like mother, she teaches him to be manipulative and insincere. He despises this game of hide-and-seek and tries to draw (grand)mother out by striking at her weak spots, for which he has a flawless intuition. He succeeds in worrying her by being indisposed, only to subsequently soothe her and proclaim his love for her. With the terrifying and desperate attacks of tightness in his chest, the narrator takes revenge on his grandmother. He makes her so anxious by exaggerating the physical symptoms of his asthma that she shows her compassion and abandons her severity. She lets go of her principles and gives him cognac to drink. She allows him the very thing she had so strenuously resisted, just as mother did with the goodnight kiss episode. The narrator still vividly recalls how, when he was a child in Combray, his grandmother used to forbid grandfather to have a glass of cognac. As soon as she abandons her discipline, upset by his asthma attack, he is able to feel compassion again and console her. After hurting her, he can briefly forget about the power struggle. This repetitive game constantly returns in all kinds of variations. His grandmother's turmoil, which means that she loves him, weighs more heavily than his gasping for breath, and over and over again he finds it appealing to defy her.

Guilt feelings and desecration also clearly overlap in the following incident. After her first cerebral haemorrhage, when the grandmother tries to hide her misery and illness from him by posing for a photograph (intended for him so he can console himself after her death, as he realises later on, which makes him feel all the more guilty), he ridicules her. This event results in a painful description of an old and helpless grandmother with a sadistic grandchild. He is happy to have her be photographed (to be used for desecration in his sexual games, just as Mlle Vinteuil does with her father's photograph) while, on the other hand, he tries to dissuade her from it by ridiculing her.

What we see here is a complicated interplay of longing and denial, characteristic of perverted love relationships. After her death, when he thinks back to this painful episode, he is filled with compassion and self-reproach. He feels that through his pestering of her, he has murdered his grandmother. And these eroticised guilt feelings are a source of sexual excitement.

The description of the illness and death of the narrator's grandmother (which stands for his mother's death as well) is marvellously poignant, yet also filled with desecration and sadism. The grandmother is doubly violated by the account of the ghastly process of dying, and the reader is forced to witness her defilement and decay. The dying grandmother has to submit to all sorts of cruel treatments such as having leeches, of which she is terrified, placed on her body. She becomes blind, deaf, paralysed from uraemia, and is in terrible pain. During this dying process, she undergoes every conceivable disfiguring humiliation:

> [....] fastened to her neck, her temples, her ears, the tiny black reptiles were writhing among her bloodstained locks, as on the head of medusa... her beautiful eyes wide open... she could not speak and must not move.[14]

Only Françoise, the maid, secretly enjoys the spectacle; the narrator, on the other hand, is appalled and filled with pity. Watching and describing this scene in every cruel detail is at one and the same time exciting and laden with guilt, touching and sadistic. The interest in watching torment and cruelties is preferably attributed to Françoise. The narrator and his mother are wholly loving and caring. Negative feelings are projected onto a third person, the father, or, in this case, the domestic servant. The narrator suspects Françoise of combing her resistant grandmother's hair just to hurt her. She merely wants to satisfy her own vanity, the way a mother dresses her child in his Sunday best to show him off proudly, thereby providing confidence to herself.

In Proust's description, grandmother is literally beaten to death:

> The blows which we aimed at the evil which had settled inside her were always wide off the mark, and it was she, it was her poor interposed body that had to bear them, without her ever uttering more than a faint groan by way of complaint.[15]

This is reminiscent of Jean's phantasy when he visits a brothel. The phantasy that his mother is beaten to a pulp is here repeated in a different form. Time and again, arousal is associated with desecration and murder; murder of the mother for whom sons have to hide their homosexuality. Homosexuals are sons without a mother, Proust writes. Their whole lives through, until they close her dying eyes, they are forced to lie to her about that which is the principal part of their life. Pretending is not only important between mother and son, but also between mother and grandmother: until her final hour, the latter uses all her energy to erase any sign of pain from her face. In turn, the family tries to conceal its grief from her to spare her any further suffering.

In the novel, father plays no role whatsoever in the three-generational game that the narrator, his mother, and his grandmother are performing. The author's father, Dr Adrien Proust, professor at the Medical School of the University of Paris, was not only famous as a fighter against cholera; he also wrote treatises on pedagogy and nervous conditions, such as those from which his son suffered. As mentioned before, he was an important man, universally respected, and of whom the writer was extremely proud. Proust had a great deal of medical knowledge, as is clear throughout his novel, which he owed to his father. But he takes merciless revenge on him by rendering every physician in his novel utterly ludicrous. Proust also describes the doctors who are called in to see his ailing grandmother with biting humour and sarcasm. They pretend to have feelings, are unable to help but, without it being noticed, they gladly slip a generous fee into their pocket. Proust himself didn't want a physician near his deathbed, not even his brother Robert who was a doctor. He had absolutely no confidence in them.

Denigration of the father is no accident and fairly characteristic of perversion: he is excluded and incapable of intervening between son and mother. He is powerless, although he sometimes loudly simulates the contrary and pretends to be authoritative.

The grandmother's death, no matter how pitiable and moving, will later be used profanely for arousal. A perverse mixture is created of weeping over her death, guilt over having hastened it, and great self-pity.

Since the son's erotic excitement signifies mother's death, the reverse can also be true: her death can generate arousal.[16] Without imaginary revenge on the parent and undoing the suffering this caused, no excitement is possible. Therein lies the meaning of the desecration that continues to surface in Proust's work. The holy mother, who tries to turn her son into a non-sexual saint, has to be defiled before there can be any question of sexual gratification.

Out of a highly personal mixture of memories and images, a phantasy tale is created that is tightly linked to the individual life story. What Moses Laufer calls the "central masturbation fantasy" acquires its final form in adolescence. The perverse sexual scenario draws its content from the same source.[17]

Mother does not want the narrator to have an intimate relationship with Albertine, whom, not unintentionally, he met while mother was absent. He gives her a taste of her own medicine: "If you don't need me and can leave me behind by myself, I will do the same, I don't need you either, I have someone else now." Mother tries to have her way by every possible means: by suffering in silence so that he will start feeling guilty, by complaining openly that he is spending too much money on Albertine. "He is to see her less frequently", in her eyes, "he is only making a fool of himself by exaggerating his interest in her", and so forth. As soon as mother has said these words, Marcel—who had just decided not to see Albertine any longer, as she was actually starting to bore him—feels a sudden fear arise that he will lose Albertine.

By her comments, his mother robs him of his intention to break off with her. By her insistent demands, she obtains the opposite of what she intended. His fear of abandonment returns in its full intensity, and he is now forced to hold on to Albertine and see her more often, indeed, see her every day.

Here, too, the conclusion is justified that the mother succeeds every time in perversely attaining the contrary of what she intends. Similarly, she had once instructed Jean to get to work at the very moment he had planned to do so. Thereupon an extra lengthy period of laziness was needed just to get the initiative on his side again, before he was able to decide to start on his homework again. He is constantly being robbed of his initiative. He becomes apathetic because he cannot realise his parents' wishes without losing his autonomy. Just to pester and punish his parents, he must do the opposite of what they desire, even though he thereby shortchanges himself. This form of resistance is characteristic of puberty. For the narrator, it ends up in his becoming a "moral masochist", extremely skilled in causing himself to suffer.

According to the psychoanalyst Reich, in a classic pioneering work still worthy of consideration, typical character traits of the moral masochist are:

> Subjectively, a chronic sensation of suffering, which appears objectively as a tendency to complain; chronic tendencies to self-damage and self-depreciation (moral masochism) and a compulsion to torture others which makes the patient suffer no less than the object. All masochistic characters show a specifically awkward, atactic behaviour in their manners and in their intercourse with others, often so marked as to give the impression of mental deficiency.[18]

We can render Proust's formulations as follows: the oversensitive nature of the child who experiences his parents as cruel makes him cruel in his attempt to protect himself. Every tender feeling is fended off by feigning the opposite, and thus two incompatible sides of the individual are created that are out of balance with each other. On the one hand, he is a masochist while, on the other hand, he behaves sadistically. The narrator believes that if he is too good-natured, the other will have too much power over him, in which his mother succeeded. In order to prevent that, he becomes as ruthless as his parents.

... in reproaching her I used the same arguments that had been so
often advanced against me by my parents when I was small, and
that had appeared so unintelligent and cruel to my misunderstood
childhood. "No, in spite of your gloomy look," I said to Albertine,
"I can't feel sorry for you; I should feel sorry for you if you were ill,
if you had suffered some bereavement; not that you would mind in
the least, I dare say, considering your expenditure of false sensibil-
ity over nothing.[19]

The child copies exactly that behaviour of his parents from which he
has most suffered. Thanks to Anna Freud, that has come to be known as
the defence mechanism called "identification with the aggressor".

As an adult, Marcel the narrator is surprised at his own coldness as it
developed after his sad and supersensitive adolescence. He looks down
on clumsy expressions of oversensitivity, such as those of Albertine,
and treats her with cool irony, just as his mother used to do with him.

Divided within ourselves, we project traits that we have repressed
because they are undesirable to us onto our partner. We then identify
with him or her and need the other's presence all the more as he or she
represents the rejected part of ourselves. This psychological mechanism,
which often appears in couples, is known as "projective identification".
Character traits you disapprove of in yourself are the very ones you
look for in the other. That is how a solid sadomasochistic relationship is
created between two individuals who mirror each other.

Proust repeatedly returns to the following theme: either we hide
our oversensitivity by behaving hard and heartlessly towards the one
we love, or else the oversensitive character looks in the partner for the
roughness and brutality that he has repressed within himself. The result
is that love becomes a martyrdom that can only bring unhappiness. The
fact that two opposite character types tend to choose each other this
way renders mutual understanding in love all but impossible, according to Proust.

We have shown how sadomasochism develops and how the respective roles, such as being cruel and enduring cruelty, become divided up
between the two partners.

The phantasy behind the narrator's perversion turns out to be a
destructive wish with regard to the mother and punishment for same:
"I am killing my mother by hurting her and to be penalised for this I
myself must die."

Proust writes exaltedly and in an idealising manner about both Jean's and the narrator's mother and grandmother. About their exceptional sensitivity, how self-effacing they are, how they conceal their emotions in order to spare the other. However, this medal has another side: with all of their goodwill, they are capable of rendering the son irate and powerless.

When the narrator says that he will keep seeing Albertine, his mother doesn't react, but her face has a tormented expression. It is her hidden intention, for his own benefit, to force him and break his will. He feels powerless, while simultaneously he is filled with feelings of hatred and revenge. However, it is impossible for him to show this since, after all, his mother is the personification of love and kindness. She wants what is best for him. All he needs to do to become a happy person is do what she wants, so why not take that small step? Mother's message is this: let go of your individuality and bliss will be yours. The appearance of solidarity must be maintained. The symbiotic mother–son illusion, from which any aggression is ousted, contains the seed of explosions of hatred and destructiveness that can lead to (phantasised) matricide. Those feelings find their way in an eroticised and stereotypical perverse ritual in which hatred, fear, lust, and revenge are safely accommodated and made harmless. In this way, the forbidden feelings, banned from consciousness, can be channelled, given free rein, and made harmless.

From his earliest writings onwards, in the youthful work of his puberty, being cruel to the parents, murdering the mother, and the guilt about this that can lead to suicide, form central themes in Proust. These phantasies represent an integral part of eroticism as described by this author.[20] The symbolic form of destruction is desecration, also known as "profanation", a key concept in Proust. Sacrilege or blasphemy, not giving a damn about the law and official morality, is one of the characteristics of the universe of perversion in which the world is effortlessly turned upside down.

In the world of Sade, laws are negated and everything sacred is mocked. "Honour thy father and thy mother" is turned into its opposite.[21] Mlle Vinteuil performs a sexual game with her woman friend who spits on her father's photograph and showers him with derision. The narrator plays exciting and forbidden games with his female cousin on the couch of his aunt. After her death, he donates this piece of furniture to a brothel. Jean and Henri become sexually aroused when they dance on the grave of a deceased nun, a nun who was also a prostitute.

The girls who work in a brothel make head coverings for the inhabitants of a convent. Thus a whole host of examples of profanation or desecration can be found in this author's work.

The message is always the same, namely that eroticism and feelings of lust can only arise on the condition that the curtailment by the parents be undone by desecrating them.

Proust and Freud agree that during our dream life, a different world is opened up wherein yearnings come to the fore to which we have no access during the day. Perversions make use of the same primary-process thinking as dreams do. Thus, in the perverse ritual, fear and hatred can more or less be brought out into the open. I should add, however, that just as in the dream, the manifest content of the frequently bizarre scenarios needs to be further interpreted in order to discern their latent meaning. Neurosis is the negative of perversion in so far as lust is lacking, while in perversion it is openly enjoyed. At least, that was Freud's formula, as we have seen. But it isn't that simple. Neurosis and perversion regularly appear together in one and the same individual. Proust calls the narrator a maniac because of his strange obsessions and his compulsive character.

The narrator's "rat dream" is reminiscent of Freud's "Ratman" who suffered from a serious obsessive-compulsive neurosis.[22] When he didn't see his beloved as often as he liked, he would have a constantly returning obsessive thought, namely that rats would penetrate her anus. When he was angry with her (something he didn't permit himself to be), he would unconsciously take revenge on her this way. The perverse phantasies that frightened the Ratman can be enjoyed openly in perversion and are accompanied by feelings of lust. In that way, neurosis can be called the negative of perversion.

The narrator dreams that his parents have changed into rats in order to be able to desecrate and humiliate them. The Ratman phantasises that his beloved is attacked by rats—his beloved, who might, I assume, stand for his mother. Freud does not mention the mother in this or any case history as he habitually concentrates on the father. I suspect he must have suppressed material pertaining to the mother, in order to prove his point about the Oedipus complex.

Just like the narrator, the obsessive-compulsive neurotic has a strong superego. Proust shows us how in perversion the superego can be circumvented. The conscience of these individuals displays lacunae. Because those who raise him are constantly meddling with the adolescent's yearnings as if he is still a little child, he has no chance of becoming independent and developing his own norms.

The superego acquires its ultimate form during adolescence. In that period of breaking free and rebelling, sexuality is central. Then the battle with parents has to do with drinking, going out, and coming home late. What is ultimately at stake is independence and autonomy. When this process is disrupted and the step to self-sufficiency cannot be taken, when the law of the father (a term of the French psychoanalyst Jacques Lacan) is missing, it can lead to psychosis, borderline personality, or perversion.

Proust's narrator is constantly watched. He must abide by his mother's wishes so that he has no chance or time to develop his own judgement. The outside world fills in what he ought to feel, how he ought to behave. Therefore he is incapable of developing a consistent personal conscience that functions independently from his parents. The narrator always feels that what is forbidden is precisely what he enjoys. The choice of his beloved is dictated by rebellion. Instead of choosing a respectable partner, his preference goes out to "lowly" and "perverse creatures". In perversion, the demands of the superego are derided by making them a part of the sexual game. Only that which is forbidden is appealing. His mother's reproaches have become an integral part of his gratification. There is no lust without the prohibition that goes with it.

That part of conscience that has remained external is readily localised in the outside world or projected onto the therapist. "I suppose you don't want me to go to the sex sauna, I'm sure you disapprove of things like that." This projected, police-like conscience is misleading because it is a vital part of the experience of lust. In the transference relationship, it functions as a barrier against intimacy, which is blocked by mistrust. This perverted caricature of the superego has something scornful, as if the subject means to say: "See, no matter how hard you beat or punish me, I'm enjoying my orgasm anyway."

Pierre describes how he has struggled with himself all evening long. He wants to go to a homosexual sauna to be able to enjoy the admiration of his erect penis and have anonymous sex. After hours of hesitation and self-reproach, he finally goes there anyway, and when he returns to his therapist he feels rejected by her beforehand. He is certain that she will condemn him. No matter what she says, and she isn't given much of a chance to speak, "he knows better". He continues to be afraid of what she thinks of him and thus anticipates condemnation. When the phantasised disapproval fails to appear, it provides him no relief at all because disapproval is indispensable as part of the sexual game.

The conditions that parents attach to their love can seriously threaten not only the superego but also the narcissistic equilibrium of a child. It is the unconditional that should characterise parental love. When the child is expected to satisfy all sorts of conditions in order to be loved, this can create "as-if behaviour" and a "false self". The antennae needed to sense what pleases the parent harm the healthy sense of self, the image of what the other one may want replaces the personal, more authentic yearnings.

The child and the subsequent adult no longer knows what he himself might want, his only desire is to please his parent(s), the other one. It's his desire to realise his mother's wishes, and he becomes panic-stricken when he doesn't succeed therein. He does not love himself, as there hardly is an undamaged self, an independent person to be loved. He is thwarted by rage and feelings of revenge, which only make him even less lovable. The narcissism of a mother who attempts to mould her son to her own image is frail, insecure, and full of gaps. He has been given the impossible task of filling those gaps and being her support in all kinds of ways in order not to lose her love. Helping to sustain his mother's self-respect is too arduous a task for a child. He will try to obey, do well in school and do his best and, more importantly, he will try not to love anyone other than his mother. In order to deserve her love, he must curtail his freedom. He cannot function independently of his mother, which degrades his sense of self-worth.

He remains bound to her in a symbiotic relationship that, at the same time, forms a threat to his masculine development. This can influence his gender identity negatively. Because of her constant obstruction of his masculine development, he hates his mother so intensely that he feels he could gladly kill her. The split-off hatred lived out in sadistic sexual actions and phantasies causes feelings of guilt and fear of retribution.

It seems that all of Proust's work revolves around this love–hate conflict. He felt that this work would signify his mother's death and, indeed, he actually only began to write seriously after she had died. He is obsessed with sadism, which was the original title of his novel. He tries to justify the sadistic sexual scenario of which he is ashamed this way: without being released from excessive scruples, excitement is impossible. Sexual gratification is possible only by playing at being the sadist that you are not.

To inexperienced Proust readers, my interpretation of Proust may seem far-fetched. What will subsequently be concealed is much more openly professed in *Jean Santeuil*. In *Remembrance of Things Past*, sadistic pleasure, hatred, and revenge are only insinuated while the love for the mother and the grandmother are accentuated. It appears to be all about admiration and positive emotions until the reader looks more closely and makes the necessary connections.

Notes

1. Freud, S. (1916–1917). *Introductory Lectures on Psycho-Analysis. S. E. 16,* p. 307.
2. Proust, M., *Jean Santeuil*. Trans. Gerald Hopkins. Harmondsworth: Penguin, 1985, p. 428.
3. "But creative writers are valuable allies, and their evidence is to be prized highly, for they are apt to know a whole host of things between heaven and earth of which our philosophy has not yet let us dream. In their knowledge of the mind they are far in advance of us everyday people, for they draw upon sources which we have not yet opened for science."
   (Delusions and dreams in Jensen's Gradiva, 1907, *S. E. 9*, p. 8)
   "The description of the human mind is indeed the domain which is most his own; he has from time immemorial been the precursor of science, and so too of scientific psychology. [….] Thus the creative writer cannot evade the psychiatrist nor the psychiatrist the creative writer" (p. 44). "He directs his attention to the unconscious in his own mind, he listens to its possible developments and lends them artistic expression instead of suppressing them by conscious criticism. Thus he experiences from himself what we learn from others—the laws which the activities of this unconscious must obey. But he need not state these laws, nor even be clearly aware of them" (p. 92). See also Freud's letters to Arthur Schnitzler (Introduction, note 21).
4. Proust, M., The end of jealousy. In: *Pleasures and Regrets*. Trans. Louise Varese. London: Crafton Books, 1988.
5. Marie Kossichef in *Jean Santeuil*, and later in *Remembrance of Things Past*, where her name is Gilberte.
6. Proust, M., *Remembrance of Things Past, The Captive*, Vol. 3, pp. 102–103.
7. Forster, E. M. (1971). *Maurice*. London: Edward Arnold.
8. Celeste Albaret, Proust's housekeeper, writes in her book *Monsieur Proust* (Paris: Laffont, 1973) that Proust did not break this vase by accident but on purpose and that, according to him, it had been the only true

outburst of rage against his mother ever. The anger was caused when he had asked his mother emphatically to buy him a pair of light yellow gloves for an outing with an elegant strumpet. Instead, she returned with a pair of grey gloves. This is characteristic of perversion: instead of doing what her son wants, she does something slightly different; she adjust his wishes to hers and he has to wear, feel, and want what she desires. His longing is perverted and made into something different.

9. Tadié, J.-Y. (1996). *Marcel Proust*. Paris: Gallimard. In his book, the author mentions the many mistresses of Proust, the father, and the unsatisfactory conjugal relationship, from which I deduce that this argues for the mother seeking refuge with her son as well.

10. *Phèdre* deals with her love for her stepson Hyppolytus, a topsy-turvy Oedipal tragedy, for Hyppolytus is terrified of this perilous love and flees from his stepmother.

11. This is reminiscent of the way in which Proust ended his life. He no longer ate at all, drank only milk, strong coffee, and freshly foaming beer that was brought to him from the Hotel Ritz. He worked nights in his cork-lined bedroom, isolated from every sound and avoiding the daylight.

12. Freud, A. (1936). *The Ego and the Mechanisms of Defence*. London: Hogarth. This signifies the defence mechanism, "turning passive into active"; that which you have endured is what you subsequently do to others.

13. Tadié, J.-Y. (1996). *Marcel Proust*. Paris: Gallimard.

14. Proust, M., *Remembrance of Things Past, The Guermantes Way*, Vol. 2, p. 346.

15. Proust, M., *Remembrance of Things Past, The Guermantes Way*, Vol. 2, p. 333.

16. The adolescent who drives the mother to her death through forbidden erotics is already described in *La confession d'une jeune fille*, a youthful work of Proust's (Chapter Three). The girl here is most likely a boy and the forbidden love is homosexuality.

17. Laufer, M. (1998). *Adolescent Breakdown and Beyond*. New York: International Universities Press. (Discusses among other things "The central masturbation fantasy, the final sexual organization and adolescence".)

18. Reich, W. (1949). *Character Analysis*. New York: The Noonday Press, 1961, pp. 218–219.

19. Proust, M., *Remembrance of Things Past, The Captive*, Vol. 3, p. 102.

20. In 1907, about ten years after his mother's death, Proust wrote an article in *Le Figaro* about his friend Henri van Blaerenberghe, who committed suicide after having killed his mother. This man lived in beautiful harmony that almost touched upon the religious with his mother. There,

where the loftiest moral standards had been pursued, this bloodbath suddenly occurred. The murderer of his mother was no criminal brute in the least but, quite the contrary, "a noble person, an enlightened spirit, a tender and devoted son". Proust compares H. v. B., who shot his eyeballs out, with Oedipus: "shooting his eyeballs out, like Oedipus who also blinded himself after her death". Gregory Zilboorg noted this in "Discovery of the Oedipus complex: episodes from Marcel Proust, (*Psychoanalytic Quarterly*, 1939: 279–302), as the simultaneous discovery of the Oedipus complex by Proust and Freud.

21. Chasseguet-Smirgel, J. (1985). *Creativity and Perversion*. London: Free Association Books. "The whole problem of perversion consists in viewing how the child—in his relationship with his mother, a relationship established in the course of the analysis, not because of his dependence on her for his survival but because of her love, that is a dependence on the desire of her desire—identifies with the imaginary object of this desire, which the mother herself symbolizes by the phallus" (p. 85). In other words, he becomes her little penis.

22. Freud, S. (1909d). Notes upon a case of obsessional neurosis. *S. E. 10*, pp. 155–319.

CHAPTER SIX

Sadomasochism according to Proust

It was not evil that gave her the idea of pleasure, that seemed to her attractive; it was pleasure, rather, that seemed evil.

—Marcel Proust[1]

The word "sadism", introduced in the field of psychiatry by Von Krafft-Ebbing around 1900, is derived from the French author the Marquis de Sade.[2] In his *Psychopathia Sexualis*, he also introduced the term "sadomasochism", resulting from the work of Sacher-Masoch.[3] It is still defined today as sexual gratification through the endurance of suffering or humiliation. In addition to sexual masochism, we also see moral masochism, a term Freud introduced.[4] Besides the physical variant, there is the equally important "mental cruelty" or "moral sadism".

In Proust's work, we find every theme from sexual to moral sadomasochism. In the Proustian universe, tormenting and suffering are indispensable ingredients of human existence. As early as the first volume of *Remembrance of Things Past*, there is a disconcerting love scene in *Combray* between two young lesbian women who are mocking the father of one of them.

In masochism, the yearning to inflict pain is carefully hidden or repressed. In fact, Proust and Freud discuss the same phenomenon,

95

namely sadomasochism. Freud wrote about patients who suffered from their symptoms, whom he referred to as "sadomasochists". In individuals who seek treatment, the masochistic component is the more conscious side of the coin, although the other, the sadistic side, is never lacking. Proust, who had originally wanted to title his novel *Sodom and Gomorrah*, in his correspondence repeatedly emphasises that the scene with the two lesbians is of crucial importance in his work. Colleagues had advised him to omit this shocking episode. Proust wrote to François Mauriac that this is a particularly key episode in the novel.[5] To me, as a beginning reader of Proust, this scene was a revelation. To be sure, Proust's explanation of sadomasochism demonstrates similarities with Freud's work, but it also forms a welcome complement to it.

Remembrance of Things Past starts off with the narrator's youth. In this *Bildungsroman*, we are witnesses to his moral and psychosexual development. The writer takes us along on an introspective expedition to Combray (called Illiers in reality, and known today as Illiers-Combray in honour of Proust). The narrator, as well as the writer, spent his summer vacations with his parents in this small town where his paternal grandparents lived. In *Combray*, we find the prelude to all the great themes of *Remembrance of Things Past*. First, there is the goodnight kiss episode. The narrator was a sad and lonely child who suffered from terrible attacks of melancholy. The feeling that he is a victim and gets attention only when he is sick and passive begins with this specific scene. This scene evokes the memory of his entire youth more than the famous cup of tea and the Madeleine cookie do. The heartrending feelings of his childhood explain his interest in the "vicissitudes" of suffering and tormenting.

One day on one of his walks outside of Combray, the narrator arrives in the area of Montjouvain where Mlle Vinteuil resides. There, he experiences that which unlocks the enigma of sadism for him.

The name *Vinteuil* surfaces regularly in *Remembrance of Things Past*. Vinteuil is a misunderstood musical genius who earns his living as a piano teacher. He is the composer of the famous sonata, the theme song, that for Swann symbolises love, art, and suffering, as it also does for the narrator later on. Mlle Vinteuil (and what she stands for) resonates throughout the novel: for her, as for the narrator whose alter-ego she is, homosexuality and sadism go back to the relationship with the parents.

Father Vinteuil is old-fashioned, strict, and demanding, but sensitive and modest as well, just like the (grand)mother of the narrator.

The mother figure is as central to Proust as the father is to Freud. But remember: here it does not concern an Oedipal father in the Freudian sense, but a pre-Oedipal parent. The narrator's mother and her son have been transposed here to father and daughter Vinteuil. This father looks very much like a controlling and overanxious mother. The beloved daughter hurts her father with gestures that seem to him to be insensitive or bad-mannered. And that while the daughter is the carbon copy of her father where oversensitivity is concerned and, just like him, she is uncommonly prudish. But she revolts with all her might against her father's demands, which thoroughly hamper her in following her own nature. She must by necessity keep her sexual preferences a secret from him. When rumours start going around that his daughter might be homosexual, they hasten her father's death. Here is a theme we have encountered before: the child's pleasure kills the parent. Mlle Vinteuil loves her father very deeply but, as the narrator does to his mother, she robs him of any hope for a "respectable future" for the daughter for whom he lives.

> There is probably no one, however rigid his virtue, who is not liable to find himself, by the complexity of circumstances, living at close quarters with the very vice which he himself has been most outspoken in condemning—without altogether recognising it beneath the disguise of ambiguous behaviour which it assumes in his presence.[6]

Mlle Vinteuil has a solid, almost masculine build, but her father treats her as if she were a frail girl. The relationship between this parent and child pair bears a striking resemblance to that of the narrator and his mother. "Mlle Vinteuil must be riddled with guilt feelings about the pain she causes her father", the mother says somewhat insinuatingly to the narrator. This remark reveals that it is a matter of transposition here: mother and narrator become Vinteuil and daughter. The perverse lesbian episode forms a sample of what awaits the reader of the novel.

The narrator is weak and feminine, while his mother does her best to make him into a strong boy by being strict and demanding. Mlle Vinteuil's father tries to do the exact opposite. Although she is sensitive by nature, she behaves in a crude and mannish fashion and is admonished to act more like a bashful girl. This child, too, is a disappointment to her parent. She has a father who apparently really wants to be proud of the very thing his daughter is not. The child must conform to the narcissistic needs of the parent, she must please the parent with forms of behaviour that do not suit her. Love and attention in exchange for passivity; in this parent–child relationship bartering reappears. The parents can be claimed and blackmailed through weakness. Parent and child claim each other, as we already saw in the goodnight kiss episode. Just as Mlle Vinteuil does, the narrator experiences the way he is being raised as cruel, even though the parent is certainly devoted. He holds a secret grudge, while at the same time almost choking with feelings of remorse and guilt. This is the oversensitivity that causes sadism; the conflicted side of the personality is indulged in secret; the sadistic side can be expressed only in a situation of altered consciousness.

The narrator is taking a solitary walk in Montjouvain, he is daydreaming and surrendering to his favourite masturbation phantasies, then lies down on the grass and takes a nap. Quite by accident, he happens to be across from the house of Vinteuil, who has died in the interim. When he wakes up, it is dark. Again by accident, he is able to look into Mlle Vinteuil's room from a short distance (we are beginning to get a glimpse of his voyeurism) and sees something that is not intended for his eyes. The entire story is reminiscent of Freud's "primal scene" in which the child observes the parents' love act from his cradle. The narrator always witnesses homosexual or sadomasochistic episodes quasi-accidentally as an uninvolved outsider. He must stay where he is lying, without moving, without letting a twig creak, in order not to be discovered. Thus he is pretty much forced to spy on Mlle Vinteuil, still in mourning for her deceased father, with her woman friend.

> Despite the brisk and hectoring familiarity with which she treated
> her companion, I could recognise in her the obsequious and reticent
> gestures and sudden scruples that had characterised her father.[7]

Just as her father used to do to her, she pretends the opposite of what she feels. She isn't very welcoming to her woman friend but acts as if she is indifferent, as if she has no interest in her whatsoever. In this regard, she is as perverse as Jean Santeuil and the narrator in *Remembrance of Things Past*.

> With an instinctive rectitude and futility beyond her control, she
> refrained from uttering the premeditated words which she had
> felt to be indispensable for the full realisation of her desire. And

perpetually, in the depths of her being, a shy and suppliant maiden entreated and reined back a rough and swaggering trooper.[8]

Mlle Vinteuil can only reach an erotic climax by transgressing the impediment of the social conventions that are so restrictive to her. She is a straitlaced girl who is able to experience pleasure and lust only when she furtively succumbs to sadistic excesses. We encounter the same thing in De Sade.[9] Overthrowing the ethical norm through inordinately shocking phantasies is the only thing that can provide orgasmic gratification. The cynical and scornful manner in which the two young girls speak together about Mlle Vinteuil's father forms an integral part of their sadomasochistic game. It concerns a ritual and a division of roles according to their stereotypical rules. Nothing is left to chance, just as with Sacher-Masoch, who drew up a contract with his wife in which he recorded in what way and to what extent she is to beat him and verbally abuse him. In his example of Mlle Vinteuil, Proust tries to illustrate his position that the proclivity for sadistic phantasies originates in its opposite: an oversensitivity that prevents excitement. He mentions nothing about the daughter's rage against her father but shifts these feelings to her woman friend who is the one who in their sexual game must humiliate the father. The daughter's spiteful feelings have been transferred to the friend, just as the narrator's guilt-laden rage at his mother is reflected only in veiled terms.

Proust describes Mlle Vinteuil's feelings and motives with great empathy, whereby he displays superb insight into her perverse behaviour.

> Her sensitive and scrupulous heart was ignorant of the words that ought to flow spontaneously from her lips to match the scene for which her eager senses clamoured. She reached out as far as she could across the limitations of her true nature to find the language appropriate to the vicious young woman she longed to be thought, but the words which she imagined such a young woman might have uttered with sincerity sounded false on her own lips. And what little she allowed herself to say was said in a strained tone, in which her ingrained timidity paralysed her impulse towards audacity.[10]

Without it being noticed, Mlle Vinteuil wants to draw her friend's attention to her father's portrait. The photograph is like a fetish that she can address with impunity as she pleases. Her attempt at pretending that the portrait just happened to be where it is instead of being placed there for their game sounds hypocritical: "Oh there's my father's picture looking at us; I can't think who can have put it there; I'm sure I've told them a dozen times that it isn't the proper place for it."[11] The portrait serves the young women for rituals of desecration as they sit on the sofa together and while the window is, not accidentally, open.

> ... for the friend replied in words which were clearly a liturgi-
> cal response. "Let him stay there. He can't bother us any longer.
> D'you think he'd start whining, and wanting to put your overcoat
> on for you, if he saw you now with the window open, the ugly
> old monkey?" To which Mlle Vinteuil replied in words of gentle
> reproach—"Come, come!"—which testified to the goodness of her
> nature, not that they were prompted by any resentment at hearing
> her father spoken of in this fashion (for that was evidently a feel-
> ing which she had trained herself, by a long course of sophistries,
> to keep in close subjection at such moments), but rather because
> they were a sort of curb which, in order not to appear selfish, she
> herself applied to the gratification which her friend was attempting
> to procure for her. It may well have been, too, that the smiling mod-
> eration with which she faced and answered these blasphemies, that
> this tender and hypocritical rebuke appeared to her frank and gen-
> erous nature as a particularly shameful and seductive form of the
> wickedness she was striving to emulate. But she could not resist the
> attraction of being treated with tenderness by a woman who had
> shown herself so implacable towards the defenceless dead, and,
> springing on to her friend's lap, she held out a chaste brow to be
> kissed precisely as a daughter would have done, with the exquisite
> sensation that they would thus, between them, inflict the last turn
> of the screw of cruelty by robbing M. Vinteuil, as though they were
> actually rifling his tomb, of the sacred rights of fatherhood. [...]
>   "Do you know what I should like to do to this old horror?" she
> said, taking up the photograph. [...] "You wouldn't dare." "Not dare
> to spit on it? On that?" said the friend with studied brutality.[12]

Thereupon the action must have been suited to the word behind closed shutters. That, the narrator states with equal sadness and hypocrisy, is the reward the father receives from his daughter for all his love and care. The father wouldn't have lost his faith in his daughter, he actually remarks, even if he had witnessed this scene.

> It was true that in Mlle Vinteuil's habits the appearance of evil was so absolute that it would have been hard to find it exhibited to such a degree of perfection save in a convinced sadist; it is behind the footlights of a Paris theatre […] that one expects to see a girl encouraging a friend to spit upon the portrait of a father who has lived and died for her alone; and when we find in real life a desire for melodramatic effect, it is generally sadism that is responsible for it. It is possible that, without being in the least inclined towards sadism, a daughter might be guilty of equally cruel offences as those of Mlle Vinteuil against the memory and the wishes of her dead father, but she would not give them deliberate expression in an act so crude in its symbolism, so lacking in subtlety; the criminal element in her behaviour would be less evident to other people, and even to herself, since she would not admit to herself that she was doing wrong.[13]

This is how Proust tries to clarify the difference between sadism as sexual perversion and actual cruelty, which sounds like an excuse. He is apparently afraid that Mlle Vinteuil and the narrator will be seen as villains.

> Sadists of Mlle Vinteuil's sort are creatures so purely sentimental, so naturally virtuous, that even sensual pleasure appears to them as something bad, the prerogative of the wicked. And when they allow themselves for a moment to enjoy it they endeavour to impersonate, to identify with, the wicked, and to make their partners do likewise, in order to gain the momentary illusion of having escaped beyond the control of their own gentle and scrupulous nature into the inhuman world of pleasure.[14]

The poor girl merely wants to escape briefly from the chaste norms her father has rammed into her head and that render lust impossible. Mlle Vinteuil identifies with her father as victim and with her friend as executioner, which provides her with the advantage of enjoying both sadistic and masochistic lust. Lust without guilt. No one is hurt, no damage is done, it's simply a game with a photograph and an innocent masturbation phantasy. The conscience can go to sleep peacefully.

Both Proust and Freud emphasise the feelings of guilt in sadomasochism. Mlle Vinteuil does her utmost to be a bad girl but she barely succeeds.

> Perhaps she would not have thought of evil as a state so rare, so abnormal, so exotic, one in which it was so refreshing to sojourn, had she been able to discern in herself, as in everyone else, that indifference to the sufferings one causes which, whatever other names one gives it, is the most terrible and lasting form of cruelty.[15]

Proust tries to ease his narrator's conscience and excuse his excesses. He explains elaborately why the players of exciting sadistic scenes and the like ought not to be confused with individuals without a conscience or empathy. Deliberate cruelty knows no empathy whatsoever, while Proust's and the narrator's compassion leave nothing to be desired, apart from the exceptional state of mind in which gratification is possible and the other can be used as a mere object.

In perverse scenarios, fears and destructive tendencies are ritualised, which limits freedom of choice in sexual matters. Sexuality is in the service of an eroticised struggle for psychic survival. The goal is to resolve emotional tension. This doesn't alter the fact that orgasm is experienced as being extraordinarily satisfying. As far superior compared to "normal sex", in fact. After a narcissistic insult, no matter how seemingly insignificant, such as a comment that threatens the subject's self-respect, the stereotypical perverse scenario is brought into play. This is then followed by a temporary release, in fact it is a form of self-esteem regulation.

Like Freud, Proust shows that sadomasochism is the result of an inner conflict. Mlle Vinteuil's masochistic nature is temporarily suspended by way of the perverse phantasy. Her masochism was generated because she never did succeed in pleasing her highly demanding father. She is reminiscent of Cordelia, King Lear's daughter and his most loving one, who nevertheless displeases her father. Like Cordelia, Mlle Vinteuil lacks a mother's love. The latter died, whereupon her father also became her mother. The frustrated love for her father, which she cannot show directly because of his strictness and their stifling symbiotic bond, creates feelings of hatred in her. Out of fear of being rejected, she conceals her need for love and her anger. She turns the repressed feelings of hate onto herself. Her masochism ties the need for punishment and lust together into a sexual ritual.

Mlle Vinteuil's story becomes more comprehensible and has a more general tenor when we see that it is a matter of transposition. In men, perversion has to do, among other things, with fear of being consumed by the female vagina, where the power of the vagina stands as a metaphor for the omnipotent mother figure.

The Montjouvain episode can be interpreted literally as a valid story about two lesbian girls and an explanation of female homosexuality in which hate towards the father regularly plays a role.[16] Let us digress briefly here to the subject of female homosexuality.

Female homosexuality can frequently be connected to a mother figure who is too distant or too cold and a father who has given equally little support to his daughter's feminine development.

Female homosexuality usually offers a less successful resolution than the male variant. Eroticism between two women is quite often problematic because it frequently suffers profoundly from a bond that is too heated, reproachful, and/or claiming, and is a reflection of a problematic mother–daughter relationship. Conflicts that women used to have with their mother, or else specifically avoided, are presented anew and have yet to be thrashed out.

A daughter's anger and accusations are commonly based on two extremes: the mother image is experienced either as too distant or as too pushy and intrusive, and sometimes it is a matter of a fateful combination of both. The result, as in Electra, is a direct but unconscious inclination towards matricide, even if only experienced through dreams or phantasies.

The not uncommon problematic eroticism between women is also caused by the fact that lesbians have a hard time accepting their female identity, while they reject male identity as well or are unable to realise it sufficiently in their own eyes. When a girl experiences the image she has of her mother or (in a few cases) of her father as being too intrusive, and in her own eyes has not been given sufficient opportunity to be in control of herself and her own body, it can result in great inner insecurity. It can even cast a doubt on her own sexuality. After all, to a large extent girls copy the art of being a woman from their mother. When those mothers are themselves insecure (about their attractiveness, their sexuality), it generally has fateful consequences for a daughter because, in that case, she has no clear model to emulate.

Another thing that causes insecurity in girls is that mothers generally enjoy daughters less than sons. For most women, the heterosexual relationship with the male child is simply more exciting, more satisfying, and less ambivalent than the relationship with a daughter.

When a woman rejects her female gender identity and her male identity rests on an unstable foundation, she finds herself empty-handed. In a lesbian couple, this often leads to a relationship without sex. More than sex or eroticism, women frequently seek a bond with a tender and loving mother. In more general terms, this holds true for both hetero- and homosexual women. Female homosexual relationships are, as a rule, less successful than male ones, as their ambivalence is hard to overcome.

When we compare the Montjouvain episode with what Freud writes in "A child is being beaten",[17] we find a number of interesting parallels and differences. Unfortunately, the article in question is primarily a theoretical work that does not delve into individual cases, their life stories are not described. Furthermore, it does not deal with men, as one might expect, but with masochism in women. Additionally, Freud never published a complete case description of either male or female perversion. "A child is being beaten" has to do with a phantasy of being beaten by the father, a phantasy the four women presented have in common. Imagining being beaten by a woman, a phantasy not described here, we see only in effeminate, sexually disturbed men.[18]

Freud, who had little time for the mother–daughter relationship, emphasises the Oedipal—in this case, the frustrated—love of the girl for the father. It's a love that is made to use all sorts of devious means because incest, even if only phantasised, rests on a grave taboo. Freud deals solely with patricide; matricide does not appear in his work. In contrast, Proust, in the Montjouvain episode, very exceptionally describes the patricidal tendencies of a woman while the rest of his work has to do with matricide in the boy and the man. Here we can clearly see what Freud and Proust have in common and what differentiates them.

Both Proust and Freud demonstrate that shame and guilt play a large role in masochism.[19] In Freud (that is to say, before 1920 when he introduced the death drive), guilt feelings are regularly the factor that turn sadism into masochism. Just as Proust writes that Mlle Vinteuil has absolutely no interest in actual cruelty, so Freud explains that his patients with sadomasochistic phantasies have a horror of violence. The patients Freud describes in "A child is being beaten" were as children never maltreated by their parents. Mlle Vinteuil's father, too, handled his daughter only lovingly. In spite of all this, children can feel harmed and frustrated by attitudes of parents that the latter do not intend as such. Both Proust and Freud posit that the girls in question are frustrated in their tender yearnings with regard to their father. Proust delves deeply into the boy's ambivalence towards the mother (the girl towards the father in the transposition). Freud mentions ambivalence and anger of girls towards the mother in connection with their lack of a penis. I believe that ambivalence towards her always plays a crucial role in girls, and sometimes in boys. On this last topic, Proust is a great deal more informed and informative than Freud.

Freud calls the mother–son relationship the most loving human relationship in existence: "A mother is only brought unlimited satisfaction by her relation to a son; this is altogether the most perfect, the most free from ambivalence of all human relationships."[20] It is possible that this highly idealised and limited view of the mother–son relationship is the reason why Freud never could delve more deeply into perversion and why, as I see it, it remained a mystery to him. To him, the key figure is the boy's Oedipal rival in the person of the father. In my opinion, the emphasis in perversion is on the mother and the missing (symbolic) father. Freud explains perversion generally and sadomasochism specifically through fixation in the phase prior to the Oedipus complex, the anal phase, or as regression back to it.

To Freud, the earliest object relationships do not yet play the role that will be attributed to them in subsequent psychoanalytic explanations of perversion. In his view, the main role is still played by the development of the drives, instead of by the object relations. A few times, Freud did allude to the early mother–child relationship from the beginning of life onwards, but during his lifetime he never completed this quest.[21]

In "The economic problem of masochism" (1924), which he calls a mysterious, baffling, and incomprehensible phenomenon, Freud maintains that the drives rather than object relationships are responsible. Masochism has already led him to replace the ego and sexual instincts by Eros and Thanatos, or life and death drives (in *Beyond the Pleasure Principle*[22]). Since then, masochism has become a primary drive that is no longer derived from sadism, a turn that has not rendered the puzzle any more comprehensible.

Nevertheless, in his *Three Essays* of 1905, Freud already mentions a form of primary masochism when he discovers that emotional tension and even pain can cause sexual excitement. Later on, in "A child is being beaten", he writes about a primary disposition to perversion, and assumes some abnormal inborn inclination or other to explain how "one of the components of the sexual drive becomes independent and a goal in and of itself early on". All of these seem desperate measures for lack of a sound explanation of perversion. He admits not to have solved the problem satisfactorily, it remains a mystery to him, although he suspects that masochism must be linked to the complete dependency of the infant and small child, and to the narcissistic insult this entails.

In the end, masochism is as difficult to explain as the repetition compulsion. Why do people always seek the very situations that have been so painful in their youth, so that one would expect them to stay far away from them? But no, they flock to people who harm them like moths to a burning flame. Why does a man who had an aloof mother fall in love with an equally aloof woman; why does a girl with an unfaithful father fall in love with men who cheat on her?; why does a man with a strict father or mother who made him suffer look for an equally stern woman?

According to Freud, the phantasy in "A child is being beaten" has its origin in the girl's malicious pleasure, when the little brother, of whom she is jealous, gets a beating. Oedipal longings with regard to the father and malicious pleasure are forbidden feelings for which she pays with a need to be punished. The essence of masochism, as Freud sees it, finds its root in the Oedipus complex: the girl wants to be loved by the father, and as its replacement she presumably wants to be beaten, just like the brother of whom she is jealous, under the guise: better to get negative attention than no attention at all. In addition, Freud assumes that longing to be beaten on the buttocks is connected to recoiling from the dangers of the Oedipal phase. That is why what takes place is a regression to the anal phase and the anal sadism that goes along with it.

To me, the reasoning concerning female masochism seems rather improbable. The more obvious solution, as I see it, may well be found in the relationship with the mother. A stern mother figure, or one who is experienced as being punishing, can in girls lead fairly directly to a masochistic character development. Martha, a patient of mine who suffered her whole life long from masochistic phantasies while making love and was therefore extremely inhibited sexually, had been frequently beaten and punished by her stern German mother. Another woman, who was equally unable to reach orgasm without masochistic phantasies, was afraid of her mother, by whom she felt unloved.

In the man, Freud derives the wish to be beaten by a woman from the negative Oedipus complex: a passive instead of a competitive attitude towards the father. Such passivity in boys is generated by a repressed aggressive attitude towards a father who is experienced as threatening. This is accompanied by inhibition of aggression and the inability to compete with other males. For Freud, it is a matter, in both men and women, of the unconscious wish to be beaten by the father. Yet, it continues to be somewhat obscure why the boy should have no desire to be beaten by the father. Here, too, it seems to me that the role of the mother and the passive attitude towards her are underexposed. I have had various homosexual men in treatment who were afraid of their father as a child and most definitely wished to be treated roughly by a man in sexualibus. Freud does not describe this variant. In my opinion, the link between the phantasy of being beaten and the relationship to the mother, experienced as a powerful, forbidding, and punishing phallic woman, is what is missing here. For Freud, the Oedipal father remains the most important (symbolic) factor in a child's life. This probably has to do with the powerlessness of women and mothers in his time, and with his preference for a male model of development, which he drafted with the aid of his self-analysis. However, no one can be blamed for not solving every psychological question in a single human lifetime.

The negative Oedipus complex, the looking up to instead of competing with the father, or more generally a more passive disposition in men, does not only and not always have to do with a strongly domineering father and with fear of him. As I see it, a clearly ambivalent and fearful attitude towards women, which seeks a perverse solution, often has more to do with the mother. In my opinion, this problem finds its origin in a much too passive, too dependent relationship with a mother figure who is experienced as being omnipotent.[23]

In Proust, as in my daily practice, I found a detailed unravelling of how parents come across in their children's experience. This is most honestly and candidly described in *Jean Santeuil*, which precedes *Remembrance of Things Past*. Proust's special subject is fixation on the symbiotic phase and the inability to attain the separation-individuation phase that, according to Margaret Mahler, the child must go through in order to become an individual.[24] His prototypical male adult is just as anxious about loss of love and abandonment as a young child *vis-à-vis* his mother.

The visible behaviour is only surface. It conceals the defence function it has and the motives that hide behind it so that its closer interpretation is essential. The triple concealment, whereby anxiety leads to aggression and aggression to shame, was clear to both Proust and Freud; sadism can mask masochism and vice versa.

Both Proust and Freud hint at problems in the development of sexual identity, which plays such an important role in the development of perversion. Father Vinteuil behaves like a mother, the daughter like a son; Marcel is more like a girl, and in disciplining her son, the mother takes on the role of the father.

Notes

1. Proust, M., *Remembrance of Things Past, Combray*, Vol. 1, p. 180.
2. Von Krafft-Ebing, R. (1903). *Psychpathia Sexualis* [12th revised and enlarged edition]. Stuttgart: Ferdinand Enke. In literature, we see examples of sadism and masochism combined. See, for example, Mario Praz (1933), *The Romantic Agony* (London: Oxford University Press, 1970), where he writes about the victim of the "femme fatale" as follows: "(…) and sadism appears under the passive aspect which is usually called masochism (as though the active and passive aspects were not usually both present in sadism and a mere change of propositions really justified a change of name)" (p. 156).

   In this connection, compare Friedrich Nietzsche; in *Ecce homo* he refers to his "Drei Abhandlungen van de Genealogie der Moral; die Psychologie des Gewissens": "Es ist der Instinkt der Grausamheit, der sich rückwärts wendet, nachdem er nicht mehr nach aussen hin sich entladen kann" (p. 1143). *Werke in drei Bände*. Münich: Zweiter Band, Carl Hanser Verlag.
3. Von Sacher-Masoch, L. (1870). *Venus im Pelz*. Stuttgart: J. G. Cotta.
4. Freud, S. (1924c). The economic problem of masochism. *S. E. 19*, pp. 159–173; *Three Essays*, p. 159.
5. Mauriac, F. (1947). *Du côté de chez Proust*. Paris: Table ronde.
6. Proust, M., *Remembrance of Things Past, Combray*, Vol. 1, p. 161.
7. Proust, M., *Remembrance of Things Past, Swann's Way*, Vol. 1, p. 175.
8. Proust, M., *Remembrance of Things Past, Combray*, Vol. 1, p. 176.
9. Bataille, G. (1957). *L'érotisme*. Paris: Éditions de Minuit. His reasoning is the same as Proust's. He compares Mlle Vinteuil with De Sade, both of them bogus sadists. The true sadist is cruel and does not explain his actions. His explanations would instantly make him into a morally driven individual and show him to be a pervert instead of a criminal.

Deleuze (see Chapter Three) and Bataille each explain why a cruel brute and De Sade do not correspond. The devil and other evildoers do not speak. They do not justify themselves, but when they speak, they use the language of power. The executioner in De Sade who speaks is a paradox, which lets us come to the conclusion that we are dealing with phantasy. De Sade was a masochist who would provoke until he landed in jail. Juliette and Justine represent the two sides of the sadomasochistic coin. De Sade could no more detach himself from his conscience than Proust, although he despises the religion and the morality of his time. The murderer and the executioner are able to enjoy their cruelty while the sadomasochist avoids reality. This is usually the case, although there are examples as well where death may be the result, such as strangulation sex, or cases in which the body's integrity is seriously injured by all kinds of deforming or life-threatening mechanical interventions.

10. Proust, M., *Remembrance of Things Past, Combray*, Vol. 1, p. 176.
11. Proust, M., *Remembrance of Things Past, Combray*, Vol. 1, p. 177.
12. Proust, M., *Remembrance of Things Past, Combray*, Vol. 1, pp. 177–178.
13. Proust, M., *Remembrance of Things Past, Combray*, Vol. 1, pp. 178–179.
14. Proust, M., *Remembrance of Things Past, Combray*, Vol. 1, p. 179.
15. Proust, M., *Remembrance of Things Past, Combray*, Vol. 1, p. 180.
16. McDougall, J. (1964). Homosexuality in women. In: J. Chasseguet-Smirgel (Ed.), *Female Sexuality*. London: Maresfield Library.
17. Freud, S. (1919e). A child is being beaten. *S. E. 17*. The biography of Anna Freud shows, among other things, that she served as the model for this article. Her masochistic masturbation phantasies contained "a child is being beaten". For many years, she was in analysis with her own father. See Elisabeth Young-Bruehl (1988). *Anna Freud: A Biography*. London: Macmillan.
18. Freud, S. (1924c). The economic problem of masochism. *S. E. 19*, pp. 159–173.
19. The following comment needs to be added here. Freud uses the terms "castration anxiety" and "guilt" in their more limited, literal meaning, closely connected to the father and the Oedipus complex. I believe that in perversion, it is a matter of a much more archaic anxiety and guilt. The perverse personality structure differs from cases in which the Oedipus complex is successfully resolved. In perversion, the fear of destruction of the self and the object are at stake. This overwhelming feeling knows no bounds, and that is precisely why perverse defence mechanisms are indispensable.
20. Freud, S. (1933a). Feminity. *New Introductory Lectures on Psycho-Analysis, S. E. 22*, pp. 112–136, 133. Freud believes that the mother–son relationship is based on narcissism, not on rivalry. Wounded narcissism can

cause hate, as is the case in the symbiotic illusion. This hate introduces some doubt about the truth of the statement: "A mother is only brought unlimited satisfaction by her relation to a son; this is altogether the most perfect, the most free from ambivalence of all human relationships."

21. Freud was, however, the first to highlight the strong bond with the mother when a father is absent, whereby an excessive identification with the mother is created, which results in a feminine development. He pointed to the pre-Oedipal bond of the girl with her mother as an important step on the road to her femininity. At the end of his life, he had some doubts about whether the Oedipus complex applied to girls at all. In the end, however, a universally valid Oedipus complex was the deciding factor above all other considerations.

22. Freud, S. (1920g). *Beyond the Pleasure Principle. S. E. 18*, pp. 7–67.

23. Proust, M. (1979). *Correspondence de 1905*. Ed. Philip Kolb. Paris: Plon. In a letter to Robert de Montesquiou, he writes that his mother, who had just died, always kept seeing him as a child of no more than about four years old. This is very obvious from their correspondence, too (he slept during the day and they wrote to each other when they didn't see each other to speak). She constantly writes to him pieces of advice concerning his health, which is her preoccupation. He, in turn, encourages this by informing her of what he ate, how he feels, how he has slept or didn't sleep, whereby he invites her to be intrusive while, at the same time, blaming her and thus hating her for it.

24. Mahler, M. S., Pine, F. and Bergmann, A. (1975). *The Psychological Birth of the Human Infant: Symbiosis and Individuation*. London: Hutchinson.

CHAPTER SEVEN

Moral and sexual masochism

No healthy person, it appears, can fail to make some addition that might be called perverse to the normal sexual aim; and the universality of this finding is in itself enough to show how inappropriate it is to use the word perversion as a term of reproach. In the sphere of the sexual life we are brought up against peculiar and, indeed, insoluble difficulties as soon as we try to draw a sharp line to distinguish mere variations within the range of what is physiological from pathological symptoms.

—Sigmund Freud[1]

Sadism and masochism occupy a special position among the perversions, since the contrast between activity and passivity which lies behind them is among the universal characteristics of sexual life.

—Sigmund Freud[2]

Erik had a cold and distant mother who was stern and disciplinary. His father had died young after a protracted illness. His mother kept him on a tight rein: nothing was possible, nothing was allowed; no friends over to the house, no going out at night. Erik always obeyed and never rebelled against his mother,

111

except for the one time when, as an adolescent on an alcoholic binge, he threatened to murder her, whereupon he was turned out of the house and placed elsewhere. His customary weapon is to keep silent and take on a reproachful, claiming attitude: whatever you do for him, it is never enough. He is and remains aggrieved, feels shortchanged, indignant about all that injustice. When he doesn't get enough attention from his wife, he pours out an avalanche of accusations at her and threatens to break up with her. The same pattern is repeated in treatment. In this, he strongly resembles Proust's narrator who continuously stages a play of rupture with his friend Albertine, whereupon reconciliation follows. Vexing the partner is taken to the greatest possible heights with the risk that an actual breach becomes almost unavoidable. The tension is increased to its maximum in order to be released in a sadomasochistic sexual game.

Generally, Erik vents his rage by projecting aggression onto the other person. He is always the weak-willed victim, while anyone else whom he deals with is the executioner and evildoer. Erik lacks initiative and self-confidence, his sense of self-worth is extremely low. He is completely passive, always anticipating something bad, and in addition suffers from frequent headaches, a sign of his repressed anger. He is still searching for the symbiosis he missed, a never-fulfilled longing that must finally be redeemed. Erik is both a moral and a sexual masochist.

Experience teaches us that moral and sexual masochism can appear in one and the same individual, although that is certainly not always the case. By no means does every moral masochist have erotic tendencies that include pain. Conversely, not every sexual masochist has a tendency to find himself in the spot where blows are delivered. The asexual form of masochism is infinitely more common than the sexual variant. The feeling of guilt plays a much greater role in the moral masochist, although it will often remain unconscious. These people do not attribute their unhappiness to their own doings but to mere chance. Having pleasure is dangerous, so you suffer most from the fear of what you may suffer, an anticipatory mechanism that prevents disappointment and avoids risk. Masochism spares narcissism in the sense that anticipating, and thereby inviting, disappointment is a self-fulfilling prophecy, in which the feeling of being right is dominant. Such individuals would rather be right than happy.

The sexual masochist, with or without moral masochism, displays character traits that are missing in the purely moral masochist. One can think of ego-splitting, a weak sexual identity, and experiencing sex in an exceptional state of mind and special situation. A problematic regulation of aggression is part of both sexual and moral masochism: anger can be directly expressed only with great difficulty and seeks all kinds of secret subterfuges.

The disposition for masochism lies in the protracted dependence of the baby on physical and emotional care, resulting in a primary helpless and passive position. Therein might lie the proclivity for hatred and vengeful feelings in humans. Without a certain amount of masochism, survival isn't possible. After all, the human child is born too soon (neoteny) because of its large cerebral capacity, with all the narcissistic offences that go along with it

Erik struggles with his intense need for constant attention, which he wrests from his partner at all costs. But it is never enough and doesn't satisfy him at all. He is like a baby that cannot tolerate it when his mother's attention isn't continuously directed at him. The minute his wife is not focusing on him, he feels rage well up inside him and initiates fierce arguments, whereby he will go to the ultimate extreme. In their sexual game, they regularly change roles and take turns being the masochist and the sadist, where coercion and surrender lead to orgasm and relaxation.

Pre-Oedipal desires were described with increasing frequency by later analysts because they realised that the child's phantasy life begins much earlier than Freud assumed. He put the emphasis on the fifth year where he placed the Oedipal phase.[3] The Kleinians always placed the Oedipus complex much earlier. The mother has gained increasingly greater importance in psychoanalytic theory. The development of masochism can now be outlined as follows: more frustration than the subject is able to handle combined with the impossibility of showing any aggression at all. Repressing all feelings of hostility, as is common in the symbiotic illusion, causes strong, pent-up, unconscious rage. When anger is directed at the self in the form of self-hatred and self-punishment, it leads to masochism.

As stated earlier, the small child is for a long time dependent on parents or caregivers. Frustration is inevitable so that a certain amount of masochism, in the sense of tolerating discomfort, becomes an almost "normal" side effect of childrearing. By turning this passivity into an active attitude, masochism can be converted into sadism, in so far as that wasn't already present as a matter of course. Is there any child who hasn't torn the legs from a fly, pulled the cat's tail, or forcefully taken away the toys from another, helpless, younger child? Sadism and masochism form a pair of opposites that belong together, just as two participants in the love act spontaneously identify with each other's position.

The phantasy of being beaten, forced, prostituted, or raped is not uncommon in women. They usually have a much closer bond with the mother than do boys and men, who are set free at a much earlier age and allowed to explore the whole wide world. Women are less capable of expressing anger, which is one of the reasons they go through a masochistic character development more often. Apart from women's position as the second sex, which makes them more vulnerable and more accustomed to being humiliated, masochism as a strictly sexual perversion appears less frequently in women.[4] On the other hand, the moral masochistic attitude of complaining and feeling aggrieved appears all the more.

One of the reasons for this could be her social position, a position that doesn't need a perverse scenario to give in to masochistic phantasies, in contrast to that of men. A woman frequently adopts her mother's masochism, even though she is just as often afraid to be like her. For a man, it is extremely frightening to resemble his mother too much, no matter what, because it may rob him of his masculinity. For the woman, who more frequently risks remaining stuck in an unresolved symbiosis with her mother, it isn't accompanied by the fear that is connected to it for men. She is less in need of the perverse sexual scenario, her femininity is already established, while the man must defend himself more often against threats to his masculinity and his potency.

However, when a girl experiences her mother as exceedingly intrusive or assertive and she isn't given enough opportunity to learn to be in control of her own body, it will result in inner uncertainty, or even doubt, about her gender identity. Herein the sexes resemble each other. In men, this is often the path that leads to homosexuality or even perversion, as is the case with Proust's narrator. For women, the consequences are less drastic since the unresolved intimacy with the mother is more "normal" for her. Generally speaking, the parasitical mother appears to get less pleasure and excitement from the girl as symbiotic object than from the heterosexual relationship with the male child, whose person or penis she can experience as object of lust or as a part of herself.

There is a clear difference between male and female homosexuality. Society is far more accepting of intimacy between women and won't be quick to label any of its forms as perverse (another proof that homosexuality and perversion are definitely not the same thing). Perverse patterns of interaction in women go unnoticed more often because their manifestations are less sexually coloured. After all, sexuality in a man is more central to his psychological make-up. On the other hand, masochistic problems in women will often hamper her sexual development, render it more difficult for her to reach orgasm, or lead to frigidity and/or vaginismus. In serious cases, masochism can even take on a self-destructive non-sexual form, such as self-mutilation (or pursuing maiming operations) and anorexia nervosa, a form of perversion in women.

For Proust's narrator, who has served as our example throughout, the pathogenic factor revolves around lesser or more subtle forms of fear. As we have seen, perverted forms of love cause archaic rage that can only be expressed indirectly so that masochism is a common solution. The lack of a sense of security and being loved imperils the self-love, self-respect, and the child's positive feelings. This occurs when a child feels desired only as long as he complies with the conditions and expectations of his parents, which they append to their love. Crippling of the sense of self-worth has a great deal to do with perversion.

Richard, a (moral) masochistic man, is a compulsive user of prostitutes. He is insecure, among other things, about his sexual identity and his motor system is clumsy. He tends towards servility and subservience. He looks to compensate for his threatened sense of self-worth, and each time he feels hurt or frustrated, which happens for the slightest reasons, he seeks his solace among call girls. His parents had waited a long time for a son: he has five older sisters. He was a sensitive child who, when he was just a baby, was already predestined to take over his father's business. It became obvious early on that, where his character was concerned, he was totally unfit for this role. He completely lacks the toughness needed for directing a large enterprise. His father, a coercive despot, who had built a great business by himself, was curt and demanding towards him. He felt more seduced and manipulated than secure and loved by his capricious and self-centred mother. Already as a child, he had always sensed that his own feelings were of no importance. From a very young age onwards, he felt constrained and coerced because his authoritarian father wanted to squeeze him into too tight a straightjacket. His own feelings and desires were of no consequence; he had to satisfy the expectations of others and the demands that his origin made on him. He always felt he was no good, which made him extremely vulnerable to being offended. He still feels instantly affronted or humiliated at any provocation. And then he boils with vehement and barely controllable rage inside. Sometimes he flares up against his wife, but mostly he grows very quiet and withdraws into the passive resistance that he put up against his parents very early on. He seeks his secret compensation elsewhere instead of expressing it and, if need be, thrashing it out.

Mario, an Italian, constantly gets himself in such difficulties that he may well be defined as masochistic. He suffers from fits of compulsive exhibitionism, which repeatedly causes him to be in trouble with the police. He presents himself for psychotherapy because he has already been sentenced several times. Each time he feels hurt, Mario reacts with the rush to expose himself. Seen objectively, it can be a matter of only the slightest offence. When he was a small child, his mother let him run around naked, only to laugh at him then with her women friends because of his little willy. It is to these events that he attributes his being so easily aggrieved.

Such frustrations in the area of narcissism in early childhood are emotionally threatening, in the sense of fearing psychic destruction, and may lead in adulthood to the continued survival of archaic, mega-lomaniacal feelings of revenge towards the love object. The very earliest childhood phantasies are crueller, cruder, and more primitive than the phantasies that develop later on. The enjoyment that children derive from the most malevolent fairy tales amply clarifies this. Anger is not yet appeased by feelings of love and appreciation for the caregiver as a complete individual, with her good and bad sides. She is experienced alternately as a kindhearted and as a wicked person. The feelings of revenge thus generated can be directed as masochism at the self. When stored in an archaic, split-off part of the personality, they can also lead to sadomasochistic perversion.

For a person with a vulnerable sense of self-worth who lacks a healthy narcissism, it is risky to display his need for love and tender-ness. "Whoever shows dependency first is out." Showing any feelings can be interpreted as weakness. In this regard, there is absolutely no difference between homosexual and heterosexual couples: when both avoid showing themselves, there will be a fight. Both see themselves as victim, accuse each other, feel shortchanged, show no desires but only vent criticism. At best, a trade is created, of love for love, in order to safeguard against rejection. The undertones of archaic aggression are avoided as much as possible. Usually in moral masochism it stops with couples fighting, without a straightforwardly sexual scenario. Acting out a perversion in sexuality is more generally a male need. However, to this end, a partner is needed who participates more or less willingly in the contract and inflicts pain in order to bring him to orgasm. Although women, too, may act out perversions, it is usually limited to masochistic masturbation phantasies or masochistic images during love-making in order to bring about orgasm.

In perversion, it is a matter of subtle, almost unnoticeable chronic frustrations, such as the impossibility of developing into an independent person. A child can unconsciously have the feeling that he is unable to realise his own desires, which happens when he has to direct himself to the wishes of his caregivers, usually the mother. A vulnerable mother elicits the feeling that she would fall completely apart emotionally if the child does not comply with her desires. In that case, a child really has to adapt, violate his feelings, and adjust, which is to say pervert himself. The child unconsciously chooses to obey, resign himself, stay close to the mother, and be loyal. It is in his own interest not to risk being (emotionally) abandoned, lose love, or be rejected. Such a child is constantly afraid of not sufficiently satisfying his mother's needs.

In the conscious realm, a child usually has the idea that his mother loved him deeply, and so, in her own way, she does. She may be well-bred, caring, and utterly sensitive, like the mother of Proust's narrator. But she gives her love exclusively on the condition that the child follows her wishes to the letter, "for his own good". The child is not allowed to decide which friends to play with, which clothes to wear, which presents to receive, whether his hair should be cut, when he wants to play outside; he must feel what his mother feels and like what she likes. When he expresses a wish that doesn't coincide with hers, she ignores it. Saïd, an Indonesian man, coming from a large close-knit family in which negative feelings and open criticism were avoided and gossip reigned supreme, always felt guilty towards his mother. He was unable to pull away from her to the extent that he always returned home with bags full of cooked food he did not want to receive. He always felt he had to live the life his mother prescribed and married a woman just as bossy as his mother. He had never known his father, and his mother had remarried with a weak and anxious man. He sought help to enable him to learn to say "no" and set limits.

In the family situation customary in perversion, the father does not intervene; at most, he is mother's helper and can thereby indulge his rivalry with, and envy of, the child. After all, the latter is a rival where the bond with his wife is concerned. More often, he stays out of everything and leaves the cumbersome business of rearing entirely to her. The father is of no support to the child with such a detached attitude, nor is he supportive when he is a brute or uninterested. Joyce McDougall emphasises the inadequate identification with the father and the failed idealisation of his power, whereby it is harder for the son to discover his own strength, not to mention using it.[5]

Of course, there are many exceptions to the rule. Thus it is certainly not always true that the symbiotic illusion exists only with the mother. Sometimes a father–son symbiosis occurs. When he was a small child, Harry was placed with a foster family for a few years because of his mother's illness. When he returned to his own family, he found he had a father who combined the most horrendous outbursts of rage with a great deal of solicitousness and warmth. The father was extremely proud and fond of his son, not of his daughter. Harry never wanted to hear a negative word about him; on the contrary, he always speaks of his father in glowing terms while his mother leaves him more or less indifferent. Harry never protested against his father's behaviour and looks exactly like him. He, too, has horrible outbursts of rage and flies into terrible tempers that border on the sadistic. His family members are afraid of him.

None of the people in the examples provided so far has ever shown any overt aggression to the parent(s), they never even considered any resistance, none of them has gone through the normal adolescent phase of protest. From early childhood onwards, they all felt forced to satisfy or endure the mostly unexpressed wishes of their mother or father. They are docile; during treatment, their concealed rage comes out bit by bit via the transference relationship. Then it turns out that they are highly suspicious and afraid of being outsmarted.

Both moral and sexual masochism serves, as it were, to make the statement: "I can only let my rage go free and only express my anger by receiving a heavy beating (symbolically in moral masochism) and experience that as sensual." The original feelings are thus perverted by first changing them into their opposite and then directing them at oneself. Moral masochists, in particular, are afraid that every well-intentioned, loving interaction will be abused. They block positive exchange because the danger threatens that their intentions, and even their whole personality, will be annexed. Sexual masochists escape from the feeling of annexation and symbiosis with (usually) the mother by means of beatings or humiliation, meant as a symbolic separation when actual separation and individuation are impossible. Thus intimacy is avoided and only then does orgasm become possible. The threat of an emotional invasion is averted by arranging for the beating oneself. In normal sexual relations, passivity, tenderness, and throwing all caution to the winds serve a healthy regression, which is impossible for those who are afraid of fusing with the object.

Perversions are extremely meticulous little "games" that have been "rehearsed" for life and are often repeated, in which fear and aggression are ritualised. Triumph plus the eroticising of fear and anger can lead to a powerful, orgasmic experience that has a manic side to it.

The conviction that one has more exciting sex than "ordinary" people comes with the fact that all kinds of things can be expressed with sexuality as a façade, problems are successfully and victoriously resolved, and depression is kept at bay.

In all the examples provided so far, passivity and dependency are problematic. The mothers of these patients invariably withheld love and tenderness from their child, unless the wholly dependent child resigned herself passively by being sick or otherwise helpless. The fathers were aloof, supported neither their wife nor their child, and were sometimes actually aggressive. Similar family constellations are most clearly and most extensively illustrated in Proust's novel.

When passivity, tenderness, and love are dangerous because with it fear of annexation is engendered, masochism is a solution for making the expression of those feelings possible, nevertheless. When relinquishing all signs of independence has been a condition for physical closeness, suffering emotional or physical pain, plus the anger directed at oneself masochistically, can become a condition for arousal. Pain becomes the price that must be paid for being loved. At the same time, it is a penance for criminal yearnings for separation and, finally, a triumph that proves that the loss of self-worth and emotional deprivation can be turned into pleasure.

The (moral) masochist attains his goals consciously or unconsciously, and usually with great subtlety. These individuals, who became accustomed to subtle manipulation in their youth, achieve great refinement in, and receptivity to, capitalising on the needs and longings of others. We will see what complicated games Proust's narrator used to play with Albertine.

My examples show both sexual and moral masochistic tendencies. The moral masochist is especially keen on arousing guilt feelings in the other: "You treat me so badly, I am so pitiable that you owe me recompense." In every case, it turns out to be of vital importance to deny aggression, which in childhood always had to be repressed. Thus the (moral) masochist lets it be known that: "I am not angry, I am just the woeful victim, and you should feel sorry for me. I am the victim of your aggression and that of others."

Rage is expressed indirectly, for example via complaints, indirect accusations, manipulation, and unacknowledged, sometimes not even conscious, blackmail projected onto the other. In moral masochism, the whole personality is typified by character traits that are better controlled in the case of sexual masochism, where they are more isolated and therefore can be indulged in a distinct ritual, apart from the rest of the personality.

The (moral) masochist won't easily ask for a favour overtly. He will say: "I wish you would do this or that for me, but you won't have any time, of course." And along with this, he'll think: of course, you don't feel like helping me, you don't like me, maybe you even hate me. He expresses this either verbally or implicitly by means of a reproachful tone or a suffering look. If you refuse him something, you have proven your lack of love; if you agree, he'll think you're only doing so because he hasn't left you any chance of saying no. You can never prove to a moral masochist that you love him. He will always keep longing for something without asking for it, and so he can always prove that you have no interest in him or even intensely dislike him. This way of asking without risking rejection is typical. Actual dependency can be avoided this way. The masochist would rather coerce a rejection than passively anticipate. He takes his fate in his own hands by staging a failure or a rejection so that the other has no chance of refusing him. Thereby he can go at it in a most coercive and manipulating manner.

The tone of the shortchanged masochist (in Chapter Eight, we shall meet the character of Saniette as a fine example of the moral masochist in the work of Proust) elicits aversion and disgust because the hidden aggression is tangible behind the submissive façade. He is the secret and unconscious organiser of his own well-directed adversities. These adversities enable him to feel he is right in thinking that he isn't loved. A classic example is the story of Eeyore in *Winnie-the-Pooh* who presents himself as victim: "Nobody thinks of me, they all forget my birthday, and I'm not getting a single present from anyone."

Disappointment is the only thing that can satisfy a masochist. This causes the well-known negative therapeutic reaction that Freud already exposed: the more progress a patient makes, the more horrible he feels, or the more adversity he runs into. Sometimes it happens, and this is true for both moral and sexual masochists, that a positive emotional current and an authentic longing get started in therapy. The ability to receive love without any conditions or preconceived pitfalls requires the ability to tolerate uncertainty and take a risk. Frequently, however, and this is true for moral but not for sexual masochists, the secondary gain of power over the one whom one reproaches is too great.

The feeling of self-worth is strengthened by always being right: "better be right than happy" is the appropriate motto here. Furthermore, being the victim can provide a sense of pride, of being unique and deserving of sympathy. Suffering can become a satisfying goal in and of itself. Moral profit can be great. The masochist surreptitiously has the initiative while grandly displaying passivity. Besides, he needn't feel guilty because he is already undergoing his punishment.

The origin lies in the childhood years and, indeed, masochists often feel they have been treated badly and have learned that negative attention is better than no attention at all. Suffering victimisation can be the only way by which to receive love from a dismissive parent. This is frequently where the moral masochistic attitude to life originates. There are vast differences between a healthy aggression by which to reach a goal, and destructiveness and unconscious aggressive phantasies that find release in masochism. The way in which one feels one is treated by one's parents shapes the way in which one learns to experience "love". Repetition compulsion makes people continue to look for the negative experiences to which they were accustomed. It is a matter of not knowing any better and being unable to recognise forms of loving that are different from the familiar and deficient ones they know.

Bringing together all destructiveness and fear into one stereotypical ritual offers certainty and security. When the feared pushiness of a woman can be symbolised by having oneself pierced by her high heel at one's own request, as Adam did, it provides the safe feeling of having the direction in one's own hands, even if it is painful, a pain moreover that is forged into excitement.

Manipulation of the love object and power are important in perversion generally, and in sadomasochism, both moral and sexual, in particular. Feelings are perverted originally during the interaction between mother and child, and later actualised with the beloved, as Proust demonstrates time and time again. A child's desire can cause discomfort in the mother, so it must be concealed, or the opposite must be simulated. Later on, it will then require a game with the partner in order to magically turn hostility into love, passivity into activity, and discomfort into desire. Nevertheless, in the end, undergoing pain and experiencing lust provide a feeling of triumphing over the rules and demands of the (imaginary) mother.

"I have to see you as more important than myself", Frank said, whereby he verbalised a role change between mother and child in which the feelings of the mother and not those of the child are central. It is in the self-interest of the child to learn to tolerate a perverted interaction, in order to protect the mother from psychic collapse and thus to safeguard his own psychic survival.

Recapitulating, we can posit that the sadomasochist avoids the intimacy of which he is afraid out of fear of narcissistic insults and loss of love. Showing feelings or tenderness entails a risk of being humiliated by the partner, a danger that must be avoided at all costs. The distance is maintained by pestering and humiliating the other or by making oneself quasi small and powerless. The archaic aggression that is sexualised in a sadomasochistic love game provides lust that is free of risk. Sexual intercourse is sidestepped and replaced by inflicting or submitting to pain, in phantasy or in reality, which leads to orgasm either directly or through masturbation. Sometimes it is a question of staging humiliation. Peter, a successful businessman, has his partner put him in nappies and can then empty his bladder or intestines like a baby, which arouses him and brings him to orgasm. Penetration is impossible for him, average sexual contact is out of the question. He takes revenge for his humiliations and regains his independence by each time rejecting her afterwards.

More indicative than a definition of perversion in terms of behaviour is the inner mental state that can exist without any overt perversion: the all-pervasive fear of a mental breakdown and being devoured by the object. The fear of disintegration, loss of identity, and loss of love. These fears, combined with the often unconscious, phantasised archaic rage at and destructiveness of the love object, can be channelled with the aid of the sexual scenarios. Sexualising feelings that originally have nothing to do with sexual relations then lead to acts that protect against loss of, or fusion with, the object. The drawback to this solution is that there is no free choice left. The sexual actions and the phantasies that accompany them acquire a compulsive character. Sexual intercourse without these laborious detours isn't possible because impotence is lurking around. The danger of direct sexual intercourse and too much intimacy is eluded with the help of all sorts of scenarios. This can be recognised as a defence mechanism by the stereotypical and the exaggeration. At times, a profound depression lies at the basis of this manic defence.

Perverse patients often complain about an all-pervasive feeling of loneliness, of emptiness, a feeling of being deprived of human warmth and intimacy. I believe that the symbiotic illusion in which the child used to live, which also characterises the functioning of the adult with regard to his (inner) object, is actually a most unsatisfactory relationship; as unsatisfactory as are cool detachment and a complete lack of symbiotic feelings. The child is frequently not cherished for who he is and how he expresses himself but, instead, must obey the object to such an extent that his own essence gets lost. The "transitional space" between mother and child, and later on between self and object, is missing. The child doesn't have the space to satisfy his own desires, he doesn't even know what they consist of any more, nor what it means to have a desire of one's own. He is dependent and subservient to the desires of the other.

Not being familiar with one's own desires and longings, separate from the desires of the love object, is depressing. It is perverse to simultaneously spoil and neglect the child, as is the case when coddling is more satisfying to the mother's needs than to those of the child. In order to counteract emptiness and the lack of an inner compass, the perverse phantasy or act becomes as indispensable as it is manic and compulsive.

Notes

1. Freud, S. (1905d). *Three Essays. S. E. 7*, pp. 160–161.
2. Freud, S. (1905d). *Three Essays. S. E. 7*, p. 159.
3. Socarides, C. W. (1979). A unitary theory of sexual perversion. In: T. B. Karasu & C. Socarides, *On Sexuality*. New York: International Universities Press. Socarides differentiates between Oedipal and

pre-Oedipal perversion. The personality structure of perversion in its strict sense, with compulsion, archaic fears such as being devoured by the demonic mother, clearly belong to pre-Oedipal development. But there are more Oedipal perversions, too. It all depends on the level of object relationships; whether these are more narcissistic or more object-directed. Whether conflicts are Oedipal or pre-Oedipal depends on fixations and regressions going back to the rapprochement sub-phase of the separation–individuation phase or to earlier symbiotic periods. In the Oedipal form, it is a matter of structural conflicts between the id, the ego, and superego, while in the pre-Oedipal form, it is a matter of conflicts around object relationships, such as fear and guilt due to a lack of differentiation between self and object. Serious regression can then be the result. Reality barely plays a role, the boundary between phantasy and reality is blurred, impulse control doesn't function very well. Obviously, the prognosis regarding removal of perversion and attaining love of the object is better in the Oedipal than in the pre-Oedipal variant. True perversions are pre-Oedipal disorders; they do not stem from an Oedipal conflict, they differ from perverse behaviour and phantasies that do not go hand in hand with a troubled gender identity (pp. 181–182).

4. That it does actually occur, however, is shown in the book by Elfriede Jelinek (1989). *The Piano Teacher*. Trans. Joachim Neugroschel. London: Serpent's Tail. Louise Kaplan writes about *Female Perversions: The Temptations of Emma Bovary* (New York: Doubleday, 1991), by which she means—among other things—a mascarade in super-femininity whereby masculine aspirations are concealed.

5. McDougall, J. (1980). *Plea for a Measure of Abnormality*. New York: International Universities Press.

CHAPTER EIGHT

Eroticism and cruel party games

But the disastrous way in which the psychopathological universe is constructed has decreed that the clumsy act, the act which we ought most sedulously to avoid, is precisely the act that will calm us, the act that, opening before us, until we discover its outcome, fresh avenues of hope, momentarily relieves us of the intolerable pain which a refusal has aroused in us.

—Marcel Proust[1]

The similarities and differences between clear-cut sadism without sexual pleasure, moral masochism, and sexual sadomasochism are confusing. Society's version of cruelty can either serve an erotic purpose or be a bald-faced exercise of power.

Proust often describes cruel party games, which he calls "the public execution". Sometimes it is merely a matter of an erotic phantasy, as is the case when Charlus asks the narrator for permission to watch while Bloch's grandfather is being severely beaten. Sometimes the action is suited to the word, as when the old baron is verbally abused in public by his former boyfriend, Charlie, and piteously jeered during a society party, which results in his departure. The victim's narcissism is destroyed through shame, derision, or desecration, which is the equivalent of the execution of his personality, or the murder of the soul.

The most explicit example is a school paper by Proust written when he was fourteen years old, describing a gladiator who dies during a battle, which serves exclusively to entertain the public.[2] As a child, Jean Santeuil can thoroughly enjoy the wind that reaches gale force, thereby creating victims. The wind can thrash people or even kill them, which for him is an exciting spectacle.

Enjoyment in the torturing of animals is equally present. *Jean Santeuil* starts off with a scene in which Jean's alter-ego drives some geese into the sea where certain death awaits them. In *Remembrance of Things Past*, cruelty to animals is attributed to Françoise, the maid, who slaughters the struggling chickens for the evening meal and then in anger yells "filthy creature" at them, as if to justify her action. We already mentioned the dream of the rats where the theme of revenge at the parents, combined with cruelty, is abundantly clear. It also reminds us of the old, malicious, bedridden Aunt Léonie in *Remembrance of Things Past*, a fascinating alter-ego of the author. She takes pleasure in tormenting her maid Françoise in every possible way and terrorises her housemates by staying in bed as if she were seriously ill. She refuses to eat, creates intrigues, phantasises about cruel calamities. She seems to represent Proust's peculiarities; he himself spent his final years in isolation in a cork-lined room, refusing food and medical care, and, in fact, slowly committed suicide. The bedridden, obsessive Aunt Léonie has a mania for order and daily routine, but at times she had:

> [...] a keen expectation of some domestic cataclysm, momentary in its duration but violent enough to compel her to put into effect, once for all, one of those changes which she knew would be beneficial to her health but to which she could never make up her mind without some such stimulus. She was genuinely fond of us; she would have enjoyed the long luxury of weeping for our untimely decease; [...] the news that the house was being destroyed by a fire in which all the rest of us had already perished [...] but from which she herself would still have plenty of time to escape without undue haste, provided that she rose at once from her bed, must often have haunted her dreams, [...] of letting her taste the full savour of her affection for us in long years of mourning, and of causing universal

> stupefaction in the village when she should sally forth to conduct
> our obsequies, crushed but courageous, moribund but erect [...][3]

She can become so intensely excited when she imagines an argument in which sharp and biting words fly back and forth while she lies in bed bathing in her sweat.

Much like his aunt, Proust enjoyed using words to ridicule; he wrote pointed, witty, and sophisticated exercises in this genre, known as "Pastiches".[4] These are humorous imitations of the style of writers such as Balzac, Flaubert, Saint-Simon, whom he liked reading and admired, but also lovingly mocked.

An everyday example of sadism via the written word and of our attitude towards the suffering of others, is the way in which we tend to read our morning paper. Proust calls this "an abominable and voluptious act", whereby, while reading, we revel in the suffering of our fellow human beings as we enjoy our breakfast. Proust gets *Le Figaro* daily, in which he reads about the matricide and suicide of Henri van Blaerenberghe. This tragedy of his friend, in which he recognises his own phantasy, troubles him profoundly (see also Chapter Five). What is for him nothing but a masturbation phantasy has here actually happened and is therefore doubly tragic.

Remembrance of Things Past is filled with scenes in which someone is ridiculed because of the way in which he speaks, his attitude, his way of receiving guests, or the peculiarities of his profession, as in the case of physicians. These descriptions are full of irony about the poignant and ludicrous sides of the people he observes.

Plots are hatched, slanderous anonymous letters are written, and ignominious newspaper articles published in order to drive a victim to despair or even to suicide. The badgering to death of poor old Saniette by the Verdurin clan, under the aegis of the sadistic and loathsome Mme Verdurin, is one of the countless examples of social sadism at the expense of the vulnerable and the insecure in Proust's work. The lack of a sense of self-worth and of the audacity to take risks irrevocably lead to inciting that which one fears, namely rejection.

Proust describes a case that everyone will recognise, with which he demonstrates how widespread moral masochism really is. That is to say, the tendency to call down misfortune upon yourself and put yourself in the very spot where the blows will fall. Moral masochist that he is, Saniette, an ageing scientist who visits the Verdurins every day, cannot stop himself from eliciting scorn and revulsion.

> But Saniette's own consciousness of being a bore had the effect that, although he was more learned, more intelligent and better than most people, it seemed impossible to feel in his company, not only any pleasure, but anything save an almost intolerable irritation which spoiled one's whole afternoon. Probably, if Saniette had frankly admitted this boredom which he was afraid of causing, one would not have dreaded his visits. But he was so anxious not to let it be seen that he was not sought after that he dared not propose himself.[5]

This character sketch furthermore describes how the man in question demeans himself in order to force his conversation partner deviously into inviting him. He causes the other one to feel uncomfortable and to purposely avoid him. On the day that he had wanted to pay him a visit but was told that the narrator wouldn't be home, he runs into someone who is on his way to see the latter. The masochist's self-pity is always confirmed and reinforces him in his role as victim. He looks for, and always finds, that he is right: no one likes him, everyone is out to harass and humiliate him. Moral masochism doesn't have any direct bearing on sexuality, it is a tendency to suffer in a much broader sense.

The crafty sadism that Mme Verdurin's guests display with regard to Saniette by constantly rejecting him and frustrating his attempts at contact as they notice his increasing need of it, is reminiscent of the Proustian motif of the child who destroys the "poor" parent by pursuing his own pleasure. The guilt feeling that causes despondency plays no role in social sadism. In these treacherous games, guilt feelings are eliminated, to the author's indignation.

> [...] the idea of deliberate unkindness being too painful for me to bear. And yet [...] unkindness has probably not in the minds of the unkind that pure and voluptious cruelty which we find so painful to imagine. Hatred inspires them (the unkind), anger prompts them to an ardour and an activity in which there is no great joy; sadism is needed to extract any pleasure from it; whereas unkind people suppose themselves to be punishing someone equally unkind.[6]

The true evildoer simply lacks sufficient imagination to put himself in the other one's shoes. A lack of empathy is what makes cruelty possible.

The narrator has a very hard time identifying with these feelings of hate and aggression, which are thus vehemently denied. Harshness or cruelty simply cannot exist in mother or grandmother, and neither can his own feelings of revenge. The oppressive guilt feeling is caused by destructive phantasies from which the narrator tries to escape. People such as Mme Verdurin or Mme de Guermantes, who enjoy malicious pleasure, do not have this sense of guilt. They choose an easy prey as victim to torment in social interaction—someone like Charles Swann, vulnerable as the daily guest in love with a celebrated regular visitor of the Verdurins, the courtesan Odette.

Proust gives numerous examples of individuals in the upper echelon whose worldly pleasures always take precedence over the interests of others. The narrator is extremely sensitive to party games at the expense of others. This crude form of pleasure is contrasted with the sadism in the hidden world of sexual perversion. He places the sadism that is performed in a split-off sphere of phantasy life in opposition to the enjoyment of senseless cruelty and violence in social interaction. Proust rightfully emphasises the difference between a cold-blooded act of violence or murder and the harmless phantasy world of the sadomasochist. He calls the latter oversensitive, just like the narrator himself who is a kind-hearted man with a great deal of compassion. Whether this is always the case, is the question.

The pleasures of the upper crust, which may not be disrupted, take priority over trouble such as illness and, yes, even the death and funeral of a close friend. Proust gives various, touching examples of this. The critically ill Swann isn't welcome at the Guermantes who are on the verge of leaving for a ball. They callously deny the fact that Swann is to die soon. Hastily saying goodbye, the duke even assures him that he is as strong and healthy as the Pont Neuf. In other words, don't you dare remind me of your misery while I'm on my way to being entertained, which takes precedence over your suffering.

At the same time, this is yet another example of the desecration of a dying person. It is particularly reminiscent of the uncompromising manner in which the narrator dealt with his grandmother. Profanation of a departed one is an ever-recurring theme. After his death, many still speak condescendingly about Swann, whereby they once again besmirch his memory. Even his own daughter disclaims her Jewish father when she sees the chance of suggesting a better origin, thanks to her aristocratic stepfather. It's like dancing on his grave when, at a ball, the duchess of Guermantes, Swann's best friend, completely denies her relationship with him to his daughter. Gilberte, Swann's daughter, accepts this because she will give anything to be received by Mme de Guermantes. The latter hadn't wanted to meet Gilberte, daughter of the courtesan Odette, Swann's wife, as long as her father was still alive, although he had more or less begged her for it. But after his death, Gilberte's chances improve when she is adopted by someone of the upper class and she has become wealthy thanks to her father's enormous inheritance.

The narrator becomes intensely captivated by the cruelty of this woman, Mme de Guermantes, who represents the reincarnation of the aristocracy. Not only does she not have any compassion for Swann, her lifelong friend and almost daily guest, but she is also cold and heartless towards her husband and her personnel. She will never take the slightest trouble for anyone and will always find excuses to refuse any help that is requested. The least little sacrifice from her end doesn't counterbalance another person's life or even death. Through her contacts, she could have rescued her cousin Robert de Saint-Loup from military service and the risk of dying in Morocco, but she chooses not to do anything for him. She loves tormenting her servants. She refuses to grant a male servant the one day off on which he could see his fiancée, giving him a different free day and suggesting that she is doing the desperate man a favour. This is like the perverse mothers I described earlier, who give something that wasn't asked for and withhold what the son would like to receive. When the servant hears his "sentence" and almost faints amidst the guests, she feels a secret pleasure. She torments and humiliates when and where she possibly can, a game whose goal it is to be the centre of attention. She is bent on being admired for her sharp tongue and her universally renowned humour.

These examples all have more to do with narcissism than with sexuality, which is also what they have in common with perversion, where sexuality is used in the service of self-esteem regulation.

Arguing, pestering, humiliating, and triumphing at the expense of others is the characteristic of all these examples. In addition, let's not forget the Dreyfus Affair, in which Proust feels strongly involved and into which he delves extensively in *Remembrance of Things Past*. The fierce discussion between those who are pro- and anti-Dreyfus turned society completely upside down. Even wealthy and prominent Jews were suddenly much less welcome in the upper circles than before. By being anti-Dreyfus, a bourgeois now can very simply climb the social ladder and work his way into the aristocracy.

Delighting in injustice, not in reality but as an exciting erotic game, is more for oversensitive, nervous maniacs such as Charlus, Proust reassures us. The aristocracy's social injustice in a case such as the Dreyfus Affair rests on pure cruelty. Captain Dreyfus was accused under false pretences, downgraded, humiliated, and banished. When a person is thus disgraced, his feeling of self-worth is violated and he is robbed of his pride completely. That is totally different from the contrite individuals who briefly step outside of their narrow emotional straightjacket for a moment of pleasure.

Proust was extremely interested in shame and being made ashamed as we already saw in the chapter on adolescence (Chapter Five). Being the son of a Jewish mother confronts him doubly with shame and self-hatred. He uses the character of Bloch, a friend of the narrator's youth, to describe a Jew who tries to conceal his lack of self-assurance through all sorts of caricatural gestures. Just like Proust and the narrator, Bloch wishes to enter aristocratic circles, although he knows that, especially after the Dreyfus Affair, they will look down on him even more. Swann alone was an exception. Although he was of Jewish descent, even if baptised in the Catholic Church like Proust, he was a successful and welcome society figure thanks to his great gifts as a connoisseur of the arts and as a conversationalist. With rightful indignation, Proust describes what Bloch must accept in humiliations and how he degrades himself, apparently without any effort, in order to attain his social aims. Proust describes how a Jew who succeeds in hiding his Jewishness becomes angry and ashamed when he is confronted with a fellow Jew who behaves in an exaggeratedly Jewish manner. Bloch's uncle is reprimanded by his family members for his overly Jewish behaviour, which turns him into a source of shame because he shows the very thing they are trying to hide. Besides, the narrator confides to the reader, Bloch's uncle is also a homosexual and a sadomasochist.

I suspect that we see Proust march, as it were, through his work in various disguises, in the incarnation of different characters. He appears not only in the character of the narrator, but also as Bloch and as Swann (the unhappy lover who doesn't get a goodnight kiss from his beloved Odette, just as the narrator didn't get one from his mother) and finally as the Baron de Charlus. The homosexual baron is an exceedingly ambiguous character. He is feared because of his brazenness, which makes him into the most explicit personage in *Remembrance of Things Past*. He expresses himself very overtly in words as someone who has a passion for attacking and insulting others with his sharp tongue; on the other hand, he can be goodness and kindheartedness itself. He is the prototype of the Proustian sadomasochist: a person whose conscience is so rigorous that he can only escape it and enjoy sex in a perverse ritual whereby cruelty is simulated. The pleasure Charlus gets from tormenting earns him the nickname "Teaser Augustus", invented by his sister-in-law, the witty and equally sharp Mme de Guermantes.

With regard to his apparently inexplicable grievances and his fierce outbursts of rage, Proust compares him to Don Quixote. Charlus writes letters and uses words—loudly, eloquently, and blasphemously—that contain the crudest insults addressed to his victim or lover, often one and the same person. In order to persuade the narrator to come and visit him, Charlus tries every trick in the book. When the visit finally takes place, the narrator is totally baffled by Charlus's insulting, unexpected, and apparently unfounded cursing and swearing. Even when he is alone reading a letter he doesn't consider sufficiently respectful, Charlus utters loud vituperations such as: "The imbecile, the scoundrel, he is too filthy even to be flung in the gutter where he'd be a danger to public health." An attack of narcissistic rage can be the result of even a minor offence. The most revealing example of Charlus's behaviour is the way in which he publicly finishes off Mme de Saint-Euverte:

> "Would you believe it, this impertinent young man" [...] indicating me "has just asked me without the slightest concern for the proper reticence in regard to such needs, whether I was going to Mme de Saint-Euverte's, in other words, I suppose, whether I was suffering from diarrhoea. I should endeavour in any case to relieve myself in some more comfortable place than the house of a person who, if my memory serves me, was celebrating her centenary when I first began to move in society, that is to say, not in her house. What a host of [...] intimate relations [she had], which certainly had nothing of the 'Saint' about them.[...] What would prevent me from questioning her about those thrilling times is the sensitiveness of my olfactory organ. The proximity of the lady is enough. I Suddenly say to myself: oh, good lord, someone has broken the lid of my cesspool, when it's simply the Marquise opening her mouth to emit some invitation. And you can imagine that if I had the misfortune to go

to her house, the cesspool would expand into a formidable sewage cart."[7]

This verbal orgy of anal excesses reveals the anal-coloured phantasies that homosexual men sometimes have about women, though they are not alone in this. In his phantasy, the "feared hole", the vagina, is an especially filthy, contagious, stinking pool, which is more likely to make one take to one's heels than to arouse a yearning to linger there.

At one point, the baron asks the narrator to arrange for a beating of old Bloch. It is neither the first nor the last example in *Remembrance of Things Past* of two homosexual men who become sexually aroused by making a fool of a third individual. This time around, it is Charlus's anti-Semitism that makes him invent a scene in which parents are desecrated. The narrator's Jewish friend is being insulted while he, together with the baron and the reader, can freely enjoy it as a voyeur.

> "Perhaps you could ask your friend to allow me to attend some great festival in the Temple, a circumcision, or some Hebrew chants. He might perhaps [...] give me some biblical entertainment, [...] You might perhaps arrange [...] a contest between your friend and his father, in which he would smite him as David smote Goliath. That would make quite an amusing farce. He might even [...] give his hag of a mother a good thrashing. That would be an excellent show, [...] my young friend, since we like exotic spectacles, and to thrash that non-European creature would be giving a well-earned punishment to that old cow."[8]

Charlus's anti-Semitism could be conceived of as a form of love, Proust writes apologetically. The mistreatment of his (Jewish!) mother isn't foreign as a phantasy to the narrator either. Charlus can elaborate on Jews who rent a house that previously belonged to Christians, or who live in a street named after a saint. He accuses them of doing so on purpose in order to desecrate that house or street and then loudly declares that such things ought to be punished. Tormenting and humiliating Jews in phantasy games brings him to a climax. The baron is erotically aroused by Bloch (and by the narrator), which is the reason why he speaks about them in such anti-Semitic ways. To me, the explanation seems a doubtful excuse.

Proust posits that everyone has two sides and that the puzzle of goodness versus evil within one and the same individual deserves explanation. It certainly is true that in cruelty the personality split is striking. The executioner who, when the murderous work is done, takes his children on his lap and pets his beloved dog was well known during the Second World War. In perversion, sadomasochism and hypersensitivity easily go hand in hand as well. Shyness and insecurity in everyday life can be combined rather well with sadistic phantasies. Feelings of narcissistic offences and the need for revenge can go together with an insecure personality, burdened with shame and guilt. When the baron is being attacked, he is incapable of defending himself, which illustrates how helpless this man actually is, despite his sadistic phantasies and his insulting utterances. Mme Verdurin can demolish the Baron de Charlus in public without any extra effort from her end. She mercilessly turns his lover, Charlie, against him by letting out the secret that the baron not only gossips about him and his lower-class birth, but also that he seeks his pleasure with criminals. Charlie immediately takes revenge and, when the baron approaches him enthusiastically, yells at him loudly and angrily: "Go away, stay away from me, I'm not the first one you're trying to pervert!" Wounded to the bone and humiliated, Charlus submits to this public execution like a completely helpless and pitiful victim.

> M. de Charlus stood speechless, dumbfounded, measuring the depths of his misery without understanding its cause, unable to think of a word to say, raising his eyes to gaze at each of the company in turn, with a questioning, outraged, suppliant air, which seemed to be asking them [...] what answer he ought to make. And yet M. de Charlus possessed all the resources, not merely of eloquence but of audacity, when seized by a rage which had been simmering for a long time, he reduced someone to despair with the most cruel words in front of a shocked society group which had never imagined that anyone could go so far [...] working himself up to a veritable frenzy which left everyone trembling. [...] not having worked himself up and concocted an imaginary rage in advance [...] he had been seized and struck down suddenly at a moment when he was unarmed [...] indeed, as I had always thought, and it was something that had rather endeared him to me, [he was] pseudo-cruel—and did not have the normal reactions [...] outraged by the violence that was being done to him. In a situation so cruelly

unforeseen, this great talker could do no more than stammer: "What does it all mean? What's wrong?"[9]

Thereupon Charlie pursues the baron in every possible way, openly accusing him of homosexuality and attempting to have him arrested. With regard to the baron's oversensitive, hysterical character, the narrator remarks:

> [...] neurotics, irritated at the slightest provocation by imaginary and inoffensive enemies, become on the contrary inoffensive as soon as anyone takes the offensive against them...[10]

Later on, in *Time Regained*, the narrator determines:

> Now in him pleasure was not unaccompanied by a certain idea of cruelty [...] the man he loved appeared to him in the guise of a delightful torturer. [...] acting as he did only in his hours of physical pleasure [...] in a manner contrary to his merciful nature, fired with passion for seductive evil and helping to crush virtuous ugliness.[11]

It seems that the narrator is using his justification of the baron's behaviour to apologise for his own sadism and to relieve his own sense of guilt about the fact that part of him hates his mother whom he loves tenderly at the same time. He repeatedly states that sadism isn't really intended that way, even though sadistic yearnings are the only path to pleasure.

This follows the tradition of De Sade, where goodness and honesty have to be destroyed in order to be able to attain sexual gratification. Strict moral principles and a deeply rooted belief in God and goodness must be annihilated for the sake of excitement and lust.

We have already seen that in Proust's work evil seems to dwell primarily in women, with the exception of the narrator's mother and grandmother. Men either aren't as malicious as they appear or else they can be easily excused. Although the mother and the grandmother are generally described as caring and virtuous, they are strict and coercive, on the other hand. Proust projects these character traits onto other women, such as Mme Verdurin and Mme de Guermantes. Despite this separation, we can easily discern the rancour against the mother that lies at its basis. Mme Verdurin is depicted as the prototype of the dominant, intrusive mother figure. Any guest in her salon who doesn't follow her rules, doesn't love what or whom she loves, is automatically damned. In contrast, the meek are crowned with affection and rewarded with loyalty. Disobedient guests who don't do precisely what she wants, such as Swann and the baron, over whom she has no hold, are ruthlessly finished off.

All the characters in *Remembrance of Things Past* more or less display the same personality structure. They have a vulnerable narcissism, they are quasi-docile while they conceal their rage and feelings of hatred. They suffer from the fear of losing love and from an unsatisfied need for tenderness and intimacy. Their mother offers love only on the condition that they are ill and/or behave obediently. The symbiotic illusion restrains the child from expressing protest or anger. He is afraid that these feelings would only destroy the mother's equilibrium, her illusion of being a good mother, her self-assurance, which would then lead to retaliation in the form of rejection. The powerless child may only show his need for love and tenderness on conditions that his mother has set. Wishes that are directly expressed frighten her, since they confront her with her own unsatisfied needs and her inability to react spontaneously. She does her utmost to avoid a direct emotional exchange with her child, and actual intimacy is out of the question. Both his erotic and aggressive feelings, which the child must manage to repress as much as possible, will consequently belong to the realm of the forbidden.

The only place where the needs and feelings that are not in harmony with the symbiotic illusion can be freely expressed is in a separate, split-off phantasy world. That is the world where laws are momentarily nullified and signs are changed into their opposite, which makes the perverted love into a caricature. Murdering your mother in an outburst of rage, like Henri van Blaerenberghe (see the next chapter), spitting on your father's photograph like Mlle Vinteuil, desecrating your parents by selling their furniture to a brothel, or having sex on their grave, all these perverse behaviours performed in a state of near-insanity, are the only way open to the spiteful, guilt-ridden child inside the adolescent and adult.

Proust provides us with a clear history of the development of perversion, which begins with the narcissistic offence to the dependent, helpless child and ends with pleasure due to cruelty. The narrator's personality forms, as it were, one entity with the other protagonists. These different personalities represent the different facets of his complicated character. Charlus, the highly cultivated, sophisticated homosexual and shameless aristocrat, displays one side; Swann, the artistic, incredibly sensitive, and subtle dandy, reflects another side. The rest of the characters, too, seem to personify hidden aspects of the narrator who, after telling the story of his youth, becomes more and more a spectator. He no longer plays an active role in the cruelty, the homosexual encounters, and the perverse behaviours he now observes only as an onlooker. Just as in dreams, various characters represent aspects of the dreamer, while he himself frequently is no more than an onlooker.

It is no coincidence that *Remembrance of Things Past* begins with a dream. We are transferred to what is in part a dream world and in part a world of the "primary process" (see Chapter One). It will be clear by now that it is difficult at times to differentiate clearly between perversion and outright cruelty. The insane, alienating dream world of perversion involuntarily displays a resemblance with the cruelty of the real world. This often makes treating such people unappealing to most psychotherapists. It is apparently difficult to repress a certain prejudice against and repugnance of these individuals. However, the therapist thereby loses sight of what Freud already realised more than a hundred years ago: that those who seek treatment are vulnerable and quite defenceless.

Notes

1. Proust, M., *Remembrance of Things Past, The Fugitive*, Vol. 3, p. 466.
2. Proust, M. (1884). Le gladiateur mourant. In: *Contre Sainte-Beuve, Essais et articles, Juvenilia*. Paris: Pléiade v, Gallimard, 1971. I am not aware of any English translation of this text.
3. Proust, M., *Remembrance of Things Past, Swann's Way*, Vol. 1, p. 126.
4. Proust, M. (1884). Pastiches et mélanges. In: *Contre Sainte-Beuve, Essais et articles, Juvenilia*. Paris: Pléiade v, Gallimard, 1971. I am not aware of any English translation of this text.
5. Proust, M., *Remembrance of Things Past, Cities of the Plain*, Vol. 2, p. 1056.
6. Proust, M., *Remembrance of Things Past, The Guermantes Way*, Vol. 2, p. 177.
7. Proust, M., *Remembrance of Things Past, Cities of the Plain*, Vol. 2, p. 726.
8. Proust, M., *Remembrance of Things Past, The Guermantes Way*, Vol. 2, p. 298.
9. Proust, M., *Remembrance of Things Past, The Captive*, Vol. 3, pp. 321–322.
10. Proust, M., *Remembrance of Things Past, The Captive*, Vol. 3, pp. 327–328.
11. Proust, M., *Remembrance of Things Past, Time Regained*, Vol. 3, p. 801.

CHAPTER NINE

Love's devious means

We are all obliged, if we are to make reality endurable, to nurse a few little follies in ourselves.

—Marcel Proust[1]

The challenge of taking the risk to love is of all ages. During our adolescence, we face this breathtaking challenge for the first time, when once again the fear of symbiosis and abandonment loom menacingly on our inner horizon.

Even in his youthful works, Proust already wrote about the Calvary that is known as love. Longing for the beloved is torment, by the mere fact that it is unattainable. Fruitless yearnings fit well with the psychology of the perversions of which this writer is the uncontested specialist.

The yearning as unconscious desire to reunite with the original love object, the mother, is well-nigh unattainable. We make do with a substitute. This old yearning dies out definitively only when life ends. While the physical needs of a baby are satisfied, the non-physical longings for the mother's undying love and everlasting attention sometimes remain unfulfilled throughout life. Whether these particulars are experienced

139

as unbearable depends on disposition and environment. It seems that in perversion the chasm between longing and fulfilment is extremely wide, and the fear of abandonment extraordinarily great.

Being in love is a subjective experience, in which the objective qualities of the beloved's persona play a fairly small role. The ideal beloved is imaginary, exists in our phantasy alone, and is the only one who can make bliss come to fruition. No one is that ideal person who can bridge the chasm between longing and reality. The early excitement and suspense of the unfamiliar in love evaporate with time. Pursuing imaginary love is an exhilarating game, which furthermore has the advantage of being less threatening than the risks of actual intimacy. But for the one who, out of fear of disillusionment, lives in a phantasy world, love is all the more disappointing.

Proustian love is a Calvary because it can never be reciprocal. The narrator chooses someone who cannot respond to his love. The beloved will keep eluding the lover, who will therefore always be afraid of losing her. Absence of the beloved is the most painful, the most inevitable. Fear of the loss of love renders the beloved indispensable, even though she doesn't satisfy the lover's ideal. The beloved is both the cause of and remedy for the unbearable fear and jealousy she arouses.

Erik, whom we encountered earlier and who met his wife as dominatrix in an SM club, knew beforehand that she liked making dates with other men. Now he watches her constantly like a jailer, just as the narrator does with Albertine. He is intolerably jealous and always afraid that he will miss out on the supposed intimacy she shares with others. She feeds the flame by regularly making him jealous and setting up appointments with other men. And yet, if the symbiotic illusion to which Erik aspires were to be realised, it would also be a torment. To solely live with and for one another, without any other pursuits such as work and friends, will soon become a stifling prison, as the narrator put it into practice with Albertine. Erik knows this very well, and yet it continues to be a yearning that he is unable to put into perspective. This dilemma rules his life. He always feels restless and can't focus his attention on anything other than his obsession. His childhood longings were never fulfilled because his mother didn't like children, although each year another child was added to the family. Erik comes from a family with five brothers and the competition for the mother's love was so fierce, the jealousy so severe, that they rarely or never see each other today. Moreover, he fulfilled a special role in his mother's phantasy: he was meant to be a daughter and for a long time was dressed as a girl.

For some people, jealousy is an essential ingredient in love. Without jealous tension, love will not catch fire or the flame will soon die out. That way, love deteriorates into a permanent narcissistic struggle that has to be thrashed out with the beloved. If you admit that you love her, you have lost face in the beloved's eyes and risk losing her. In order to excite her, a game must be played: telling lies and showing the opposite of your innermost feelings; pretending you don't care for her at all, or acting as if you're in love with someone else.

When jealousy is continuously fed, love becomes a torment.

When a man chooses a whorish or vulgar love object, it can satisfy a need for superiority, while it simultaneously feeds jealousy. The anxiety and tension that are thus generated in turn provide the necessary excitement. At the end of *Swann in Love*, when he looks back on his life with the courtesan Odette de Crécy, Swann exclaims: "To think that I've wasted years of my life, that I've longed to die, that I've experienced my greatest love, for a woman who didn't appeal to me, who wasn't even my type!"[2]

Edmund Wilson expressed it as follows:

> This tragic subjectivity of love is even more striking in the case of the sexual inverts; for here [...] there is nothing romantic to be seen at all, and the grotesque disparity between the ideal which is exalting or tormenting the lover and the object in which he has located it becomes ludicrous or disgusting.[3]

For Proust, love is *"cette maladie"* (that illness) that is always closely connected to being physically and mentally ill.[4] Love is the torment that, from his earliest work on, is always linked to ruin and damnation. Thereby, he finds himself in the company of Denis de Rougemont, who puts the myth of romantic love coupled as it is with suffering in an historic perspective.[5] Not forgetting Mario Praz, who demonstrates that love as a concept reaches its apex during the period of Romanticism.[6] De Sade was popular and the decadents were fascinated by the perverse pleasures of lust combined with pain.

Richard has a steady partner but keeps longing for whores and massage parlours, which he does, indeed, visit regularly. He also attends live sex shows. At first, he'd sometimes bring his wife along, but she's not that interested and doesn't really understand his obsession. Richard was never allowed to enter his parents' bedroom and was so scared of his father that he never dared do anything that was forbidden. Anything enjoyable had to happen clandestinely, in a secret little phantasy world to which his parents had no access. His father was menacing and strict, while his mother was both seductive and rejecting. His father wanted him to be a brave, strong man, while his mother preferred to see an unmanly ally in her son. Now, as a voyeur, he can witness the scenes from which he felt excluded as a small child. Now he can enjoy sex surreptitiously while no one knows where he is or what he is doing. He spends his life being preoccupied with skirting his parents' taboos and prohibitions that have frustrated him since early childhood. Although Richard can look like a guilty, beaten dog, he is scarcely ashamed of his perverse escapades, nor does he feel any guilt about them. On the contrary, they are the only moments when he feels free and happy. The quantity of guilt feelings in Proust is much greater than usual because he is, at heart, a moralist.

In perversion, love and hate are badly integrated. In the primitive, vehement phantasies of the young child, hostility towards the parent is not yet alleviated by the love for that same parent. The good and the evil sides of the parents are not yet integrated into one and the same person. In later development, when the child discovers that the parents share something that excludes him, it turns out that he is the third person in the triangle and not the only one for either one of them. Accepting this is a mental process: triumphing over narcissistic offences and disappointments. It means gaining more insight into reality, which Melanie Klein calls the "depressive position". Sadder and wiser, not living in illusions any longer, is the direction in which it is hoped that growing older and/or psychotherapy help to move forward. But what holds for perversion is that archaic representations are maintained in part of the consciousness; imaginary omnipotence, killing or being killed, all of it as ferocious as in the fairy tales.

The narrator's perverse phantasy play serves to create erotic scenes that undo what used to torment him as a child. Actively staging that which was once passively suffered helps to ferret out pleasure from a defeat. The roles of traumatised childhood, when he suffered insult after insult, are now turned around. Gratification lies in the manic flush of victory that is thus created. The relationship of the narrator with Albertine is determined by his earliest experiences, but in the reversal of changing passive into active. Proust illustrates what Freud calls "transference" by showing that the feelings originally meant for the mother are now projected onto Albertine.

In Proust's early work, we already read about the ritual scenario that is the indispensable condition for excitement. The love object's untrustworthiness that causes fear of abandonment is acted out and ritualised in a perverse scenario. The two protagonists each take up their respective positions in tacit and implicit mutual agreement. The beloved must be taught what she ought to do and say in order to summon the right amount of tension and fear, after which the love game can begin. The lover has to humbly implore the beloved to tell him about her relationships and unfaithfulness to him. Initially she refuses but, after pleading with her ever more humbly, she finally yields to his wishes. She has to torment him the way a toreador provokes a bull.

Humiliation generates love in the narrator, who doesn't fall in love with Gilberte until he feels she has treated him rudely. That inspires him with the sadistic phantasy to curse and humiliate her in turn. In Jean Santeuil, the ritual game displays the same scenario as in Swann and, finally, in the narrator and his girlfriend Albertine. At first, beatings—the ultimate outcome of this game—are mentioned only in passing. This topic doesn't come up for full discussion until the end of *Remembrance of Things Past*, namely in *Time Regained*, where the Baron de Charlus has himself severely beaten in a male brothel in order to come to climax.

Albertine, the narrator's girlfriend, also goes to a brothel, at least in his imagination, in order to meet other lesbians. There, she is "beaten on her bottom", an expression that is neither haphazard nor without significance. It is jargon for anal sex and suggests a transposition, namely that behind Albertine a man is lurking. Thus it is a partial reversal just like the one the writer applies to Mlle Vinteuil. Marcel exerts endless pressure on Albertine to force her to tell the "truth" about her alleged lesbian adventures, which arouse him. The narrator is fascinated by lesbians and phantasises about two women who violently thrash each other. The heterosexual relationship in the novel conceals a homosexual phantasy, not between two women, but between two men.

The lover spies on his beloved so he can indulge his averted, split-off, and projected homosexual phantasies. Then the narrator appeals to Albertine's honour and tries to make her feel guilty. He demonstrates the combination of masochistic humility and sadistic coercion.

The entire game is reminiscent of how the narrator's mother treated him when he was a little boy.

Just like Swann, the narrator becomes frantic when his beloved isn't there at a time when he expects her. He has to know from hour to hour, day and night, where she is, what she is doing, and whose company she keeps. Any third person entering or disturbing the dyadic relationship raises panic and fear of loss of love. Her presence is the only balm for his tortured soul. Hence his constant interrogation of her and why he drives her into a corner with his questions: homosexual unfaithfulness is what goads him before all else. This causes endlessly repeated scenes of reproach and supplication, as Proust calls them, in which the lover's intentions are skilfully hidden behind a smokescreen of hypocrisy. The interrogation stops only when the victim caves in. When Albertine wants to go out against her lover's will, he blackmails her: "Either you do what I want, and won't go out, or I'll no longer love you." Everything in love is perverted.

> Among all the methods by which love is brought into being, among all the agents which disseminate that blessed bane, there are few so efficacious as this gust of feverish agitation that sweeps over us from time to time. For then the die is cast, the person whose company we enjoy at that moment is the person we shall henceforward love. It is not even necessary for that person to have attracted us, up till then, more than or even as much as others. All that was needed was that our predilection should become exclusive. And that condition is fulfilled when—in this moment of deprivation—the quest for the pleasures we enjoyed in his or her company are suddenly replaced by an anxious, torturing need, whose object is the person alone, an absurd, irrational need which the laws of this world make it impossible to satisfy and difficult to assuage—the insensate, agonising need to possess exclusively.[7]

From this, we must draw the conclusion that the jealousy of which Proust speaks is actually a more primary narcissistic envy, not the longing for love, but the desire to possess the other completely and exclusively in a dyadic relationship, in short: longing for the symbiotic illusion.

In perversion, the fear is not so much "Can I, as one of the rivals in an Oedipal triangle, be successful?" It has more to do with the anxious question: "Am I really the only one she loves?" At stake are archaic feelings of all-or-nothing. If it is a matter of loss or abandonment, either the lover or the beloved will be guilty and will have to pay with punishment by death. It isn't clear who will have to suffer. Will the narrator commit suicide, as he often plans to do, or will he cause Albertine's death?

In following the fortunes of the successive protagonists in *Remembrance of Things Past*, the perverse scenario not only becomes very clear but even stereotypical. Furthermore, we mustn't forget that this isn't a general template and that the emphases vary in every individual case.

Swann and Odette have a daughter, Gilberte, who plays the same role in the life of the young narrator as Odette does in Swann's life: teasing and bewildering by being as elusive as possible. The jealousy that elicits love is a recurring paradox. The pattern is later repeated with Albertine. The narrator first sees her on the beach of Balbec where she is one in a group of tomboyish girls. They fascinate him because they are both shy and rough and, what's more, unattainable to him. Captivated, he watches as they tease an old man who is quietly dozing on a bench.

Back in Paris, he forgets about the girls and falls in love with the unapproachable, aristocratic Mme de Guermantes. What really irks him is that, although they live on the same block, she cuts him dead. She pretends not to see him while he shadows her on her daily walks like a stalker. He phantasises that one day she will be poor and humiliated and come begging to him for help. The exact opposite of what she presently is: unattainable, cold, and haughty, whereby he feels small and insignificant.

At the same time, he knows he annoys her, the same way he previously used to annoy Gilberte by visiting her every day. But he persists nevertheless, and thus engenders the rejection that he fears. Proust compares humiliation in love to an unmanageable child who is beaten. The battle over his bad habits that he used to wage with his parents earlier is transformed into a struggle with himself, the same way that Zeno fights with himself throughout an entire book about his smoking addiction.[8]

When the narrator starts to meet with Albertine regularly, he becomes enthralled with the combination of timidity and insolence in her character. Once she lives with him, he keeps her locked up at home like a prisoner, just as his mother did with him. He feels the same tormenting need to keep Albertine close to him, as during the goodnight kiss episode with his mother. He plucks at Albertine's heartstrings until he has power over her. He demonstrates how miserable, how bewildered, shortchanged, ill, and frightened he is until she finally gives in. It all becomes very heated and Albertine accuses him of being cruel to her. She is deeply sad and insulted, and threatens suicide. The narrator hates her because of her supposed homosexual affairs and secretly wishes her nothing but the worst. He feels wronged and hurt, although he knows perfectly well that he is morbid, oversensitive, and maniacal, and has problems with his nerves. He realises that he invites his own suffering, just as Swann used to do when he was in love with Odette. He recognises that his being in love is an inner condition that has little connection to the objective qualities of the beloved. Although he is aware of the fact that it actually has nothing to do with Albertine, he wants his fears to be soothed by her.[9]

The narrator secretly enjoys the suffering he causes Albertine every time he makes her cry with his insistent grilling. In fact, he hates her more than he loves her, which doesn't make her any less indispensable to his peace of mind. When Albertine grows frightened, worried, and restless, afraid that their relationship will be broken off, he has reached his goal. He has her in his power. He could now calm down but, instead, puts even more pressure on her by forcing her to tell him in even greater detail about her supposed secret love relationships. Once he is sure that she doesn't want to lose him, he knows no mercy. She has to submit to him totally and be brought to her knees. He uses every method, every trick and ruse he can think of, to gain absolute power over her. Once that has been achieved, his mood changes: he suddenly feels filled with love and emotion when he sees how Albertine suffers by his doing. However, in order not to betray his feelings, he must lead her up the garden path. Being in love and admitting to it is dangerous in the narcissistic power struggle that lovers must wage. He claims he no longer loves her but is, instead, madly in love with her friend, Andrée.

With this game, the narrator has apparently won the battle. He would rather pervert his feelings than risk rejection and abandonment. Tenderness cannot be asked for openly, but only after a fight and under false pretences. Albertine seems to be completely aware of the game that is being played and helps the narrator to save face by pretending she isn't wise to it. She even seems to be touched by his twisting reality and the cunning he uses to hold on to her love.

Because the narrator is terrified of losing control, he forces Albertine into a subservient position. The lovers are like two frightened children looking for solace from each other. Although in this case the depiction of the state of affairs is extreme, nevertheless, in reading Proust's revelations we all recognise something of our own fears and devious ways when in love, which makes his work so fascinating and cherished.

At a certain point, the relationship between the narrator and Albertine seems to be better than ever. Of her own accord, she expresses her desire to stay with him, which makes it possible for him to continue to be with her like two lovers while pretending he no longer loves her. When Albertine reacts benevolently to his plea to be forgiven for the scenes he's made and for starting fights, he feels like the little boy back in his mother's good graces. A few expressions of tenderness actually follow, exactly the way things went between the narrator and his mother in earlier days. She would only give in and be tender after the most heartrending scenes wherein he showed himself to be helpless. Then the narrator comments wistfully:

> I ought to have gone away that evening and never seen her again. I sensed there and then that in a love that is not shared—one might almost say in love, for there are people for whom there is no such thing as shared love—we can enjoy only that simulacrum of happiness which had been given to me at one of those unique moments in which a woman's good nature, or her caprice, or mere chance, respond to our desires, in perfect coincidence, with the same words, the same actions, as if we were really loved.[10]

When love cannot be trusted, a carefully designed scenario of behaviour performed according to a fixed ritual will help against fear of abandonment. It will help to keep the fear of annihilation of one of the two partners under control. Hate is not openly expressed and fear stays on a manageable level so that the path to excitement and suspense is open. In this comedy of rupture, as Proust calls the fights with Albertine, you can take the risk of getting closer to the other person more than would be possible without it. This game can be endlessly repeated: always watching how far you can go, always just to the edge of a real catastrophe, followed by the usual reconciliation.

Enjoying love and tenderness straightforwardly is dangerous because you can be rejected completely and without warning. The masochist can avoid threatening danger by putting on a mask of suffering while having pleasure. That is what the narrator learned and has taken to heart from his youth onwards. The love between the narrator and Albertine consists of a never-ending game of mutual defiance. What it resembles most is a prolonged caricature of normal foreplay. A complicated web of lies is created that conceals the truth. Not only Albertine, but the reader, too, is taken for a ride. With so many affirmations and denials following each other, we lose the thread of the story.

The psychoanalyst also doesn't always know where the truth lies. He is sometimes led astray by the patient's need to run the show. The latter can tell him in tears how much he will be missed while on vacation and, at the same time, convey the feeling that he is merely play-acting this sadness.

In the end, Albertine caves in and feels sorry for Marcel when she hears about his (invented) hopeless love for her girlfriend Andrée. His self-confidence is rescued by this lie and he can now devote himself to her without any risk. Piteously diminishing yourself and thereby manipulating the object is a stealthy exertion of power. Marcel still doesn't know whether he loves Albertine or simply feels sorry for her because he has been tormenting and imprisoning her for so long. The difference doesn't matter to him because he is only able to love a person with whom he plays this cat-and-mouse game.

We now come to the final development in the relationship of the narrator and Albertine, the climax of *Remembrance of Things Past*. Proust himself draws all the parallels between the relationship of the narrator as a child with his mother and as an adult with Albertine. He even sends her to a performance of *Phèdre* and then gets angry with her afterwards. Thus her repeats the struggle with her that he used to have as a child with his mother where going out was concerned. Suddenly he feels a renewed and vehement rage at her and has an uncontrollable need to aggravate her. He wants her to be afraid of his retaliations, of being rejected and abandoned by him. In short, he makes her tread the same road of Calvary that he himself walked as a little boy.

The only way to keep Albertine in his grasp is to make her into a prisoner, especially when he discovers to his horror that Albertine knows Mlle Vinteuil, with all that this implies for him about her secret homosexual life, which he had long surmised. He had just decided to break off with her when, because of this disquieting information, he suddenly feels totally captivated by her again. Heartrending memories of his grandmother come back to him: the images of his awful behaviour towards her torture him so much that it drives him to complete despair.

He thinks he caused his (grand)mother's death and that he needs to be punished for it.

After his feelings for (grand)mother and Albertine have become interwoven, a new abyss of suffering inevitably opens up for him. It is now really impossible to let Albertine go. In his imagination, his independence, that is to say his homosexuality with its accompanying hostile rituals, has killed his (grand)mother.

The only way in which to shield the inner image of Albertine and himself from destruction is to stay close to her and keep a sharp eye on her at all times. He must prevent Albertine's independence from becoming fatal to him.

Marcel is prepared to corner his girlfriend to such an extent that she simply won't be able to leave him. As a result of her life with the narrator, Albertine goes through a complete character change. She loses her spontaneity because of his constant inquisition. Afraid to make him jealous, she hides as much as she can from him, which only results in his ever-increasing jealousy. Sadism is the answer to our powerlessness, the impossibility of possessing the other. Now the tormenting relationship between Marcel and Albertine is complete. Albertine feels aggrieved, accused, and persecuted. Any normal conversation between them has become impossible. But they are well matched. They are both extremely skilled manipulators who never openly show their feelings or desires.

Marcel and Albertine are cool to each other and withhold from each other the tenderness they both need. Love is perverted to barely hidden mutual torments and lies told back and forth. Being hard and dishonest becomes synonymous with loving. The narrator alternates between the position of mother and child. Albertine gives the goodnight kiss or else withholds it, just like mother, and then he weeps all night, just as before.

In the final phase of the relationship with Albertine, the narrator constantly thinks about death. He cannot expect the same from a partner as he used to from his mother, although he still feels that same child inside him. This dilemma makes the entire situation with Albertine increasingly unbearable: the more he is her master, the more he is her slave. Things are bound to come to a head before long.

Until the day when Albertine accidentally lets something slip about an event (anal sex, thus another transposition) in a brothel, a reconciliation has always occurred after a comedy of rupture. Up to this point, Albertine always follows the implicit instruction to bring the narrator to the edge of despair, a game from which both derive pleasure. Now the unanticipated truth shocks the narrator so much that he falls apart entirely. After this "slip of the tongue", he is so bewildered and desperate that, scarcely able to hide his tears, he asks her to leave the following day. He feigns anger, but Albertine believes him and this time no reconciliation ensues.

He has gone too far: the game has become reality. She leaves at the crack of dawn, exactly as he had requested. In sadomasochistic relationships, misunderstandings can lead to a climax from which there is no way back. The narrator supposedly sends Albertine away out of fear that she wants greater freedom, but she takes him seriously and departs for good, as it turns out. By suppressing the homosexuality in Albertine that his mother wanted to ward off in him, he pushes her towards death. The interrogations and lies that started with his mother grow into a war of attrition that ends in death and destruction.

For the narrator, Montjouvain, homosexuality and sadomasochism finally lead to a work of art that brings him the only true happiness. But he isn't there yet, first he has to process the loss of Albertine.

A few weeks pass in which the "lovers" write each other letters full of deception. The narrator phantasises that he is going to commit suicide on her stoop if she doesn't come back to him. But he actually only misses her as long as he thinks he can be sure she won't return. He actually prefers this tension to her presence. In the meantime, he tries to feed his ravenous jealousy and thereby maintain his love for her. He pines less with love for an individual than that he needs the fear of abandonment in order to be able to love at all. The danger of forgetting her makes him as sad as when he is truly losing her. In order to bring his sorrow to an end, he ultimately wishes her dead, while he sends her a telegram imploring her to come back. He promises that from time to time he will hereafter do everything she asks in exchange for a goodnight kiss. In response, he receives a telegram with the message that Albertine has had a fatal fall off her horse. This dreadful news does not end his jealous preoccupations in any way whatsoever; in reality she may well be dead, but in his imagination she is all the more alive.

After Albertine's death, Marcel wallows in ceaseless melancholy and is far more fiercely preoccupied with her than he ever was during her lifetime. In his mind, hate, tenderness, and suspicion alternate with each other. This reminds us of Freud's "Mourning and melancholia"[11] where he explains how, as a result of identifying with the deceased, sadism and hostility towards the love object are transformed into irate reproaches against the self. Mourning the loss of Albertine is like the longing for his unattainable mother, while his inner image of her comes back to life. Now he can no longer lose Albertine, which brings him a dubious peace of mind. But before this salvation is complete, he once again has to go through all the feelings around boundless fear and despair about Albertine's unfaithfulness. He feels a profound pity for her and is ashamed of having survived her. It is as if his phantasy world benefits from her death: a dead beloved is better than a living one who causes suffering instead of bringing happiness. Not until she is dead do we come to know her deeper truths.

He now feels guilty as if he has two deaths on his conscience: that of his grandmother and of Albertine. At the same time, he has now become the victim of Montjouvain instead of the innocent onlooker he once was. Even posthumously, Albertine causes him to suffer by her excesses, the same way that Mlle Vinteuil made her father suffer, the same way he made his mother and grandmother suffer. He continues to wallow obsessively in the voyeuristic pleasure of watching how Albertine diverts herself with someone else in his mind's eye. The careful reader understands that all this lust around a dead person at the same time contains the gratification of a desecration, the by now well-known theme of profanation.

As time goes by, he finally no longer thinks about Albertine, which gives him an empty, desolate feeling, as if he were recuperating from a serious illness. In the end, he comes to the conclusion that a masochist's choice of partner amounts to a choice of an object that is in league with the need to suffer.

> [...] desire, reaching out always towards what is most opposite to oneself, forces one to love what makes one suffer. [...] In the midst of the most complete blindness, perspicacity subsists in the form of predilection and tenderness; so that it is a mistake to speak of bad choice in love, since as soon as there is a choice it can only be a bad one.[12]

Experience teaches us that people often blindly choose the one who complements their personal traumatic experiences most perfectly so that they really must lapse into repeated patterns. It is striking how in relationships, when the transference from early days onto each other becomes complete, the mutual problems suddenly turn out to fit like a well-placed zipper. The partners think they recognise the detested traits of their own mother or father in the other one. Both partners suffer from the choice that, in retrospect, turns out to be anything but free. We cannot say that love is blind, it actually has an extraordinarily sharp eye. How else could it succeed in having us choose the exactly fitting partner who has the traits that are so familiar to us, which we were unconsciously seeking because those traits represent the only forms of love that we are able to recognise as such. This is how we have to repeat our history, especially if traumatic.

Freud said it before now: finding a love object is not finding but retrieving. We are victim of the repetition compulsion that prescribes us to repeat in our later relationships what we experienced in our original bonds. Our unconscious needs are clairvoyant and lead us to choices of which we can say years later: "What, in the name of God, ever made me choose this partner who doesn't match me at all? At least not match my conscious desires."

In order to have some idea of what has remained untold about the narrator's perversion, we need to turn to the character of the Baron de Charlus. The youthful narrator discovered homosexuality to his great surprise when he surreptitiously witnessed Charlus seducing another man. That man was Jupien, a servant, who later becomes the boss of a male brothel, which Charlus frequents. From that moment on, the narrator understands Charlus's advances to himself. Charlus, always a difficult character to gauge, can display the most unimaginable attacks of rage, as we have already seen. He enjoys intimidating his adversary. He once tried to impose his will on the youthful narrator, just as the latter will do to Albertine. The baron invited him, has him wait interminably in the antechamber, and, when he finally receives him, addresses him in the most insulting way and with unprecedented ferocity in an interior filled with theatrical opulence. The baron is incensed when the narrator declines his generous offer to become his personal "prisoner". He shouts at him, abuses him verbally, and humiliates him in every possible way.

The entire scene is as theatrically and wittily described as a simulated break between two lovers. The baron claims, as the narrator does to Albertine, that these are the very last words he'll ever say to him. Initially, the narrator is as meek to the baron as Albertine is to him, but in the end, he becomes so irate that he tramples on the baron's hat and takes to his heels. However, he lets the baron persuade him to come back again when he is told that: "One chastises what one loves and so, if I chastised you it is because I love you." Whereupon the baron starts all over again, just as the narrator does with Albertine. He accuses him of all things nasty and gets him to make the false confession that he has spoken ill of the baron behind his back. In all of this, Charlus is obviously dishonest and merely play-acting. Moreover, he constantly contradicts himself, oscillating between rage and melancholy. Finally, he invites the narrator to spend the night, as he assures him he no longer loves him, while caressing his cheek. The narrator refuses and Charlus tries to draw out the goodbye with all sorts of complicated ruses. The narrator has the daunting feeling that, although he lards his hate with fine words, Charlus might be capable of committing murder. The latter's hurt pride and resentment feed his sadism to such an extent that he is capable of anything. But let us not forget that in Proust's jargon, murder can be a metaphor for making love. Desecration, possessive jealousy, and voyeurism all get their chance in this perverse orgy as a means to excite both the baron and the narrator. During the entire scene, two of the baron's servants have secretly stood listening at the door, in their turn joining in the excitement as quasi-inadvertent participants.

In *Cities of the Plain*, Charlus has a relationship with the pianist Morel that leads to a violent end through his own fault. The fact is that Charlus gets a demonic pleasure from treating Charlie like a little boy and humiliating him, the son of a servant, in every possible way. His lowly birth is an important factor in the act of lovemaking. That is, the lovers like to switch roles whereby Charlus pretends to be a servant and Morel an aristocrat. They entertain themselves with this by discussing how they can take others for a ride. The baron showers Charlie with expensive gifts, just as the narrator does with Albertine. And they argue incessantly, as do all couples in *Remembrance of Things Past*. Charlus uses every line of attack, even slander—the worst thing for a performing artist—to get power over Charlie and convince him to come and visit him, although he will never manage to make him his prisoner.

The narrator, who keeps his distance, notices that the baron is very keen on combing the streets at night when one runs the risk of being murdered (loved sadistically). But this risk is precisely what the baron, a sexual masochist, finds exciting.

It is striking that through the baron, Proust illustrates those aspects of homosexuality that he finds reprehensible. In his old age, Charlus increasingly resembles a carping old crone. In *Time Regained*, we see the baron again in the pathetic figure of an ageing sadomasochist. A negative depiction of homosexuality that André Gide, also a homosexual, strongly holds against the author and leads to a rejection of his manuscript.

When the narrator walks through Paris at night during the blackout in the First World War and feels thirsty, he goes into a random (!) establishment. It's not hard to guess what, to his surprise, he finds there. For it turns out that he has landed in Jupien's brothel. The latter shows him, through a peephole, how Charlus, chained to a bed, is being severely beaten by young men from the slaughterhouse. Now all three can surreptitiously share the excitement of watching this extraordinary scene. This form of sexual gratification exists by the grace of anonymity and nocturnal cruising in search of adventure.

Proust declares, like Freud, that there is but a gradual difference between so-called "normal" love and perversion. Phantasy must provide the gratification that is missing in reality. One is always pursuing a dream, a chimera.

> And if there is something of aberration or perversion in all our loves, perversions in the narrower sense of the word are like loves in which the germ of disease has spread victoriously to every part. Even in the maddest of them love may still be recognised. [...] In short his desire to be bound in chains and beaten, with all its ugliness, betrayed a dream as poetical as, in other men, the longing to go to Venice or to keep ballet-dancers.[13]

Compare this with Freud's remarkably similar formulation:

> It is perhaps in connection precisely with the most repulsive perversions that the mental factor must be regarded as playing its largest part in the transformation of the sexual instinct. It is impossible to deny that in their case a piece of mental work has been performed which in spite of its horrifying result, is the equivalent of an idealization of the instinct. The omnipotence of love is perhaps never more strongly proved than in such of its aberrations as these. The highest and the lowest are always closest to each other in the sphere of sexuality.[14]

Proust and Freud, who frequently have the same opinion, both resemble Old Testament prophets and gloomy moralists.

Proust was extremely pessimistic about love, but not much more so than Freud, although the latter was not struggling with personal pathology like the former. In 1820, preceding them both, Stendhal already determined that we see our beloved before us in our imagination without taking their actual character traits into account.[15] Love, fear, and unfulfilled longing have become almost synonymous in the Western tradition of romantic love. With that comes the repression of, or control over, feelings for the sake of postponing instant gratification, which in turn leads to a rich phantasy world.

Despite *Civilisation and its Discontents*, the paradox is that without cultural effects, such as commands and taboos, we would only have straight-up-and-down sexuality, as is the case with animals. The sometimes indeed dubious pleasures that the stimulated phantasy adds, are an indispensable ingredient for suspense and excitement. The cold reality will never be capable of satisfying the images of our dreams.

Notes

1. Proust, M., *Remembrance of Things Past, Within a Budding Grove*, Vol. 1, p. 636.
2. Proust, M., *Remembrance of Things Past, Swann in Love*, Vol. 1, p. 415.
3. Wilson, E. (1931). *Axel's Castle: A Study in Imaginative Literature.* Glasgow: Fontana Collins, 1959. Chapter Five, where he writes, among other things: "The episode of Albertine does not supply us with any of the things we ordinarily expect from love affairs in novels. It is quite without tenderness, glamour or romance to involve neither idealism nor enjoyment. But this is also its peculiar strength: it is one of the most original studies of love in fiction and in spite of the rather highly special conditions under which it is made to take place, we recognize in it an unescapable truth. (...) The tragedy of Albertine is the tragedy of the little we know and the little we are able to care about those persons whom we know best and for whom we care most (...) gives us that impression of bolder honesty, of a closer approach to reality, which we get only from deep and original genius" (pp. 126–127).
4. Proust, M. (1896). La fin de la jalousie. In: *Les plaisirs et les jours.* Paris Pléiade IV, Gallimard, 1971. To my knowledge, this has not been translated. The story forms a foretaste of the subsequent one with Albertine, complete with jealousy, spying on the beloved, and coercing confessions of unfaithfulness; in short, all the sadistic indignities that turn her into his prisoner and victim. The mother who, beautifully dressed, leaves with her husband for a ball, causes catastrophic fears of abandonment in

her son. Whereupon Honoré, an asthmatic who has regularly recurring and critical attacks of near suffocation, dies after falling off a horse, as will happen to Albertine later on.

5. De Rougemont, D. (1939). *L'amour et l'occident*. Paris: Plon.
6. Praz, M. (1933). *The Romantic Agony*. London: Oxford University Press, 1970.
7. Proust, M., *Remembrance of Things Past, Swann's Way*, Vol. 1, p. 252.
8. Svevo, I. (2001). *Zeno's Conscience*. New York: Everyman's Library.
9. This reminds us of Freud's article on narcissism (1914c), where he explains that the more love there is for the object, the less there remains for yourself. In this line of thinking, love is dangerous. Actually, Proust and Freud describe an unhealthy narcissistic love. Normally, loving someone should increase rather than threaten the sense of self.
10. Proust, M., *Remembrance of Things Past, Cities of the Plain*, Vol. 2, p. 864.
11. Freud, S. (1917e). Mourning and melancholia, *S. E. 14*, pp. 243–259.
12. Proust, M., *Remembrance of Things Past, The Fugitive*, Vol. 3, p. 624.
13. Proust, M., *Remembrance of Things Past, Time Regained*, Vol. 3, p. 870.
14. Freud, S. (1905d). *Three Essays*, p. 161.
15. Stendhal (1957). *De l'Amour*. Paris: La Renaissance du Livre.

CHAPTER TEN

What does the son want? Conclusion

The facts of life do not penetrate to the sphere in which our beliefs are cherished; they did not engender those beliefs, and they are powerless to destroy them.

—Marcel Proust[1]

Of all the mammals, the human child is by far the most aggressive, which undoubtedly is closely connected to his prolonged dependence on parents and educators. The inevitable frustrations during the period of upbringing are beneficial to the development within certain parameters, provided they are not too serious and that the parents' attitude is sufficiently positive.

For Proust's narrator, who has been our example throughout, it is a matter of subtle fear combined with a perverted form of love that creates an archaic rage, which can be expressed only indirectly. This results from a lack of a sense of security because his mother does not love him unconditionally. The child's self-love, self-respect, and his feelings of well-being are endangered when he only feels wanted as long as he satisfies his parents' conditions and expectations. A crippled feeling of self-worth is an important factor in the origin of a deviation such as perversion.

Sadism without empathy and finding lust in that belongs to the realm of cruelty and criminality. Power and abuse of power outside of the eroticism between two people belong to the area where violence and cruelty are used for gain or for the profit it delivers. In many cases that, too, is a matter of revenge due to hurt pride. Abuse of power not only plays a role between individuals or couples, but also between groups or is practised by the state. These forms of sadism go hand in hand with a complete insensitivity to the fate of the other. Here private and public roles are kept carefully separated, the executioner puts his children on his lap at night, pets his dog, listens to classical music. Projection leads to demonising and excluding the other as inferior. And it is the latter who turns into the barbarian, the heathen, the sex maniac, the profiteer.

Indoctrination and the anonymity of collective aggression result in lacking any feeling of guilt. However, criminal sadism is not our subject; what we are dealing with here are the vicissitudes of hate and fear, lived out in the phantasy or by means of ritual sexual scenarios between two consenting adults.

Not until the 1970s and 1980s did psychoanalysis gain a greater understanding of perversion. In my opinion, there are assorted reasons why, after a promising start, the interest in perversion stagnated. I will mention four of these.

The first reason why psychoanalysis comes back to perversion after all these years is a shift in emphasis in the theory. The child's earliest development has supplanted the Oedipal phase as shibboleth. More important still is the shift in emphasis in the theory from drives to object relations. Freud's opinion that the Oedipal phase forms the core of both neurosis and perversion has hampered the study of perversion. In the Oedipus complex and its resolution, or lack thereof, the father's image was central. Little was as yet known about the child's experience, and especially about the way in which the mother experiences her child.

Since the 1920s, a number of parallel developments have influenced the history of psychoanalysis. After Freud, the most significant changes in the theory have come from female researchers. Often, these were women who were also child psychoanalysts, such as Melanie Klein, Anna Freud, and Margaret Mahler. Thanks to their contributions, and despite their differences of opinion, we now know a great deal more about the development of the young child.

Generally, acknowledging the fact that, psychologically speaking, everything occurs much earlier in the child's life than Freud had assumed was not accepted for a long time because Anna Freud continued to adhere to her father's opinions.

Her rival, Melanie Klein, the other Viennese child psychoanalyst who later settled in London just like Anna Freud, was quickly aware that the psyche of the young child is shaped extremely early in life.[2] In the 1920s, Klein was already interested in the phantasy world of the very young child. She believed that an Oedipus complex, in the sense of triangulation, occurred much sooner than Freud presumed. However, it would still be a long time before her revolutionary ideas would be integrated in mainstream psychoanalysis. In any case, it became ever more obvious that the formative influence of the relationship with the parents starts with life itself. The so-called "pre-Oedipal development", a term meant to allow the Oedipus complex to maintain its validity, was intensely examined from the 1940s onwards. In Anna Freud's Hampstead Clinic (since her death, known as the Anna Freud Centre), the world of the child was researched empirically for the first time in history. As a result of the Second World War, the emphasis was now placed on the influence of loss and abandonment. The mother was seen increasingly as the instrument of both normality and pathology.

The term "transitional object", the teddy bear or the "blankie" that has to come to bed with the child, was created by Donald Winnicott, paediatrician and psychoanalyst.[3] This comforting item, which facilitates the transition from being with mother to being alone, is reminiscent of the fetish of the adult. Its absence in childhood could be an indication that the symbolic representation of the person of the mother has not been properly established. That lack of representation becomes visible when the child cannot tolerate his mother being absent and displays severe separation fears.

In the United States, Margaret Mahler and her colleagues did extensive empiric observational research in the reactions of babies to their mothers. Observation without introspection or interpretation of invisible and unconscious motives has objections attached to it. Moreover, the unconscious fears and longings of the mother were still not getting much attention, while fathers were hardly included in the research at all. For a long time, the father remained just the symbolic Oedipal father that he had been for Freud. Until the 1970s, his actual daily influence on the formation of the child hardly played any role. This now changed.

For the above-mentioned researchers, the emphasis shifted from the symbolic father to the concrete mother. In addition, it was followed by a revolution in psychoanalytically oriented child psychiatry, by means of carefully designed experiments.[4] Gradually, the subtleties of early parent–child interactions now acquired full attention in the field known as infant research. Video techniques and the possibility of repeating, reviewing, and studying images have had a great influence.

These new developments made it increasingly clearer that the child's personality is formed long before he attains the Oedipal phase, as conceived of in classical theory. His gender identity, his level of fear, his aggression regulation, and his self-confidence have already been put into effect.

The small child sees the mother as a powerful figure with male and female attributes, like Pallas Athena. Thus Proust speaks of *autoféconda-tion* (self-fertilisation) when he talks about the "race" of homosexuals: they are both man and woman.

Narcissism, which Freud once linked to homosexualtiy and perversion, in the 1970s again became the centre of attention.[5] This development led to a different view of perversion as well. The Oedipal father was no longer merely a mythical figure, he also possessed the symbolic phallus that provides power in the child's phantasy. It began to be obvious—and in this context the influence of the French psychoanalyst Jacques Lacan and his "Law of the Father" deserves to be mentioned—that in a psychic family constellation that contributes to the genesis of perversion and psychosis, the phallus is not represented by the father. More simply stated: when the father doesn't claim his place in the family and doesn't fulfil his fatherly role, when his disinterest, his weak position, or his absence, combined with a dominating mother whose self-confidence is weak and who needs her child as narcissistic support, this can promote a perverse personality structure.[6]

When the father is absent in the mother's conceptual universe and, as a result, also in that of the child—and this can also occur when the father is physically present—pathology lies ahead. The father doesn't only play a role in the direct relationship. How the mother sees him, or sees men in general, is equally decisive for the conception that her son has of men and masculinity. Both the conscious and the unconscious family constellation are important in perverse development.

A second obstacle in perversion research is the taboo, the undesirable idea that a mother not only can love her (male) child, but can also hate him, and that the son can hate the mother or wish her dead. After all, Freud declared that the most perfect of all human relationships, characterised by unconditional love, the most devoid of ambivalence and unspoiled by any egoistic considerations, exists only between mother and son. He does point out that the mother may try to realise her repressed ambitions via her son but he doesn't mention the parasitical relationship. I have created the term "symbiotic illusion" for that specific situation. With this, I mean a mutual, stifling dependency that replaces the normal, temporary dependency of the child. Since the mother is not dependent upon the child, the term "symbiotic phase", which implies a symmetrical relationship, strictly speaking in normal development, is not applicable. It is, in fact, always a pathological form of relationship. The parasitical infantilising attitude of the mother towards her child arises from her need for affirmation. She makes her well-being dependent on her child. Thus an unhealthy, two-sided dependency is created. The symbiosis functions as a defence mechanism. The symbiotic cocoon in which a baby initially finds himself with his mother is not resolved. The temporary symbiotic illusion becomes permanent. The struggle with love and hate that every child experiences when gratification isn't forthcoming is disavowed. Hate is pushed aside so that a false idyll between mother and son is created.

His yearning to share in the mother's power and deny the inevitable separation between them is a defence mechanism that serves to protect his sense of self-worth. Thus a bilateral contract based on illusion is created. When the symbiosis is not dissolved by a third person, it will continue to exist in the son's inner world alongside a reality that is incompatible with it.

For this reason, I use the word "symbiosis" in the sense of an unhealthy and imaginary bond, and therefore connect it with the word "illusion". The symbiotic phase as a blissful, untroubled period of life is romanticised by adults who seek to idealise childhood as the lost paradise. The concept "symbiotic illusion" can help to explain perversion. Upholding the mutual dependency of mother and son is both gratifying and frightening for the latter. In order to protect her sense of self, the mother has a tendency to create a false idyll with her child, so that he can support her narcissism. When a mother is emotionally dependent on her child, he has to help protect her from mental breakdown. In an interaction of that sort, both parties much prefer to deny anything that might allude to ambivalence and hate.

Let us take Freud's most appealing case description of Little Hans as an example[7] not of the Oedipus complex, but of a lack thereof, which can lead to perversion. Hans' phobia of horses seems to be linked more to the fear of his mother—so powerful in his eyes—who threatens him with castration when he touches his pecker, and to his unfinished, symbiotic, ambivalent bond with her, than to his father and the Oedipus complex. Freud's account of his consultations with the father as therapist of his young son Hans renders this alternative interpretation possible.

The moment that Hans' father consults Freud about his son's phobia of horses, Freud becomes the until then missing symbolic father figure for Hans. The boy appears to thrive under this double interest in him. Apparently, Hans' father feels supported as he attempts to behave more like a father to his son. After deciding to ask for Freud's help, he provides the child with a more directed attention. I assume that, possibly for the first time, Hans distinctly experiences the feeling of having a father. This helps him in loosening the symbiosis with his mother. Up to that point, he had to repress his anger at her, fearful of revenge. He transposed that anger to a phobia of (pregnant) horses. Thus the quasi-idyll with his mother is brought to an end. When Hans has a little sister and, thanks to Freud, is enlightened, it becomes clear to him that his mother is unfaithful to him with his father, which helps even more to loosen the bond with her. Partly due to this, Hans discovers the existence of an Oedipal triangle and a connection between his parents that excludes him. Now the exclusive bond with his mother can come to an end. Finally, Hans can relinquish his all too strong feminine identity and identify with his father. Thanks to the assistance of "grandfather" Freud, who helps his father to be a true father, it is now easier for him to acquire a masculine identity.

A third factor that may be important in explaining why perversion didn't, by a long shot, receive the attention it deserves, due to its by no means rare occurrence, could be the fact that Freud prematurely abandoned the seduction theory. What it boils down to in this theory is that a trauma in the childhood years—such as sexual abuse of the child by an adult (usually a father, an uncle, or an acquaintance of the parents)—is the only reason for the origin of neuroses. This outside influence as the determining factor in development was later replaced by the discovery of the influence of the child's own phantasy world, such as his Oedipal longings. These days, we pay attention to both factors, both trauma and the inner phantasy world, as significant in the development of pathology.

Perversion has to do with a form of seduction that amounts to a quasi-incestuous relationship between mother and son. Incest need not consist of the actual occurrence of physical sexual contact. An ambiance, a suggestion that floats in the air and is complemented and nourished by the imagination, can be equally incestuous.

The differences in generation and sex are ignored by the mother–son couple in the "contract" that I have called the symbiotic illusion. The father (the man, the third party) is excluded, or by his own choosing doesn't participate in the family triad. The relationship between the parents is problematic and sexually unsatisfying. This father would rather leave the care of his son to his wife than himself assume his position and responsibility as father. He does not affirm his child and fails to help in resolving the symbiosis between mother and son. He would rather not intervene.

The fourth, primarily unconscious, reason for neglecting perversion could be the fact that psychoanalysts as well as psychotherapists have a difficult time in emotional, practical, even moral, and—more importantly—theoretical regard with deviant forms of sexuality, especially with the aggressive hatred-driven or insalubrious variants. The aggressively shaded or distasteful erotic phantasies might be openly entrusted to the therapist, often without any shame or reserve. Not infrequent attempts at seducing him to take part in a perverse transference relationship create aversion.

When we study perversion, we are studying anxiety and the need of someone with a vulnerable sense of self to destroy an imaginary adversary, to make him an accomplice or turn him into a lifeless object, at least in phantasy. The slightest narcissistic offence is already sufficient to mobilise this defence mechanism.

We are living in a world ruled by a terrifying drive to destroy and kill, which can be seen on television every day. From a tender age on, children much prefer to watch violent movies. But we, as therapists, would rather avoid direct confrontation with fiercely sexual and aggressive themes. Psychotherapy is not concerned only with the patient who learns to take his aggression seriously, examine it more closely, and take responsibility for it. Needed also is a therapist who can handle negative emotions without discomfort. For the two individuals who are involved in a therapeutic process, the boundary between aggressive phantasies and reality isn't always equally clear, which can summon fear in both, while the therapist must keep watch over the sense of security in himself and his patient.

Violent phantasies can stir fear in therapists, just as actions do, although the philosophers have determined that evil doesn't speak but keeps mum at all times and works in silence. Perversions between consenting adults do not harm anybody. When someone seeks therapy for his perversion, it is mostly because he cannot find a consenting adult, or because he is in a relationship with someone who does not agree to his sexual wishes. People who go into therapy often do so for problems other than their perverse preferences. Perversion is usually not something that can be cured as it is a vital defence mechanism that protects against disintegration and mental breakdown. Psychoanalysis has always paid more attention to moral masochism, which is a more general phenomenon and easier to confront than is its opposite: sadistic manifestations. People seek treatment because something makes them suffer. Not everyone with a sexual life that could be called perverse suffers from it. Perversion can provide gratification without creating problems.

Perhaps all these factors combined contribute to the fact that good insight into perversion, paraphilia, or neosexuality was unable to take hold for such a long time. The theory still needs to be completed. Even its designation changes from "perversion" to "neosexuality" to "paraphilia" because the word carries a negative connotation. A sound definition is equally difficult to offer. Perversion must have a compulsive and obsessional instead of a voluntary character, and is a condition for potency and reaching orgasm. In any case, the combination of inhibition and sublimation, in addition to the staging of a dream world, is characteristic.

Proust provides a different explanation of the Oedipus myth. He shows the importance of the matricide that, for him, replaces the patricide of Freud. That concept helped me to better understand perversion.

Detachment from the symbiotic bond with the mother, letting go of the dyad with her, or of its failure, determines the psychosexual development of men. At any rate, that is what I have tried to demonstrate, without excluding other types of explanation, such as disposition and heredity. However, nothing definitive has been proven about the latter, nor does is entail any possibility of therapeutic influence.

It is my contention that Proust and Freud can be seen as complementary; Proust writes more about the mother, Freud about the father. Freud's preoccupation with fathers is probably connected to the equilibrium in the family from which he came. King Oedipus was powerful and strong: worthy of being defeated. This did not hold true for Freud's father, who was a traditional Jewish patriarch, on the one hand, and socially weak, on the other. His mother was a strong personality, from whom it was difficult to become detached. He survived her by only eight years, which could explain his aversion to writing about the mother's psychological influence. Freud who, like any man, needed a strong father figure, was able to "correct" his family situation with the Oedipus story and represent a strong father in his phantasy world.

Proust and Freud both had to accomplish their self-analysis by breaking the command: "Honour thy father and thy mother." In Proust, that led to desecration of the mother and matricide, and in Freud to patricide, as in *The Interpretation of Dreams*[8] where his recently deceased father appears repeatedly in less than flattering terms. I suspect that Freud was able to neutralise his domineering mother by giving the successful father, for whom he yearned, a central position in his phantasy. He was in quest of a father who was more worthy of his unconscious desire to symbolically conquer or kill him. Thus he gave us the myth of Oedipus as development's central paradigm. Proust, who created more of an oresteian than Oedipal drama, does not place the emphasis on the father but on the influence of the powerful mother figure. In this regard, he wrote a valuable supplement to Freud's theory, which helps us to better understand perversion.[9]

Freud, in contrast, tended to omit material that concerned the mother, as he did in his case histories of the "Ratman" and "Dora".[10] The treatment, and certainly the written account of the Ratman, had to deal with the imaginary, symbolic father–son relationship if Freud wanted to be able to substantiate his theory about the Oedipus complex. In Dora,[11] the mother, too, was probably a far more important factor in her pathology than Freud intimates.

By not delving into the relationship with the mother, Freud could maintain the idyll between mother and son. Freud attributed the negative feelings between parents and children to the father–son relationship or, for girls, to the mother–daughter relationship. This was the case for Dora, whose love for the father was firmly established for Freud. That love was represented as having shifted to Mr K. Her negative feelings towards her father and her yearning for the love of her mother were ignored by him.

For Freud, the son's positive emotions were reserved for the mother, the negative ones for the father. Together, this formed the male Oedipus complex. The mother–son relationship remained vague in Freud's writings, since the Oedipal symbolic father was the key figure on which he focused his attention. Early in his career, Freud looked in his immediate environment for strong father figures with whom to identify. These were colleagues such as Josef Breuer and Wilhelm Fliess, later on it was Joseph the interpreter of dreams, Hannibal who took a stand against the Romans, and finally Moses, the leader of the Jewish people. Freud paid little attention to the failed or non-established Oedipal relationship.

Proust, on the other hand, was particularly concerned with love and hate in the symbiotic bond between mother and son. In a family setting where the father doesn't have a role and the triad is lacking, the son is afraid of being devoured by her. Non-committal perverse games poke fun at coercion and bondage towards the mother, a solution whereby a heterosexual relationship remains possible. In homosexuality, we see a different solution to the problem with the powerful mother: there, the woman as love object is shunned. In some cases, however, fear can still arise, which can be resolved through alternative games. In perversion in the strict sense, it is a matter of stereotypical, compulsive scenarios. There revenge is unconsciously taken on the mother image by symbolically killing her in preparation for, or instead of, intimate intercourse.

The renewed interest in the psychology of perversion has caused a revival of the interest in the psychology of love life.[12] The wave of publications about narcissism and early object relationships has given love back its status as a special subject in psychoanalysis.

Despite the fact that Proust writes primarily about love combined with perversion, his ideas about love are relevant and comparable to those of Freud. It is clear that Proust is preoccupied with love in a more pathological sense. A love that brings unhappiness because it can never provide gratification. A healthy, lasting bond of love demands that partners share the available narcissistic space, have common interests, augment each other's sense of self-worth, and can experience the tenderness that is coupled with sexual attraction.

It isn't hard to describe the ideal love relationship, but in reality there is a gradual difference, or hierarchy, in the more primitive to the more developed forms of object relations. The roots always lie in the emotional world of the young child. Archaic characteristics are recognisable in even the most flourishing love relationships. Just like heterosexual relationships, homosexual ones display different levels that range from less to more successful emotional relations. In both cases, perverse solutions are sometimes necessary to maintain a fragile equilibium.

Freud believed that hate was always present in every relationship with the exception of that between mother and son. In the meantime, this point of view has been abandoned. The consequences of the ambivalent mother–son relationship have become more obvious. Hatred and ambivalence create the longing to incorporate the feared object, to possess it and turn it into a lifeless object, a "thing", as can be seen in perversion.

Love is based on retrieving the lost object of the earliest years, the mother, but also on the projection of our ego-ideal onto the beloved. Once the boundaries between ego and non-ego have been discovered, self-love can more easily grow into love for the other. This condition is not met in ego-alien compulsive forms of perversion.

Erik requires constant attention from his partner, but when she gives him too much attention, he must deserve it and live up to it, and then he begins to feel insecure again. Everything is aimed at supporting his frail sense of self-worth. A sadomasochistic scenario offers a solution to this dead-end, destructive path.

Love and narcissism are intimately connected: the active form of loving always goes hand in hand with the passive one, the longing to be loved. In every love relationship, object love and narcissistic love are intermingled in different proportions. In perversion, the amount of narcissism is disproportionate and sexuality is used to serve the sense of self and to re-establish a psychic equilibrium. A threat to one's self-esteem causes tension, which is subsequently eroticised. Then sexuality is used for non-erotic purposes, namely in service of the denying and suppressing undesirable feelings. As we have seen, sexual scenarios serve to protect the threatened self by means of eroticising fear and aggression.

In every love relationship, the same reciprocity exists, the identification with the other that is to be found in perversion. The man imagines himself in the woman's role and vice versa, just as the voyeur identifies with the one being watched and the exhibitionist with the one watching. From the very earliest beginning, with the infant sucking its thumb (auto-eroticism), before its libido is directed at the object, this circular movement from self to object and back again is characteristic. Thus it is a characteristic of both perversion and love. Narcissus can be replaced by someone with whom he identifies, who in turn keeps looking at Narcissus. Identification with the object onto which the ego-ideal has been projected, is characteristic of both love and perversion; the difference between them is gradual rather than absolute. The yearning to remove the separation and be absorbed in the other is not possible until a stage of development has been reached where fusional desires don't arouse the fear of being devoured or of losing one's own identity. Love is nourished by symbiotic yearnings, but these can only be realised without the fear of being devoured or of fusion, when the development level of separation has been attained. Yet, everyone is familiar with the longing for symbiosis and the fear of loss of love. That is what makes being in love the fierce and urgent situation that it is.

It is only in the deviations from the norm that we see what is considered to be normal. This was Freud's adage, which we follow in analysing the problems that the fictional Proustian characters encounter in their quest for happiness.

In conclusion, a few remarks to summarise one last time the main theme of this book. What I have asserted about the role of the more or less typical family pattern in the development of perversion is, of course, merely schematic and hypothetical. Although it cannot be proven that the traditional nuclear family is a vital condition for psychic well-being (we aren't very clear on what promotes good health, but we do know what causes problems), nevertheless, it seems desirable that certain requirements be satisfied. These are necessary to provide the child with the needed triangulation and the possibility of mentalisation (learning to understand that one's own thoughts do not coincide with those of the other) to stimulate his mental development. Today, there are alternative family constellations or lifestyles as well, such as homosexual couples who adopt a child or sire one by a third person. It has not been shown that such constellations have a negative influence on the development of the child's gender identity. Definitive conclusions about the effects of such family constellations cannot yet be drawn because research data, especially from a depth psychology perspective where the inner reality is also of concern, are to a large extent missing. Perhaps the emotional and psychological character differences between two parents is more important than their gender.

Today, one-parent families are numerous. Marriage, or even having a partner, isn't crucial in raising a child. The indispensable factor seems to be that the mother, whether she is alone with the child or not, has a conceptual universe that encompasses more than herself and the child created in her own image. A third individual, symbolic or real, seems necessary to procure a perception of the environment in the child's mind that offers sufficient perspective to look at life from different points of view. When the mother has interests and activities other than her child alone, she won't draw her narcissistic gratification exclusively from motherhood. If the latter is the case, she will threaten to smother her child with love, use him to satisfy her (unconscious) desires, or hate him in so far as he doesn't affirm her and satisfy her longings and emotional needs.

More than his sister, the boy lends himself to the parasitical role of fulfilling the mother's longings and becoming the object of seduction. Furthermore, he is often more hurt by such a situation than a girl. Fully developed heterosexuality will be less easily attainable. His gender identity will be less clearly established. The primary identification with the mother will be more difficult to resolve, the sexual difference will be more easily denied. Consequently, a pathological symbiosis in the form of an apparently conflict-free, blissful but false idyll will have a better chance of developing.

I assume that perversion will thrive less quickly in a fully fledged (Oedipal) triangle with a father and a mother who each fulfil their own role with respect to the child. In my experience as a practitioner, perversion issues forth from the unresolved mother–child dyad, in which there is room for one "prima donna" only: the mother. She suggests there is just one person to whom she is attached and whom she claims to love most. And that person is not the denigrated object, the father, but her own blood, the son, towards whom she will behave in an overprotective, possessive manner.

Proust rightly compares the jealous lover with this kind of mother. The son finds himself in an insecure position because he lives in an unstable illusion that prevents his sense of reality from developing.

Unconsciously, the mother suggests that her son is a part of her and her exclusive love object. She is both seductive and frustrating to him in order to thereby stimulate the illusion of exclusivity. To the child, her preferences remain obscure. She and her son seem to be partners, while in the meantime she is connected to an adult man, by whom she can replace him any time she chooses. To her son, she continues to be the woman with a concealed penis, man and woman rolled into one, who has made the father superfluous and can fertilise herself.

Stephan's mother kept her pregnancies hidden, sexuality didn't exist, any sexual education was out of the question. That way his mother maintained the illusion of their dyad without any sexual or generational difference. He didn't discover his own genitals until he was twenty-five, when he married (more because it was expected of him than that he longed for it). Until that time, he had accepted the implicit definition of himself as a genderless being. The marriage ended up in a sadomasochistic sexual relationship with bizarre stagings in an otherwise solid marriage and a successful life for both partners.

In the case of perversion, we are in the world of early childhood, where envy and paranoid fears predominate. The mother is feared and envied. She can cause frustration by denying gratification. Just like the child's ego, her image can easily become split into a good object that offers gratification and a bad object that intentionally denies it. Proust's personages always have two sides to their character. The conflicting ego-sides are badly integrated. They cover up aggression with its opposite. They use the partner as supplement and as vehicle to contain undesirable traits. Thus they form a psychological dyad with their beloved. Her bad side gives the lover a reason to torment her. The two partners become a more closely knit couple by identifying with those sides in the other that they deny in themselves. This creates a unity by means of "projective identification", namely projecting onto the other what you yourself do not want to be. The narrator combats the homosexuality in Albertine that he denies in himself.

When a man with an insecure sexual identity is heterosexually active, he has no other choice than to manipulate the woman's image in order to suppress his fear of her imaginary power. As a masochist, he can let her beat him, or play the sadomasochistic games that Proust describes, whereby he continues to exercise a hidden power.

Everything that Freud and his disciples call pre-Oedipal, the ambivalence of the anal phase, the feelings of fear, hatred, and revenge of the early mother–child relationship followed by depression, it can all be found in Proust's work. He describes every problem around the demonised mother of perversion.

We have to assume that the more serious pathology is generated by the lack of the Oedipal triangle. In the father–mother–child triangle, love, jealousy, rivalry, heterosexuality, and the sexual and generational differences are more easily resolved. Pathology, such as the compulsive performance of bizarre perverse scenarios, stems from being unable to distinguish adequately between the self-image and the inner image of the mother, from not acknowledging the pertinent differences between the sexes and generations, and from being consumed by archaic fears of and longing for and fear of fusion with the image of the proto-mother. Denial of the sexual attraction between father and mother and of their ability to procreate, of seeing the mother as a phallic woman, are factors that tend to intensify the fear of heterosexuality. As Jacob, one of my perverse patients, said in his bewilderment: "For me, the question has always been: what is it that mother really likes about father? She indicates that she doesn't have any high opinion of him. I wonder how you can be attracted to an ogre, for that is what she thought he was, unless that is exciting to you." He apparently thought his mother was perverse and masochistic, in which he was probably not entirely wrong. A result of the changed thinking about perversion is that psychoanalysts have gained an increased interest in "the perverse solution". That may or may not be why there are today more people with perversions who seek treatment than before, when, if they did show up, were considered to be untreatable. In the meantime, it is recognised that perversion need not be a counter-indication and that treatment makes sense, even if it is not to make perversion vanish.

Notes

1. Proust, M., *Remembrance of Things Past, Swann's Way*, Vol. 1, p. 162.
2. Klein, M. (1932). *The Psychoanalysis of Children*. London: Hogarth, 1973; Klein, M. (1946). Envy and Gratitude, *Notes on Some Schizoid Mechanisms*. London: Hogarth, 1975. Even before the Second World War, Melanie Klein already worked with seriously disturbed children and psychotics. She assumed that the baby knows fear and rage very early on. She called the first phase of life the "schizoid position". Klein had a great influence on the subsequent development of psychoanalysis and the thinking about perversion.
3. Winnicott, D. W. (1951). Transitional objects and transitional phenomena. In: *Collected Papers*. London: Tavistock Publications, 1958.

4. Stern, D. (1985). *The Interpersonal World of the Infant: A View from Psychoanalysis and Developmental Psychology*. New York: Basic Books.
5. Kohut, H. (1971). *The Analysis of the Self: A Systematic Approach to the Psychoanalytic Treatment of Narcissistic Personality Disorders*. London: Hogarth; Kernberg, O. (1975). *Borderline Conditions and Pathological Narcissism*. New York: Jason Aronson.
6. Kristeva, J. (1983). *Histoires d'amour*. Paris: Denoël.
7. Freud, S. (1909b). Analysis of a phobia in a five-year-old boy. *S. E. 10*, pp. 5–149.
8. Freud, S. (1900a). *The Interpretation of Dreams, S. E. 4 and 5*.
9. Zilboorg, G. (1939). Discovery of the Oedipus complex: episodes from Marcel Proust. *The Psychoanalytic Quarterly*, 8: 279–302.
10. Freud, S. (1909d). Notes upon a case of obsessional neurosis. *S. E. 10*, pp. 155–318.
11. Freud, S. (1905e). Fragment of an analysis of a case of hysteria. *S. E. 8*, pp. 7–125.
12. Otto Kernberg (1988). *Love Relations: Normality and Pathology*. New Haven: Yale University Press.

REFERENCES

Please note that all citations from Freud and Proust are taken from the following editions:

Freud, S. (1891–1939). *The Standard Edition of the Complete Psychological Works of Sigmund Freud, Volumes I–XXIV*, Trans. J. Strachey, in collaboration with A. Freud. London: Hogarth, 1971.

Proust, M (1913–1927). *À la recherche du temps perdu. In Search of Lost Time* (or *Remembrance of Things Past*), *Volumes I, II, III*, Trans. C. K. Scott Moncrieff and T. Kilmartin. New York: Random House, 1981.

* * *

Albaret, C. (1973). *Monsieur Proust*. Paris: Laffont.

Bach, S. (1994). *The Language of Perversion and the Language of Love*. New York: Jason Aronson.

Bataille, G. (1957). *L'érotisme*. Paris: Éditions de Minuit.

Baudry, J. -L. (1984). *Proust, Freud et l'áutre*. Paris: L'écrit du temps, Éditions de Minuit.

Blos, P. (1985). *Son and Father, before and beyond the Oedipus Complex*. New York: The Free Press/Macmillan.

Bowie, M. (1987). *Freud, Proust and Lacan: Theory as Fiction*. Cambridge: Cambridge University Press.

Chasseguet-Smirgel, J. (1985). *Creativity and Perversion*. London: Free Association Books.

De Rougemont, D. (1939). *L'amour et l'occident*. Paris: Plon.

Deleuze, G. (1967). *Présentation de Sacher-Masoch, La Vénus à la Fourrure*. Paris: Éditions de Minuit.

Deleuze, G. & Guattari, F. (1972). *L'Anti-Oedipe*. Paris: Éditions de Minuit.

Dolto, F. (1971). *Le cas Dominique*. Paris: Éditions du Seuil.

Ellenberger, H. (1970). *The Discovery of the Unconscious: The History and Evolution of Dynamic Psychology*. New York: Basic Books.

Forster, E. M. (1971). *Maurice*. London: Edward Arnold.

Freud, A. (1936). *The Ego and the Mechanisms of Defence*. London: Hogarth.

Freud, E. L. (Ed.) (1961). *Letters of Sigmund Freud, 1973–1939*. Translated by Tania and James Stern. London: Hogarth, 1975.

Freud, H. C. (2010). *Electra vs Oedipus: The Drama of the Mother–Daughter Relationship*. London: Routledge.

Freud, S. (1899a). Screen memories. *S. E. 3*: 301–322. London: Hogarth.

Freud, S. (1900a). *The Interpretation of Dreams. S. E. 4 and 5*. London: Hogarth.

Freud, S. (1905d). *Three Essays on the Theory of Sexuality. S. E. 7*: 130–243. London: Hogarth.

Freud, S. (1905e). Fragment of an analysis of a case of hysteria. *S. E. 8*: 7–125. London: Hogarth.

Freud, S. (1907a). Delusions and dreams in Jensen's Gradiva. *S. E. 9*: 7–95. London: Hogarth.

Freud, S. (1909b). Analysis of a phobia in a five-year-old boy. *S. E. 10*: 5–149. London: Hogarth.

Freud, S. (1909d). Notes upon a case of obsessional neurosis. *S. E. 10*: 155–319. London: Hogarth.

Freud, S. (1910c). *Leonardo Da Vinci and a Memory of His Childhood. S. E. 11*: 63–137. London: Hogarth.

Freud, S. (1910h). A special type of choice of object made by men. (*Contributions to the Theory of Love*, I). *S. E. 11*: 165–175. London: Hogarth.

Freud, S. (1912d). On the universal tendency to debasement in the sphere of love. (*Contributions to the Theory of Love*, II), *S. E. 11*: 179–190. London: Hogarth.

Freud, S. (1914c). On narcissism: an introduction. *S. E. 14*: 73–107. London: Hogarth.

Freud, S. (1915–1916). *Introductory Lectures on Psycho-Analysis*, Parts I, II. *S. E. 15*. London: Hogarth.

Freud, S. (1916–1917). *Introductory Lectures on Psycho-Analysis* (Part III). *S. E. 16*. London: Hogarth.

Freud, S. (1917e). Mourning and melancholia. *S. E. 14*: 243–258. London: Hogarth.

Freud, S. (1919e). A child is being beaten: a contribution to the study of the origin of sexual perversions. *S. E. 17*: 177–204. London: Hogarth.

Freud, S. (1920g). *Beyond the Pleasure Principle. S. E. 18*: 7–64. London: Hogarth.

Freud, S. (1924c). The economic problem of masochism. *S. E. 19*: 159–173. London: Hogarth.

Freud, S. (1927e). Fetishism. *S. E. 21*: 149–159. London: Hogarth.

Freud, S. (1930a). *Civilisation and Its Discontents. S. E. 21*: 64–145. London: Hogarth.

Freud, S. (1931b). Female sexuality. *S. E. 21*: 223–243. London: Hogarth.

Freud, S. (1933a). Femininity. In: *New Introductory Lectures on Psycho-Analysis, S. E. 22*: 112–135. London: Hogarth.

Freud, S. (1940e). Splitting of the ego in the process of defence. *S. E. 23*: 275–278. London: Hogarth.

Friedman, R. C. (1988). *Male Homosexuality: A Contemporary Psychoanalytic Perspective*. New Haven: Yale University Press.

Gay, P. (1987). *A Godless Jew*. New Haven: Yale University Press.

Girard, R. (1978). Narcissism, demythified by Proust. In: A. Roland (Ed.), *Psychoanalysis, Creativity and Literature*. New York: Columbia University Press.

Halberstadt-Freud, H. C. (1991). *Proust, Perversion and Love*. London: Taylor & Francis.

Halberstadt-Freud, H. C. (1999). Pertinence psychanalytique de Marcel Proust. Perversion et homosexualité: patricide ou matricide? In: *Revue Française de Psychanalyse*, Vol. LXIII: 285–602.

Isay, R. (1989a). The development of sexual identity in homosexual men. In: *Psychoanalytic Study of the Child, 41*: 467–489.

Isay, R. (1989b). Fathers and their homosexually inclined sons in childhood. *Psychoanalytic Study of the Child*: 275–294.

Isay, R. (1989c). *Being Homosexual: Gay Men and Their Development*. London: Penguin.

Jelinek, E. (1989). *The Piano Teacher*. Trans. Joachim Neugroschel. London: Serpent's Tail.

Kaplan, L. (1991). *Female Perversions: The Temptations of Emma Bovary*. New York: Doubleday.

Kernberg, O. (1975). *Borderline Conditions and Pathological Narcissism*. New York: Jason Aronson.

Kernberg, O. (1988). *Love Relations: Normality and Pathology*. New Haven: Yale University Press.

Khan, M. M. R. (1979). *Alienation in Perversions*. London: Hogarth.

Klein, M. (1932). *The Psychoanalysis of Children*. London: Hogarth, 1973.

Klein, M. (1946). Envy and Gratitude. In: *Notes on Some Schizoid Mechanisms*. London: Hogarth, 1975.

Kohut, H. (1971). *The Analysis of the Self: A Systematic Approach to the Psychoanalytic Treatment of Narcissistic Personality Disorders*. London: Hogarth.

Kohut, H. (1977). *The Restoration of the Self*. New York: International Universities Press.

Kristeva, J. (1983). *Histoires d'amour*. Paris: Denoël.

Kristeva, J. (1993). *Proust and the Sense of Time*. London: Faber and Faber.

Kristeva, J. (1994). *Le temps sensible*. Paris: Gallimard.

Lacan, J. & Granoff, W. (1956). Fetishism: the Symbolic, the Imaginary and the Real. In: S. Lorand & M. Balint (Eds.), *Perversion* (pp. 265–278). London: Ortolan Press.

Lasch, C. (1978). *The Culture of Narcissism: American Life in an Age of Diminishing Expectations*. New York: W. W. Norton.

Laufer, M. (1998). *Adolescent Breakdown and Beyond*. New York: International Universities Press.

Mahler, M. S., Pine, F. & Bergmann, A. (1975). *The Psychological Birth of the Human Infant: Symbiosis and Individuation*. London: Hutchinson.

Mauriac, F. (1947). *Du côté de chez Proust*. Paris: Table ronde.

May, U. (2001). Abraham's discovery of the "bad mother": a contribution to the history of the theory of depression. *International Journal of Psycho-Analysis, 82, 2*: 283–305.

McDougall, J. (1964). Homosexuality in women. In: J. Chasseguet-Smirgel (Ed.), *Female Sexuality: New Psychoanalytic Views* (pp. 171–212). London: Maresfield Library.

McDougall, J. (1980). *Plea for a Measure of Abnormality*. New York: International Universities Press.

McDougall, J. (1985). *Theaters of the Mind: Illusion and Truth on the Psychoanalytic Stage*. New York: Basic Books.

Meyer, J. (2011). The development and organizing function of perversion: the example of transvestitism. *International Journal of Psychoanalysis, 92*: 311–332.

Miller, M. (1956). *A Psychoanalytic Study of Marcel Proust*. Boston: Houghton Mifflin.

Mitscherlich, A. (1973). *Auf dem Weg zur vaterlosen Gesellschaft*. Munich: Piper.

Money, J. (1980). *Love and Love Sickness: The Science of Sex, Gender Difference, and Pair-Bonding*. Baltimore: The Johns Hopkins University Press.

Money, J. (1984). Paraphilias: phenomenology and classification. *American Journal of Psychotherapy, 38*: 164–179.

Nietzsche, F. (1888). *Ecce Homo*. In: *Werke in drei Bände*. Münich: Zweiter Band, Carl Hanser Verlag.

Praz, M. (1933). *The Romantic Agony*. London: Oxford University Press, 1970.

Proust, M. (1884). Juvenilia, Le gladiateur mourant. In: *Contre Sainte-Beuve, Précédé de pastiches et mélanges et suivi de Essais et articles*: 321–322. Édition établie par Pierre Clarac avec la collaboration d'Yves Sandre. Paris: Pléiade v, Gallimard, 1971.

Proust, M. (1896a). La fin de la jalousie. In: Jean Santeuil précédé de *Les plaisirs et les jours*: 146–155. Édition établie par Pierre Clarac avec la collaboration d'Yves Sandre. Paris: Pléiade iv, Gallimard, 1971.

Proust, M. (1896b). *La confessions d'une jeune fille*. In: Jean Santeuil, précédé de *Les plaisirs et les jours*, pp. 85–96. Édition établi par Pierre Clarac avec la collaboration d'Yves Sandre. Paris: Gallimard, 1971.

Proust, M. 1971. L'Affaire Lemoine: 12–16 and: Sentiments filiaux d'un parricide: 150–160. In: Contre Sainte-Beuve, précédé de Pastiches et Mélanges et suivi de Essais et articles. Édition établie par Pierre Clarac avec la collaboration d'Yves Sandre. Paris : Gallimard.

Proust, M. (1905). *Correspondence de 1905*. Ed. P. Kolb. Paris: Plon, 1979.

Proust, M. (1913–1927). *Remembrance of Things Past*. Volumes I, II, III. Trans. C. K. Scott Moncrieff and T. Kilmartin. New York: Random House, 1981.

Proust, M. 1983. *Selected Letters* 1880–1903. Ed. P. Kolb. London: Collins.

Proust, M. 1985. *Jean Santeuil*. Trans. Gerald Hopkins with a preface by André Maurois. Middlesex: Penguin; New York: Viking Press.

Proust, M. 1988. A Young Girl's Confession. In: *Pleasures and Regrets*, Trans. Louise Varese. London: Crafton Books.

Reich, W. (1949). *Character Analysis*. New York: The Noonday Press, 1961.

Richards, A. K. (2003). A fresh look at perversions. *International Journal of Psychoanalysis, 51*: 1199–1217.

Rivière, J. (1972). *Quelques progrès dans l'étude du coeur humain*. Paris: Librairie de France.

Rosolato, G. (1967). Étude des Perversions sexuelles à partir du fétichisme. In: *Le désir et la perversion*. Collection dirigée par Jacques Lacan. Paris: Éditions du Seuil.

Roudinesco, E. (2009). *Our Dark Side: A History of Perversions*. Cambridge: Polity Press.

Rousseau, J. -J. (1914). *Les Confessions*, tome 1. Paris: Georges Crès.

Sartre, J. -P. (1943). *L'être et le néant*. Paris: Gallimard.

Schatzman, M. (1976). *Soul Murder: Persecution in the Family*. Harmondsworth: Penguin.

Schneider, M. (1999). *Maman: L'un et l'autre*. Paris: Gallimard.

Socarides, C. W. (1979). A unitary theory of sexual perversion. In: T. B. Karasu & C. Socarides (Eds.), *On Sexuality*. New York: International Universities Press.

Stendhal (1957). *De l'Amour*. Paris: La Renaissance du Livre.

Stern, D. (1985). *The Interpersonal World of the Infant: A View from Psychoanalysis and Developmental Psychology*. New York: Basic Books.

Stoller, R. (1968). *Sex and Gender*. London: Hogarth.

Stoller, R. (1976). *Perversion: The Erotic Form of Hatred*. New York: Harvester Press/Random House.

Stoller, R. (1979). *Sexual Excitement, Dynamics of Erotic Life*. New York: Pantheon Books.

Svevo, I. (2001). *Zeno's Conscience*. New York: Everyman's Library.

Tadié, J. -Y. (1996). *Marcel Proust*. Paris: Gallimard.

Tournier, M. (1983). The fetishist. In: *The Fetishist and Other Stories* (pp. 195–216). London: Collins.

Von Krafft-Ebing, R. (1903). *Psychopathia Sexualis, Zwölfte verbesserte und vermehrte Auflage*. Stuttgart: Ferdinand Enke.

Von Sacher-Masoch, L. (1870). *Venus im Pelz*. Stuttgart: J. G. Cotta.

Welldon, E. V. (1989). *Mother, Madonna, Whore: The Idealization and Denigration of Motherhood*. London: Heinemann.

Wieland, C. (2000). *The Undead Mother: Psychoanalytic Explorations of Masculinity, Femininity and Matricide*. London: Rebus Press.

Wilson, E. (1931). *Axel's Castle: A Study in Imaginative Literature*. Glasgow: Fontana. Collins.

Winnicott, D. W. (1951). Transitional objects and transitional phenomena. In: *Collected Papers* (pp. 219–228). London: Tavistock Publications, 1958.

Winnicott, D. W. (1972). Ego distortion in terms of true and false self. In: *The Maturational Processes and the Facilitating Environment* (pp. 140–152). London: Hogarth.

Young-Bruehl, E. (1988). *Anna Freud: A Biography*. London: Macmillan.

Zilboorg, G. (1939). Discovery of the Oedipus complex: episodes from Marcel Proust. *The Psychoanalytic Quarterly, 8*: 279–302.

INDEX